KU-482-816

INGLORIOUS EMPIRE

SHASHI THAROOR

Inglorious Empire

What the British Did to India

HURST & COMPANY, LONDON

ALSO BY SHASHI THAROOR

NON-FICTION

FICTION

First Published under the title *An Era of Darkness: the British Empire in India*
in India in 2016
by Aleph Book Company, 7/16 Ansari Road,
Daryaganj, New Delhi 110 002,
Copyright © Shashi Tharoor 2016

This edition first published in the United Kingdom in 2017 by
C. Hurst & Co. (Publishers) Ltd.,
41 Great Russell Street, London, WC1B 3PL

Fifth impression, 2017

All rights reserved.
Printed in the United Kingdom by Bell & Bain Ltd.

The right of Shashi Tharoor to be identified as the author of
this publication is asserted by him in accordance with the
Copyright, Designs and Patents Act, 1988.

A Cataloguing-in-Publication data record for this book
is available from the British Library.

ISBN: 9781849048088

This book is printed using paper from registered sustainable
and managed sources.

www.hurstpublishers.com

For
my sons, Ishaan and Kanishk,
whose love of history equals,
and knowledge of it exceeds,
my own

But 'tis strange.
And oftentimes, to win us to our harm,
The instruments of darkness tell us truths…

William Shakespeare, *Macbeth*, Act I, scene iii

Thy hand, great Anarch! lets the curtain fall;
And universal darkness buries all.

Alexander Pope, *The Dunciad*

We live in the flicker—may it last as long as the old earth keeps rolling!
But darkness was here yesterday.

Joseph Conrad, *Heart of Darkness*

India—a hundred Indias—whispered outside beneath the indifferent moon,
but for the time India seemed one and their own,
and they regained their departed greatness by hearing its departure
lamented…

E. M. Forster, *A Passage to India*

CONTENTS

CHRONOLOGY

1600 British Royal Charter forms the East India Company, beginning the process that will lead to the subjugation of India under British rule.

1613–14 British East India Company sets up a factory in Masulipatnam and a trading post at Surat under William Hawkins. Sir Thomas Roe presents his credentials as ambassador of King James I to the Mughal Emperor Jehangir.

1615–18 Mughals grant Britain the right to trade and establish factories.

1700 India, under Mughal Emperor Aurangzeb, accounts for 27 per cent of the world economy.

1702 Thomas Pitt, Governor of Madras, acquires the Pitt Diamond, later sold to the Regent of France, the Duc d'Orléans, for £135,000.

1739 Sacking of Delhi by the Persian Nadir Shah and the loot of all its treasures.

1751 Robert Clive (1725–74), aged twenty-six, seizes Arcot in modern-day Tamil Nadu as French and British fight for control of South India.

1757 British under Clive defeat Nawab Siraj-ud-Daula to become rulers of Bengal, the richest province of India.

1765 Weakened Mughal Emperor Shah Alam II issues a *diwani* that replaces his own revenue officials in the provinces of Bengal, Bihar and Orissa with the East India Company's.

CHRONOLOGY

1767	First Anglo-Mysore War begins, in which Hyder Ali of Mysore defeats the combined armies of the East India Company, the Marathas and the Nizam of Hyderabad.
1771	Marathas recapture Delhi.
1772	Birth of Rammohan Roy (d. 1833). British establish their capital in Calcutta.
1773	British East India Company obtains monopoly on the production and sale of opium in Bengal. Lord North's Regulating Act passed in Parliament. Warren Hastings appointed as first Governor-General of India.
1781	Hyder Ali's son, Tipu Sultan, defeats British forces.
1784	Pitt the Younger passes the India Act to bring the East India Company under Parliament's control. Judge and linguist Sir William Jones founds Calcutta's Royal Asiatic Society.
1787–95	British Parliament impeaches Warren Hastings, Governor-General of Bengal (1774–85), for misconduct.
1793	British under Lord Cornwallis introduce the 'permanent settlement' of the land revenue system.
1799	Tipu Sultan is killed in battle against 5,000 British soldiers who storm and raze his capital, Srirangapatna (Seringapatam).
1803	Second Anglo-Maratha War results in British capture of Delhi and control of large parts of India.
1806	Vellore mutiny ruthlessly suppressed.
1825	First massive migration of Indian workers from Madras to Reunion and Mauritius.
1828	Rammohan Roy founds Adi Brahmo Samaj in Calcutta, first movement to initiate socio-religious reform. Influenced by Islam and Christianity, he denounces polytheism, idol worship and more.
1835	Macaulay's *Minute* furthers Western education in India. English is made official government and court language.
1835	Mauritius receives 19,000 migrant indentured labourers from India. Workers continued to be shipped to Mauritius till 1922.

CHRONOLOGY

1837	Kali-worshipping thugs suppressed by the British.
1839	Preacher William Howitt attacks British rule in India.
1843	British conquer Sindh (present-day Pakistan). British promulgate 'doctrine of lapse', under which a state is taken over by the British whenever a ruler dies without an heir.
1853	First railway built between Bombay and Thane.
1857	First major Indian revolt, called the Sepoy Mutiny or Great Indian Mutiny by the British, ends in a few months with the fall of Delhi and Lucknow.
1858	Queen Victoria's Proclamation taking over in the name of the Crown the governance of India from the East India Company. Civil service jobs in India are opened to Indians.
1858	India completes first 200 miles of railway track.
1860	SS *Truro* and SS *Belvedere* dock in Durban, South Africa, carrying first indentured servants (from Madras and Calcutta) to work in sugar plantations.
1861	Rabindranath Tagore is born (d. 1941).
1863	Swami Vivekananda is born (d. 1902).
1866	At least a million and a half Indians die in the Orissa Famine.
1869–1948	Lifetime of Mohandas Karamchand Gandhi, Indian nationalist and political activist who develops the strategy of non-violent disobedience that forces Britain to grant independence to India (1947).
1872	First British census conducted in India.
1876	Queen Victoria (1819–1901) is proclaimed Empress of India (1876–1901). Major famine of 1876–77 mishandled by Viceroy Lord Lytton.
1879	The *Leonidas*, first emigrant ship to Fiji, adds 498 Indian indentured labourers to the nearly 340,000 already working in other British empire colonies.
1885	A group of middle-class intellectuals in India, some of them British, establish the Indian National Congress to be a voice of Indian opinion to the British government.
1889	Jawaharlal Nehru is born (d. 1964).
1891	B. R. Ambedkar is born (d. 1956).

1893	Swami Vivekananda represents Hinduism at Chicago's Parliament of the World's Religions, and achieves great success with his stirring addresses.
1896	Nationalist leader and Marathi scholar Bal Gangadhar Tilak (1856–1920) initiates Ganesha Visarjan and Shivaji festivals to fan Indian nationalism. He is the first to demand 'purna swaraj' or complete independence from Britain.
1897	Queen Victoria's Diamond Jubilee celebrated amid yet another famine in British India.
1900	India's tea exports to Britain reach £137 million.
1901	Herbert Risley conducts first ethnographic census of India.
1903	Lord Curzon's grand Delhi Durbar.
1905	Partition of Bengal rouses strong opposition. Swadeshi movement and boycott of British goods initiated. Lord Curzon, prominent British viceroy of India, resigns.
1906	The Muslim League political party is formed in India at British instigation.
1909	Minto–Morley Reforms announced.
1911	Final imperial durbar in Delhi; India's capital changed from Calcutta to Delhi. Cancellation of Partition of Bengal.
1913	Rabindranath Tagore wins Nobel Prize in Literature.
1914	Indian troops rushed to France and Mesopotamia to fight in World War I.
1915	Mahatma Gandhi returns to India from South Africa.
1916	*Komagata Maru* incident: Canadian government excludes Indian citizens from immigration. Lucknow Pact between Congress and Muslim League.
1917	Last Indian indentured labourers are brought to British colonies of Fiji and Trinidad.
1918	Spanish Influenza epidemic kills 12.5 million in India, 21.6 million worldwide.
1918	World War I ends.
1919	Jallianwala Bagh massacre. General Dyer orders Gurkha troops to shoot unarmed demonstrators in Amritsar,

killing at least 379. Massacre convinces Gandhi that India must demand full independence from oppressive British rule. Montagu–Chelmsford Reforms promulgated. Rowlatt Acts passed.

1920   Gandhi formulates the *satyagraha* strategy of non-cooperation and non-violence. Khilafat movement launched.

1922   Non-cooperation movement called off by Mahatma Gandhi after Chauri Chaura violence.

1927 & 1934   Indians permitted to sit as jurors and court magistrates.

1930   Jawaharlal Nehru becomes president of the Congress party. Purna Swaraj Resolution passed in Lahore. Will Durant arrives in India and is shocked by what he discovers of British rule. Mahatma Gandhi conducts the Salt March.

1935   Government of India Act.

1937   Provincial elections in eleven provinces; Congress wins eight.

1939   World War II breaks out. Resignation of Congress ministries in protest against not being consulted by viceroy before declaration of war by India.

1940   Lahore Resolution of Muslim League calls for the creation of Pakistan.

1942   Cripps Mission. Quit India movement. Congress leaders jailed. Establishment of Indian National Army (Azad Hind Fauj) by Subhas Chandra Bose to fight the British.

1945   Congress leaders released. Simla Conference under Lord Wavell.

1946   Royal Indian Navy Mutiny. Elections nationwide; Muslim League wins majority of Muslim seats. Cabinet Mission. Interim government formed under Jawaharlal Nehru. Jinnah calls Direct Action Day. Violence erupts in Calcutta.

1947   India gains independence on 15 August. Partition of the country amid mass killings and displacement. Britain exits India.

ACKNOWLEDGEMENTS

There are many wonderful people I would like to thank for helping me with this book. First of all, my friend and publisher David Davidar, who talked me into undertaking this project—a decision I made rashly without fully realizing how much work it would involve—and guided the manuscript to the form in which it is before you now. His colleague Simar Puneet, for her diligent and painstaking assistance throughout the editing process, deserves a special word of appreciation. I greatly appreciate the thoughtful editorial advice of Michael Dwyer in the preparation of the Hurst edition.

Inglorious Empire required an extraordinary amount of research and reading (in many cases, re-reading) of source material on the British Raj in India. In this endeavour Professor Sheeba Thattil was invaluable, digging up digitized versions of original documents, texts and books from the eighteenth and nineteenth centuries, as well as finding academic material of more recent provenance in the form of books and journal articles relating to my subjects of enquiry. My two tireless researchers, Abhimanyu Dadu, who bore the brunt of the load, and Ben Langley, unearthed valuable insights and substantiated them meticulously. Abhimanyu stayed involved with the preparation of the manuscript, including crosschecking its many references and citations, for which I am most grateful.

A handful of close friends read the manuscript and offered useful comments: my son Kanishk Tharoor, a better historian and writer than his father; my close aide Manu Pillai, author of a superb history of the period himself; my friend, and sometime collaborator, the writer and

ACKNOWLEDGEMENTS

polymath Keerthik Sasidharan; and my 'sister from another womb', the historian Dr Nanditha Krishna. My schoolmate and now parliamentary colleague Professor Sugata Bose, the eminent Harvard historian, read a late draft of the manuscript and gave me the benefit of his wisdom. While their thoughts and ideas were most valuable, I remain solely responsible for the substance and the conclusions in this book.

Above all, my profound gratitude to His Majesty Jigme Khesar Namgyel Wangchuck, King of Bhutan, without whose generous hospitality and support I would have been unable to write this book or finish it within deadline. Thanks to his kindness and help I was able to escape into the mountains of his beautiful country and write undisturbed, without interruptions, calls or visitors, at considerable speed. My thanks, too, to Dasho Zimpon Ugyen Namgyel, Chamberlain to His Majesty, Captain Jattu Tshering and Tsedon Dorji for their unfailing courtesy and assistance in my endeavour.

My staff has backed me up in a hundred vital ways throughout the writing of this book, no one more so than Narayan Singh to whom I remain eternally grateful.

And for the special friend who left me alone to write, but supported and encouraged me daily, no words are necessary, nor will suffice.

Shashi Tharoor   *Paro, Bhutan*
August 2016

PREFACE

This book, somewhat unusually, began as a speech.

At the end of May 2015, I was invited by the Oxford Union to speak on the proposition 'Britain Owes Reparations to Her Former Colonies'. Since I was already scheduled to speak at the Hay Festival of Literature later that week, I thought it might be pleasant to stop in Oxford on the way and debate there again (as I had once done, on behalf of the United Nations, a decade earlier). The event, in the Union's impressive wood-panelled premises, dating back to 1879, was a success and I left pleased enough, but without giving the proceedings a second thought.

In early July, however, the Union posted the debate on the web, and sent me a video copy of my own speech. I promptly tweeted a link to it—and watched in astonishment as it went viral. Within hours it was being downloaded and replicated on hundreds of sites, sent out on WhatsApp and forwarded by email. One site swiftly crossed over three million views; others did not keep track, but reported record numbers of hits. Right-wing critics of mine suspended their 'trolling' of me on social media to hail my speech. The Speaker of the lower house of the Indian parliament, the Lok Sabha, went out of her way to laud me at a function attended by the Prime Minister, Narendra Modi, who then congratulated me for having said 'the right things at the right place'. Schools and colleges played the speech to their students; one university, the Central University of Jammu, organized a day-long seminar at which eminent scholars addressed specific points I had raised. Hundreds of articles were written, for and against what I had said. For months, I kept meeting strangers who came up to me in public places to praise my 'Oxford speech'.

I was pleasantly surprised but also a bit perplexed. For one thing, though I had spoken well enough for my side to win the debate by a two-thirds majority of the audience, I knew I had made better speeches that had not acquired a tenth of the fan following this one had. For another, I honestly did not think I had said anything terribly new. My analysis of the iniquities of British colonialism was based on what I had read and studied since my childhood, and I thought the arguments I was making were so basic that they constituted what Americans would call 'Indian Nationalism 101'—the fundamental, foundational arguments that justified the Indian struggle for freedom from British rule. Similar things had been said by Indian nationalists in the late nineteenth century, and by Jawaharlal Nehru and a host of others in the twentieth.

Yet the fact that my speech struck such a chord with so many listeners suggested that what I considered basic was unfamiliar to many, perhaps most, educated Indians. They reacted as if I had opened their eyes, instead of merely reiterating what they had already known.

It was this realization that prompted David Davidar to insist I convert my speech into a short book—something that could be read and digested by the layman but also be a valuable source of reference to students and others looking for the basic facts about India's experience with British colonialism. The moral urgency of explaining to today's Indians—and Britons—why colonialism was the horror it turned out to be could not be put aside.

The book differs from the speech in some crucial respects. It is not about reparations, for one thing. My speech led up to that argument because that was the topic the Oxford Union had announced, not because I was personally wedded to the case for reparations. I was convinced about the wrongs inflicted on colonial subjects by the British empire, but I suggested at the end of my speech that India should be content with a symbolic reparation of one pound a year, payable for 200 years to atone for 200 years of imperial rule. I felt that atonement was the point—a simple 'sorry' would do as well—rather than cash. Indeed, the attempt by one Indian commentator, Minhaz Merchant, to compute what a fair sum of reparations would amount to, came up with a figure so astronomical—$3 trillion in today's money—that no one could ever reasonably be expected to pay it. (The sum would be larger than Britain's entire GDP in 2015.)

This book is also not about British colonialism as a whole, but simply about India's experience of it. This is partially because discussing the entire history of British colonialism, as the speakers at the Oxford Union did, would have made for a huge and unwieldy book, but also because I simply don't know enough about it, whereas Indian history is a field I have delved into since my student days. I do not mean to discount the horrors of the British colonization of Africa, or the monstrosity of the slave trade, for which reparations may well be justified (it is striking that when slavery was abolished, the British government paid compensation, not to the men and women so inhumanely pressed into bondage, but to their former owners, for their 'loss of property'!) There are others who can do justice to those issues; I hope I have done justice in this volume to the specific case of British rule in India.[1]

There is a third respect in which this book differs from my speech. At Oxford I was arguing one side of a debate; there was little room for nuance or acknowledgement of counter-arguments. In a book laying out the 'Evils of Empire', however, I feel duty-bound to take into account the arguments for the British Raj as well. This I have done in each chapter, especially in chapter 2, and in chapters 3 to 7 in which I consider and reject most of the well-worn remaining arguments in favour of the British empire in India. I have supplemented my own years of reading with extensive research both into colonial-era texts and into more recent scholarly work on the British in India, all duly cited in the notes at the end. I hope my arguments have sufficient expert backing, therefore, to be regarded seriously even by those who may disagree with me.

Finally, this book makes an argument; it does not tell a story. Readers looking for a chronological narrative account of the rise and fall of the British empire in India will not find it here; the sequence of events is outlined only in the chronology preceding this Preface. The purpose of this volume is to examine the legacy of the Raj, to critically study the claims made for its alleged benefits, and to present the evidence and the arguments against it.

[1] As I was typing this last sentence, somewhat hastily, my spellcheck offered 'Brutish' as an acceptable substitute for 'British' rule in India.

My speech did not, of course, arouse universal approbation. For one thing, in the context of the debate I could scarcely acknowledge that many aspects of Empire were far more complicated in nature or ambiguous in impact than any generalization of good or evil could do sufficient justice to. This book is built on the premise that many of the issues involved require more complex treatment and substantiation than is possible in a debating chamber. In addition, several other arguments were made in response to my speech that should be acknowledged here, even though they do not fit directly into the themes of any of my chapters.

The most common of these criticisms is that India's postcolonial failings invalidate my attacks on Britain's colonial cruelties. 'Tharoor might have won the debate—but moral victory eludes India' wrote a columnist in *TIME* magazine, arguing that the Indian government's performance since Independence indicates that there is no evidence that any reparations paid to India would be spent well, or would reach the intended beneficiaries. One blogger added, for good measure, that the deplorable attitude of India's post-Independence authorities is evident from over millions of tons of food grains that were found damaged in the government's storage depots in 2010, as if incompetence after Independence justified the famines that occurred before it.

My position as a Member of Parliament for the Indian National Congress party, which had ruled India for fifty-two of its sixty-eight years of independence (at the time I made my Oxford speech), left me vulnerable to another line of attack. Commentator Jonathan Foreman put it most bluntly: '[T]he Congress Party,' he declaimed somewhat intemperately, 'misruled India for more than six decades, all the time becoming increasingly arrogant and corrupt, and seeming almost as insulated from ordinary Indians as their British predecessors had been.' Indian leaders from the Congress were responsible for India's woeful 'Hindu rate of growth', and 'because of the ruling elite's neglect of basic education and literacy, their obsession with socialist planning, their fostering of the "Licence Raj", and their corrupt deals with a handful of monopolistic business families, countries like South Korea and even Mexico overtook India in per capita GDP between 1950 and 1980.'

Some of these criticisms are legitimate—indeed, I have made variants of them myself in my own books, though not in such extreme or trenchant terms—but one set of failings do not invalidate another. Nor can twenty decades of colonial oppression be undone in six; the record of Indian, indeed Congress, governments is in most respects vastly better than that of their British colonial predecessors in India, especially on such indices as GDP growth, literacy, poverty eradication, life expectancy and overcoming droughts and crop failures. History, in any case, cannot be reduced to some sort of game of comparing misdeeds in different eras; each period must be judged in itself and for its own successes and transgressions.

The fact that reparations were a centrepiece of the Oxford debate added fuel to my critics' fire. One Indian commentator argued that the claim for reparation revealed India's insecurities and low self-esteem; Indians making this argument were transferring responsibility to the British for the subsequent failures of Indian rule. Others pointed out that it would be impossible to identify the beneficiaries who genuinely deserved to receive compensation for colonial exactions.

In any case, some averred, Britain has in effect provided reparations in the form of aid to India over the years—not, by any means, as acceptance of guilt, but out of British generosity to their former colonial subjects. More than enough has been unilaterally transferred from Britain to India post-independence, and not just as aid; according to historian John MacKenzie, one of my adversaries at Oxford, British companies 'can be said to have fostered part of the outsourcing boom that India experienced which can be considered a form of reparations'. Another debater against the Oxford motion, Sir Richard Ottaway, MP, argued that given the voluntary aid extended by wealthier countries to poorer ones, 'to demand even more is to maintain the old inferiority complex'.

I need scarcely point out, of course, that I did not demand more; I demanded less—just a symbolic one pound a year. But that is also beside the point. I used Oxford's reparations motion to raise the issue of the moral debt Britain owed her former colonies, not a financial one. And as for aid, British aid amounts to less than 0.02 per cent of India's GDP, and somewhat less than the Government of India spends on fertilizer subsidies—an appropriate metaphor, perhaps, for the aid argument.

Many pointed out that today's Britons bore no responsibility for the transgressions of their forebears and should not be expected to bear the burden of reparations for sins in which they played no part. Nor, for that matter, were today's Indians worthy of being compensated for the sufferings of their ancestors. Compensation should be paid to the victims, not to their grandchildren, and by the wrongdoers, not by their grandchildren.

Fair enough, but this elides the sense of national identity and responsibility that characterizes most countries. When Willy Brandt was chancellor of Germany, he sank to his knees at the Warsaw Ghetto in 1970 to apologize to Polish Jews for the Holocaust. There were hardly any Jews left in Poland, and Brandt, who as a socialist was persecuted by the Nazis, was completely innocent of the crimes for which he was apologizing. But in doing so—with his historic *Kniefall von Warschau* (Warsaw Genuflection), he was recognizing the moral responsibility of the German people, whom he led as chancellor. That is precisely why I called for atonement rather than financial aid.

Of course, not everyone agrees that even atonement is due. Historian John Keay put it best: 'The conduct of states, as of individuals, can only be assessed by the standards of their age, not by today's litigious criteria. Otherwise, we'd all be down on the government of Italy for feeding Christians to the lions.' Amusing, but indefensible. The British Raj is scarcely ancient history. It is part of the memories of people still alive. According to a recent UN Population Division report, the number of Indians over the age of eighty is six million: British rule was an inescapable part of their childhoods. If you add to their number, their first-generation descendants, Indians in their fifties and sixties, whose parents would have told them stories about their experiences of the Raj, the numbers with an intimate knowledge of the period would swell to over 100 million Indians.

It is getting late for atonement, but not too late: I, for one, dearly hope that a British prime minister will find the heart, and the spirit, to get on his or her knees at Jallianwala Bagh in 2019 and beg forgiveness from Indians in the name of his or her people for the unforgivable massacre that was perpetrated at that site a century earlier. David Cameron's rather mealy-mouthed description of the massacre in 2013 as a 'deeply shameful event' does not, in my view, constitute an apology. Nor does the ceremonial visit to the site in 1997 by Queen Elizabeth and the Duke of Edinburgh, who merely left their signatures in the visitors' book, without even a redeeming comment. Whoever the PM is on the centenary of that awful crime will not have been alive when the atrocity was committed, and certainly no British government of 2019 bears a shred of responsibility for that tragedy, but as a symbol of the nation that once allowed it to happen, the PM could atone for the past sins of his or her nation. That is what Prime Minister Justin Trudeau did in 2016 when he apologized on behalf of Canada for the actions of his country's authorities a century earlier in denying permission for the Indian immigrants on the *Komagata Maru* to land in Vancouver, thereby sending many of them to their deaths. Trudeau's Willy Brandt moment needs to find its British echo.

Indeed, the best form of atonement by the British might be, as Labour leader Jeremy Corbyn has suggested, to start teaching unromanticized colonial history in British schools. The British public is woefully ignorant of the realities of the British empire, and what it meant to its subject peoples. These days there appears to be a return in England to yearning for the Raj: the success of the television series *Indian Summers*, building upon earlier Anglo-nostalgic productions like *The Far Pavilions* and *The Jewel in the Crown*, epitomize what the British-domiciled Dutch writer Ian Buruma saw as an attempt to remind the English 'of their collective dreams of Englishness, so glorious, so poignant, so bittersweet in the resentful seediness of contemporary little England.' If British schoolchildren can learn how those dreams of the English turned out to be nightmares for their subject peoples, true atonement—of the purely moral kind, involving a serious consideration of historical responsibility rather than mere admission of guilt—might be achieved.

Buruma was, of course, echoing what the Indian-born British writer Salman Rushdie had said a few years earlier: 'The continuing decline, the growing poverty and the meanness of spirit of much of Thatcherite Britain encourages many Britons to turn their eyes nostalgically to the lost hour of their precedence. The recrudescence of imperialist ideology and the popularity of Raj fictions put one in mind of the phantom twitchings of an amputated limb... The jewel in the crown is made, these days, of paste.'

Britain is no longer 'Thatcherite', though in the aftermath of 'Brexit', it may even be worse. The need to temper British imperial nostalgia with postcolonial responsibility has never been greater.

And then there's the issue of Indian complicity in British rule. The Indian columnist Aakar Patel suggested that we are unable to come to terms with the fact that the British 'takeover was facilitated and encouraged by Indians'. Indeed, Indians were active collaborators in many, if not most, of the misdeeds that I will spell out in this book. This was especially true of Indian princes who, once British rule was well established, accepted a Faustian bargain to protect their wealth and their comforts in exchange for mortgaging their integrity to the British. These nominal 'rulers' went out of their way to demonstrate their loyalty to the Crown—thus the cricketer-prince Ranjitsinhji obliged his peasantry, in the midst of a crippling drought, to contribute to the British coffers during World War I; and as his state choked in the grip of famine, he literally burned up a month's revenues in a fireworks display for a visiting Viceroy. Such episodes were by no means untypical of the complicity shown by the compromised Indian aristocracy with the colonial project.

There were other well-known Indian supporters of Empire, most notably the Bengali intellectual and unabashed Anglophile, Nirad C. Chaudhuri, who in a series of books extolled the virtues of the British empire and lamented its passing. (We will discuss specific examples later in this book.) Many ordinary Indians, too, went along with the British; many never felt they had a choice in the matter. But when a marauder destroys your house and takes away your cash and jewellery, his responsibility for his actions far exceeds that of the servant who opened the door to him, whether out of fear, cupidity or because he simply didn't know any better.

In describing and confronting what the British did to us, are we refusing to admit our own responsibility for our situation today? Are we implying that the British alone are responsible for everything that is wrong with us? Of course not. Some writers have pointed out that growth and development requires sound institution-building and wise macro-economic policies, not a recitation of past injustices. I wish to stress that I agree. I do not look to history to absolve my country of the need to do things right today. Rather I seek to understand the wrongs of yesterday, both to grasp what has brought us to our present reality and to understand the past for itself. The past is not necessarily a guide to the future, but it does partly help explain the present. One cannot, as I have written elsewhere, take revenge upon history; history is its own revenge.

One final caveat about this book. I write of British rule in India, fully conscious of the fact that the 'India' I am referring to no longer exists but has become three separate states. Much of what I have to say also applies to what are today the independent states of Bangladesh and Pakistan. This is not to associate any unwilling foreigners with my arguments, but to grant that my case is theirs too, should they wish to adopt it. Still, I write as an Indian of 2016 about the India of two centuries ago and less, animated by a sense of belonging morally and geographically to the land that was once so tragically oppressed by the Raj. India is my country, and in that sense my outrage is personal. But I seek nothing from history—only an account of itself.

This book has no pretensions to infallibility, let alone to omniscience. There may well be facts of which I am unaware that undermine or discredit some of my arguments. Still, the volume before you conveys in essence what I understand of my country's recent past. As India approaches the seventieth anniversary of its independence from the British empire, it is worthwhile for us to examine what brought us to our new departure point in 1947 and the legacy that has helped shape the India we have been seeking to rebuild. That, to me, is this book's principal reason for existence.

'[W]hen we kill people,' a British sea-captain says in the Indian novelist Amitav Ghosh's *Sea of Poppies*, 'we feel compelled to pretend that it is for some higher cause. It is this pretence of virtue, I promise you, that will never be forgiven by history.' I cannot presume to write on behalf of history, but as an Indian, I find it far easier to forgive than to forget.

1

THE LOOTING OF INDIA

In 1930, a young American historian and philosopher, Will Durant, stepped onto the shores of India for the first time. He had embarked on a journey around the world to write what became the magnificent eleven-volume *The Story of Civilization*. But he was, in his own words, so 'filled with astonishment and indignation' at what he saw and read of Britain's 'conscious and deliberate bleeding of India' that he set aside his research into the past to write a passionate denunciation of this 'greatest crime in all history'. His short book, *The Case for India*, remains a classic, a profoundly empathetic work of compassion and outrage that tore apart the self-serving justifications of the British for their long and shameless record of rapacity in India.

As Durant wrote:

> The British conquest of India was the invasion and destruction of a high civilization by a trading company [the British East India Company] utterly without scruple or principle, careless of art and greedy of gain, over-running with fire and sword a country temporarily disordered and help-less, bribing and murdering, annexing and stealing, and beginning that career of illegal and 'legal' plunder which has now [1930] gone on ruth-lessly for one hundred and seventy-three years.

The Conquest of India by a Corporation

Taking advantage of the collapse of the Mughal empire and the rise of a number of warring principalities contending for authority across

1

eighteenth-century India, the British had subjugated a vast land through the power of their artillery and the cynicism of their amorality. They displaced nawabs and maharajas for a price, emptied their treasuries as it pleased them, took over their states through various methods (including, from the 1840s, the cynical 'doctrine of lapse' whenever a ruler died without an heir), and stripped farmers of their ownership of the lands they had tilled for generations. With the absorption of each native state, the Company official John Sullivan (better known as the founder of the 'hill-station' of Ootacamund, or 'Ooty') observed in the 1840s: 'The little court disappears—trade languishes—the capital decays—the people are impoverished—the Englishman flourishes, and acts like a sponge, drawing up riches from the banks of the Ganges, and squeezing them down upon the banks of the Thames.'

The India that the British East India Company conquered was no primitive or barren land, but the glittering jewel of the medieval world. Its accomplishments and prosperity—'the wealth created by vast and varied industries'—were succinctly described by a Yorkshire-born American Unitarian minister, J. T. Sunderland:

> Nearly every kind of manufacture or product known to the civilized world—nearly every kind of creation of man's brain and hand, existing anywhere, and prized either for its utility or beauty—had long been produced in India. India was a far greater industrial and manufacturing nation than any in Europe or any other in Asia. Her textile goods—the fine products of her looms, in cotton, wool, linen and silk—were famous over the civilized world; so were her exquisite jewellery and her precious stones cut in every lovely form; so were her pottery, porcelains, ceramics of every kind, quality, color and beautiful shape; so were her fine works in metal—iron, steel, silver and gold.
>
> She had great architecture—equal in beauty to any in the world. She had great engineering works. She had great merchants, great businessmen, great bankers and financiers. Not only was she the greatest shipbuilding nation, but she had great commerce and trade by land and sea which extended to all known civilized countries. Such was the India which the British found when they came.

At the beginning of the eighteenth century, as the British economic historian Angus Maddison has demonstrated, India's share of the world economy was 23 per cent, as large as all of Europe put together. (It had been 27 per cent in 1700, when the Mughal Emperor Aurangzeb's treasury raked in £100 million in tax revenues alone.) By the time the British departed India, it had dropped to just over 3 per cent. The reason was simple: India was governed for the benefit of Britain. Britain's rise for 200 years was financed by its depredations in India.

It all began with the East India Company, incorporated by royal charter from Her Majesty Queen Elizabeth I in 1600 to trade in silk and spices, and other profitable Indian commodities. The Company, in furtherance of its trade, established outposts or 'factories' along the Indian coast, notably in Calcutta, Madras and Bombay; increasingly this involved the need to defend its premises, personnel and trade by military means, including recruiting soldiers in an increasingly strife-torn land (its charter granted it the right to 'wage war' in pursuit of its aims). A commercial business quickly became a business of conquest, trading posts were reinforced by forts, merchants supplanted by armies.

The first British 'factor', William Hawkins, found himself treated with scant respect, his king mocked and his assets scorned. When the first British ambassador, Sir Thomas Roe, presented his credentials in 1615 at the court of the Mughal Emperor, Jehangir, the Englishman was a supplicant at the feet of the world's mightiest and most opulent monarch. The Mughal empire stretched from Kabul to the eastern extremities of Bengal, and from Kashmir in the north to Karnataka in the south. But less than a century and a half later, this Mughal empire was in a state of collapse after the spectacular sacking of Delhi by the Persian Nadir Shah in 1739 and the loot of all its treasures. The Mughal capital was pillaged and burned over eight long weeks; gold, silver, jewels and finery, worth over 500 million rupees, were seized, along with the entire contents of the imperial treasury and the emperor's fabled Peacock Throne; elephants and horses were commandeered; and 50,000 corpses littered the streets. It is said that when Nadir Shah and his forces returned home, they had stolen so much from India that all taxes were eliminated in Persia for the next three years.

Amid the ensuing anarchy, provincial satraps asserted control over their own regions, and rivals for power (notably the Maratha and later the Peshwa dynasties) asserted themselves at the expense of the central authority, many calling themselves maharajas and nawabs while owing nominal allegiance to the Mughal emperor in Delhi. In 1757, under the command of Robert, later Lord, Clive, the Company won a famous victory in Plassey over a ruling nawab, Siraj-ud-Daula of Bengal, through a combination of superior artillery and even more superior chicanery, involving the betrayal of the nawab by one of his closest nobles, Mir Jafar, whom the Company duly placed on his throne, in exchange for de facto control of Bengal. Clive soon transferred the princely sum of £2.5 million (£250 million in today's money, the entire contents of the nawab's treasury) to the Company's coffers in England as the spoils of conquest.

In August 1765, the young and weakened Mughal emperor, Shah Alam II, was browbeaten into issuing an imperial edict whereby his own revenue officials in the provinces of Bengal, Bihar and Orissa were replaced with the Company's. An international corporation with its own private army and princes paying deference to it had now officially become a revenue-collecting enterprise. India would never be the same again.

In the hundred years after Plassey, the East India Company, with an army of 260,000 men at the start of the nineteenth century and the backing of the British government and Parliament (many of whose members were shareholders in the enterprise), extended its control over most of India. The Company conquered and absorbed a number of hitherto independent or autonomous states, imposed executive authority through a series of high-born governors-general appointed from London, regulated the country's trade, collected taxes and imposed its fiat on most aspects of Indian life. In 1803, Company forces marched into Delhi to find the old and terrified Mughal monarch cowering under a royal canopy. During the following decades the Company's domains absorbed several Indian principalities. In the eight years after he took over as the Company's Governor-General in 1847, Lord Dalhousie annexed a quarter of a million square miles of territory from Indian rulers.

Till an open revolt occurred against them in 1857—the so-called 'Indian Mutiny'—leading to the takeover of British domains by the Crown in the following year, the East India Company presided over the destinies of more than 200 million people, determining their economic, social and political life, reshaping society and education, introducing railways and financing the inauguration of the Industrial Revolution in Britain. It was a startling and unrivalled example of what, in a later era, Marxists in the 1970s grimly foretold for the world: rule of, by and for a multinational corporation.

Though the Mughal emperor's edict referred to the directors of the East India Company as 'the high and mighty, the noblest of exalted nobles, the chief of illustrious warriors, our faithful servants and sincere well-wishers, worthy of our royal favours, the English Company', no royal favours were required, other than signing on the dotted line. Shah Alam II and his successors lived on the sufferance of the Company, prisoners and pensioners in all but name. 'What honour is left to us?', the historian William Dalrymple quotes a Mughal official named Narayan Singh as asking after 1765, 'when we have to take orders from a handful of traders who have not yet learned to wash their bottoms?' But honour was an irrelevant concern for his emperor's 'faithful servants and sincere well-wishers'. The Company ran India, and like all companies, it had one principal concern, shared by its capitalist overlords in London: the bottom line.

The Deindustrialization of India: Taxation, Corruption & The 'Nabobs'

The British government assisted the Company's rise with military and naval resources, enabling legislation (prompted, in many cases, by the Company's stockholders in Parliament), loans from the Bank of England and a supportive foreign policy that sought both to overcome local resistance and to counter foreign competitors like the French and Dutch. But as the Company's principal motive was economic, so too were the major consequences of its rule, both for India and for Britain itself.

Britain's Industrial Revolution was built on the destruction of India's thriving manufacturing industries. Textiles were an emblematic case in point: the British systematically set about destroying India's textile manufacturing and exports, substituting Indian textiles by British ones manufactured in England. Ironically, the British used Indian raw material and exported the finished products back to India and the rest of the world, the industrial equivalent of adding insult to injury.

The British destruction of textile competition from India led to the first great deindustrialization of the modern world. Indian handloom fabrics were much in demand in England; it was no accident that the Company established its first 'factory' in 1613 in the southern port town of Masulipatnam, famous for its Kalamkari block-printed textiles. For centuries the handloom weavers of Bengal had produced some of the world's most desirable fabrics, especially the fine muslins, light as 'woven air', that were coveted by European dressmakers. As late as the mid-eighteenth century, Bengal's textiles were still being exported to Egypt, Turkey and Persia in the West, and to Java, China and Japan in the East, along well-established trade routes, as well as to Europe. The value of Bengal's textile exports alone is estimated to have been around 16 million rupees annually in the 1750s, of which some 5 to 6 million rupees' worth was exported by European traders in India. (At those days' rates of exchange, this sum was equivalent to almost £2 million, a considerable sum in an era when to earn a pound a week was to be a rich man.) In addition, silk exports from Bengal were worth another 6.5 million rupees annually till 1753, declining to some 5 million thereafter. During the century to 1757, while the British were just traders and not rulers, their demand is estimated to have raised Bengal's textile and silk production by as much as 33 per cent. The Indian textile industry became more creative, innovative and productive; exports boomed. But when the British traders took power, everything changed.

In power, the British were, in a word, ruthless. They stopped paying for textiles and silk in pounds brought from Britain, preferring to pay from revenues extracted from Bengal, and pushing prices still lower. They squeezed out other foreign buyers and instituted a Company monopoly. They cut off the export markets for Indian textiles, interrupting long-standing independent trading links. As British manufacturing grew, they went further. Indian textiles were remarkably cheap—so much so that Britain's cloth manufacturers, unable to compete, wanted them eliminated. The soldiers of the East India Company obliged, systematically smashing the looms of some Bengali weavers and, according to at least one contemporary account (as well as widespread, if unverifiable, belief), breaking their thumbs so they could not ply their craft.

Crude destruction, however, was not all. More sophisticated modern techniques were available in the form of the imposition of duties and tariffs of 70 to 80 per cent on whatever Indian textiles survived, making their export to Britain unviable. Indian cloth was thus no longer cheap. Meanwhile, bales of cheap British fabric—cheaper even than poorly paid Bengali artisans could make—flooded the Indian market from the new steam mills of Britain. Indians could hardly impose retaliatory tariffs on British goods, since the British controlled the ports and the government, and decided the terms of trade to their own advantage.

India had enjoyed a 25 per cent share of the global trade in textiles in the early eighteenth century. But this was destroyed; the Company's own stalwart administrator Lord William Bentinck wrote that 'the bones of the cotton weavers were bleaching the plains of India'.

India still grew cotton, but mainly to send to Britain. The country no longer wove or spun much of it; master weavers became beggars. A stark illustration of the devastation this caused could be seen in Dhaka, once the great centre of muslin production, whose population fell from several hundred thousand in 1760 to about fifty thousand by the 1820s. (Fittingly, Dhaka, now the capital of Bangladesh, is once again a thriving centre of textile and garment production.)

British exports of textiles to India, of course, soared. By 1830 these had reached 60 million yards of cotton goods a year; in 1858 this mounted to 968 million yards; the billion yard mark was crossed in 1870—more than three yards a year for every single Indian, man, woman or child.

The destruction of artisanal industries by colonial trade policies did not just impact the artisans themselves. The British monopoly of industrial production drove Indians to agriculture beyond levels the land could sustain. This in turn had a knock-on effect on the peasants who worked the land, by causing an influx of newly disenfranchised people, formerly artisans, who drove down rural wages. In many rural families, women had spun and woven at home while their men tilled the fields; suddenly both were affected, and if weather or drought reduced their agricultural work, there was no back-up source of income from cloth. Rural poverty was a direct result of British actions.

Apologists for Empire suggest that Indian textiles were wiped out by the machines of Britain's Industrial Revolution, in the same way that traditional handmade textiles disappeared in Europe and the rest of the world, rather than by deliberate British policy: in this reading, if they hadn't collapsed to British power, the weavers would have been replaced within fifty years by Indian textile mills using modern machinery. India's weavers were, thus, merely the victims of technological obsolescence.

7

It is plausible that, in due course, handlooms would have found it difficult to compete with mass-produced machine-made textiles, but they would surely have been able to hold on to a niche market, as they do to this day in India. At least the process would have occurred naturally and gradually in a free India, perhaps even delayed by favourable protective tariffs on English imports of mill-made textiles, rather than being executed brutally by British fiat. And many Indian manufacturers would surely have imported technology themselves, given the chance to upgrade their textile units; the lower wages of Indian workers would always have given them a comparative advantage over their European competitors on a level playing field. Under colonialism, of course, the playing field was not level, and the nineteenth century told the sad tale of the extinction of Indian textiles and their replacement by British ones.

Still, inevitably, Indian entrepreneurs began to set up their own modern textile mills after 1850 and to produce cloth that could compete with the British imports. The American Civil War, by interrupting supplies of cotton from the New World, set off a brief boom in Indian cotton, but once American supplies resumed in 1865, India again suffered. As late as 1896, Indian mills produced only 8 per cent of the total cloth consumed in India. By 1913, this had grown to 20 per cent, and the setbacks faced by Britain with the disruptions of the World War I allowed Indian textile manufacturers to slowly recapture the domestic market. In 1936, 62 per cent of the cloth sold in India was made by Indians; and by the time the British left the country, 76 per cent (in 1945).

But for most of the colonial era, the story of Indian manufacturing was of dispossession, displacement and defeat. What happened to India's textiles was replicated across the board. From the great manufacturing nation described by Sunderland, India became a mere exporter of raw materials and foodstuffs, raw cotton, as well as jute, silk, coal, opium, rice, spices and tea. With the collapse of its manufacturing and the elimination of manufactured goods from its export rosters, India's share of world manufacturing exports fell from 27 per cent to 2 per cent under British rule. Exports from Britain to India, of course, soared, as India's balance of trade reversed and a major exporting nation became an importer of British goods forced upon the Indian market duty-free while British laws and regulations strangled Indian products they could not have fairly competed against for quality or price.

The deindustrialization of India, begun in the late eighteenth century, was completed in the nineteenth and only slowly reversed in the twentieth. Under the British, the share of industry in India's GDP was only 3.8 per cent in 1913, and at its peak reached 7.5 per cent when the British left in 1947. Similarly, the share of manufactured goods in India's exports climbed only slowly to a high of 30 per cent in 1947. And at the end of British rule, modern industry employed only 2.5 million people out of India's population of 350 million.

Extraction, Taxation and Diamonds

But the ill effects of British rule did not stop there. Taxation (and theft labelled as taxation) became a favourite British form of exaction. India was treated as a cash cow; the revenues that flowed into London's treasury were described by the Earl of Chatham as 'the redemption of a nation…a kind of gift from heaven'. The British extracted from India approximately £18,000,000 each year between 1765 and 1815. 'There are few kings in Europe', wrote the Comte de Châtelet, French ambassador to London, 'richer than the Directors of the English East India Company.'

Taxation by the Company—usually at a minimum of 50 per cent of income—was so onerous that two-thirds of the population ruled by the British in the late eighteenth century fled their lands. Durant writes that '[tax] defaulters were confined in cages, and exposed to the burning sun; fathers sold their children to meet the rising rates'. Unpaid taxes meant being tortured to pay up, and the wretched victim's land being confiscated by the British. The East India Company created, for the first time in Indian history, the landless peasant, deprived of his traditional source of sustenance.

Ironically, Indian rulers in the past had largely funded their regimes not from taxing cultivators but from tapping into networks of trade, both regional and global. The Company's rapacity was a striking departure from the prevailing norm.

Corruption, though not unknown in India, plumbed new depths under the British, especially since the Company exacted payments from Indians beyond what they could afford, and the rest had to be obtained by bribery, robbery and even murder. Everybody and everything, as the 1923 edition of the *Oxford History of India* noted, was on sale.

Colonialists like Robert Clive, victor of the seminal Battle of Plassey in 1757 that is seen as decisively inaugurating British rule in India, were unashamed of their cupidity and corruption. On his first return to England Clive took home £234,000 from his Indian exploits (£23 million pounds in today's money, making him one of the richest men in Europe). He and his followers bought their 'rotten boroughs' in England with the proceeds of their loot in India ('loot' being a Hindustani word they took into their dictionaries as well as their habits), while publicly marvelling at their own self-restraint in not stealing even more than they did.

Clive came back to India in 1765 and returned two years later to England with a fortune estimated at £400,000 (£40 million today). After accepting millions of rupees in 'presents', levying an annual tribute, helping himself to any jewels that caught his fancy from the treasuries of those he had subjugated, and reselling items in England at five times their price in India, Clive declared: 'an opulent city lay at my mercy; its richest bankers bid against each other for my smiles; I walked through vaults which were thrown open to me alone, piled on either hand with gold and jewels... When I think of the marvellous riches of that country, and the comparatively small part which I took away, I am astonished at my own moderation.' And the British had the gall to call him 'Clive of India', as if he belonged to the country, when all he really did was to ensure that a good portion of the country belonged to him.

The scale and extent of British theft in India can be gauged by the impact of Indian-acquired wealth upon England itself. In his biographical essay on Clive, the nineteenth-century politician and historian Lord Thomas Babington Macaulay went beyond the details of Clive's life to inveigh against some of the larger forces his success had set in motion. (This is not to say Macaulay was an opponent of Empire. He served the East India Company in various capacities, and called it 'the greatest corporation in the world'.) His diatribe was aimed at the 'nabobs', the term applied to East India Company employees who returned to England after making fortunes in India. It was a term famously given currency by Edmund Burke in his ferocious denunciation of the Company's Governor-General, Warren Hastings, who was impeached by Parliament in 1788 for rampant corruption and abuse of power. The word 'nabob', Macaulay knew, was a mispronounced transliteration of a high Indian title, nawab or prince, carrying associations of aristocracy and authority that Macaulay found problematic. Nabobs, he wrote, 'had sprung from obscurity...they acquired great wealth...they exhibited it insolently...they spent it extravagantly' and demonstrated the 'awkwardness and some of the pomposity of upstarts'. They 'raised the price of everything in their neighbourhoods, from fresh eggs to rotten boroughs...their lives outshone those of dukes...their coaches were finer than that of the Lord Mayor...the examples of their large and ill-governed households corrupted half the servants of the country...but, in spite of the stud and the crowd of menials, of the plate and the Dresden china, of the venison and Burgundy, [they] were still low men'.

It didn't take much to make money if you were a Briton in India. Company official Richard Barwell boasted to his father in 1765 that 'India is a sure path to [prosperity]. A moderate share of attention and your being not quite an idiot are (in the present situation of things) ample qualities for the attainment of riches.' Nabobs were often Company officials who indulged in private trade on their own account while on the Company's business. This was extraordinarily lucrative, given the Company's monopoly on its own territories: profits of 25 per cent were regarded as signs of a moderate man, and vastly higher sums were the norm.

Clive's father followed his son's career in India closely, recognizing that the family's fortunes depended on Indian loot. 'As your conduct and bravery is become the publick [sic] talk of the nation,' he wrote to his son in 1752, 'this is the time to increase your fortune, make use of the present opportunity before you quit the Country." He did, buying his father and himself seats in Parliament, and acquiring a peerage (it was only in Ireland, so he renamed his County Clare estate 'Plassey'.) The Whig politician and author Horace Walpole wrote: 'Here was Lord Clive's diamond house; this is Leadenhall Street, and this broken column was part of the palace of a company of merchants who were sovereigns of Bengal! They starved millions in India by monopolies and plunder, and almost raised a famine at home by the luxury occasioned by their opulence, and by that opulence raising the prices of everything, till the poor could not purchase bread!'

The Cockerell brothers, John and Charles, both of whom served the East India Company in the second half of the eighteenth century, built an extraordinary Indian palace in the heart of the Cotswolds, complete with a green onion-shaped dome, umbrella-shaped *chhatris* and over-hanging *chhajjas* (eaves), Mughal gardens, serpent fountains, a Surya temple, Shiva *lingams*—and with Nandi bulls guarding the estate. The mansion, Sezincote, designed by a third Cockerell brother, the architect Samuel Pepys Cockerell (who, unlike his siblings, had never been to India), still stands today, an incongruous monument to the opulence of the nabobs' loot.

But it was Indian diamonds, which the nabobs brought back to Britain with them, that made the Empire real to the British public. They were the insignia of new money, indications that as Britain was becoming an imperial power, the country was being transformed. But old money was contemptuous of the new; many in the establishment did not want diamonds to sully the hands of good Englishmen. As Horace Walpole sneered in 1790: 'What is England now? A sink of Indian wealth.' Walpole hoped his nation would endeavour to act 'more honestly' than the nabobs did in bringing home 'the diamonds of Bengal'. He would not, he wrote, behave like the nabobs 'for all Lord Clive's diamonds'.

In the late eighteenth and early nineteenth centuries, the nabobs' diamonds were not hailed as jewels in Britain's imperial crown or prized imperial symbols, as the famed Kohinoor diamond would later be. Instead they were both envied and attacked as imports that pinched the purses of domestic Britons—and threatened to change British politics fundamentally.

Perhaps the earliest Company employee to bring Indian diamonds into the headlines (and thereby consecrate Indian diamonds as an imperial trope) was Thomas Pitt, the governor of Madras. In 1702, Pitt acquired (for £24,000, it was said, itself a considerable sum beyond the reach of 99 per cent of Englishmen) a diamond said to be 'the finest jewel in the world'. Pitt shipped the 400–carat gem to Britain, referring to it in his letters as 'my greatest concern' and 'my all'.

Soon after his diamond's safe arrival in Britain, he gave up his governorship, purchased a grand estate and paid handsomely for a seat in Parliament. The British historian John Keay tells us that 'wild rumours' swirled around Pitt's diamond, one suggesting that it had been 'snatched from the eye socket of a Hindu deity or smuggled from the mines by a slave who hid it in a self-inflicted gash in his thigh'. Like the purloined jewel in the title of Wilkie Collins's 1868 novel *The Moonstone*, the Pitt Diamond became a legend. It represented the wealth that was widespread in India, Britain's power to extract that wealth, and the luxury that came with power in India—especially if you were British.

The traditional British view of wealth based it on the ownership of land, which, through its solidity, connoted an earthy stability, and since land was held for a long time, reflected hierarchy and implied a sense of permanence. This had changed somewhat thanks to the advent of the mercantile classes, but the Pitt Diamond represented a dramatically alternative model, based on something far more adventurous—colonial exploits, if not exploitation. The owners of these diamonds escaped the confinement of traditional sources of wealth for something that could be acquired by colonial enterprise rather than traditional inheritance. Fifteen years after he had brought the diamond from India, Thomas Pitt sold it to the Regent of France, the Duc d'Orléans, for the princely sum of £135,000, almost six times what he had paid for it. The astronomical amount (worth multiple millions in today's money) bought the Pitt family a new place in English society. An Indian diamond thus gave a financial springboard to a British dynasty that would, in very short order, produce two prime ministers—his grandson William Pitt, the 1st Earl of Chatham, and Chatham's own son, William Pitt 'the Younger'.

In other words, the nabobs and their money were changing British politics during the late eighteenth-century expansion of Britain's Indian empire. As an essay in *The Gentleman's Magazine* reported in 1786, 'the Company providentially brings us home every year a sufficient number of a new sort of gentlemen, with new customs, manners, and principles, who fill the offices of the old country gentlemen [*sic*].' The danger was that these new men would remake Britain: 'It is plain that our constitution, if not altered, is altering at a great rate.' The East India Company was no longer just a trading concern and had gone well beyond the terms of its original charter. Some in Britain were concerned and alarmed: they summoned Clive before Parliament to explain his actions in India and the fortune he had made there. In impeaching Hastings, Burke commented pointedly: 'Today the Commons of Great Britain prosecutes the delinquents of India. Tomorrow these delinquents of India may be the Commons of Great Britain.'

The government of the Earl of Chatham, Pitt's descendant, sought to assert parliamentary supremacy over the Company in 1766, but thanks to his own ill health and since many MPs were in fact East India Company shareholders, this attempt was not too successful. Indeed, it was not until the passage of Lord North's Regulating Act of 1773 that Parliament gained some measure of control over the Company's activities in India. But even then, a majority of MPs stood to gain from the Company's successes, and they passed enabling legislation rather than restrictive laws. William Pitt the Younger would finally pass an India Act in 1784, establishing a Board of Control with power to endorse or dictate orders to the Company, to bring to heel the kinds of practices that had enriched his own ancestor. However, for all the talk of reform, the *London Chronicle* listed, in 1784, the names of twenty-nine members of Parliament with direct Indian connections; there were many more who owned shares in the Company.

The playwright Richard Sheridan was scathing in his denunciation of the Company, whose operations 'combined the meanness of a pedlar with the profligacy of a pirate... Thus it was [that] they united the mock majesty of a bloody sceptre with the little traffic of a merchant's counting-house, wielding a truncheon with the one hand, and picking a pocket with the other'.

Nor were Company officials unaware of the impact of their actions. Baron Teignmouth, who as John Shore went on to serve as governor-general of India from 1793–97, pointed out in a Minute as early as 1789 that the East India Company were both merchants and sovereigns in India: 'in the former capacity, they engross its trade, whilst in the latter, they appropriate its revenues'. Teignmouth pointed to the iniquity of the policies of extraction, the drain of currency (silver) and resources from the country to Europe, and the resultant collapse of India's internal trade, which had flourished before the Company's depredations.

There are many accounts of the perfidy, chicanery and cupidity with which the Company extracted wealth from the native princes, and went on to overthrow them and take over their territories; it would be tiresome today to regurgitate stories that have been in circulation since the late eighteenth century, when the British Parliament unsuccessfully impeached Warren Hastings, arguably one of the most rapacious of the Company's many venal governors-general. But a couple of examples will serve to illustrate the point I'm making. Hastings accepted substantial personal bribes and then went on to wage war against the bribe-giver (one wonders whether to deplore his avarice or admire him for the fact that despite being 'paid for', he refused to be 'bought'). His brazenness in such matters compels admiration: when he tortured and exacted every last ounce of treasure from the assets of the widowed Begums of Oude, Hastings duly informed the Council that he had received a 'gift' of 10 lakh rupees (£100,000 in those days, a considerable fortune) from the spoils and requested their formal permission to keep it for himself. The Council, mindful no doubt of the larger sum that would go on the Company's balance sheet, readily concurred.

Burke, in his opening speech at the impeachment of Hastings, also accused the East India Company of 'cruelties unheard of and devastations almost without name...crimes which have their rise in the wicked dispositions of men in avarice, rapacity, pride, cruelty, malignity, haughtiness, insolence'. He described in colourfully painful detail the violation of Bengali women by the British-assigned tax collectors— 'they were dragged out, naked and exposed to the public view, and scourged before all the people...they put the nipples of the women into the sharp edges of split bamboos and tore them from their bodies'—leading Sheridan's wife to swoon in horror in Parliament, from where she had to be carried out in distress. More indictments followed in the mellifluous and stentorian voices of Sheridan and Charles James Fox, but in the end, Hastings was acquitted, restoring the image of the Empire in the eyes of the British public and serving to justify its continuing rapacity for a century and a half more.

But the problem went well beyond Hastings. The preacher William Howitt speaking in 1839, while the Company was still in power, lamented that 'the scene of exaction, rapacity, and plunder which India became in our hands, and that upon the whole body of the population, forms one of the most disgraceful portions of human history... There was but one object in going thither, and one interest when there. It was a soil made sacred, or rather, doomed, to the exclusive plunder of a privileged number. The highest officers in the government had the strongest motives to corruption, and therefore could by no possibility attempt to check the same corruption in those below them... Every man, in every department, whether civil, military, or mercantile, was in the certain receipt of splendid presents.'

Even Lord Macaulay (who, as we have seen, thought very highly of the Company, and was employed by it for several years) was moved to write: 'the misgovernment of the English was carried to such a point as seemed incompatible with the existence of society... The servants of the Company forced the natives to buy dear and sell cheap... Enormous fortunes were thus rapidly accumulated at Calcutta, while thirty millions of human beings were reduced to the extremity of wretchedness. They had never [had to live] under tyranny like this...' Macaulay added that whereas evil regimes could be overthrown by an oppressed people, the English were not so easily dislodged. Such an indictment, coming from a liberal Englishman and an architect of the Empire, with whom we will have other bones to pick later, is impossible to contradict.

Revenue Collection and the Drain of Resources

It is instructive to see both the extent to which House of Commons debates on India were dominated by figures of the revenues from India, which seemed to many to justify every expediency the East India Company's officers resorted to and the extent to which, at the same time, contemporary observers were horrified by the excesses occurring in their country's name.

The prelate Bishop Heber (whose contempt for idol-worship led him to author the famous lines about a land 'where every prospect pleases / And only Man is vile') wrote in 1826 that 'the peasantry in the Company's provinces are, on the whole, worse off, poorer, and more dispirited, than the subjects of the Native princes'. In an extraordinary confession, a British administrator in Bengal, F. J. Shore, testified before the House of Commons in 1857: 'The fundamental principle of the English has been to make the whole Indian nation subservient, in every possible way, to the interests and benefits of themselves. They have been taxed to the utmost limit; every successive province, as it has fallen into our possession, has been made a field for higher exaction; and it has always been our boast how greatly we have raised the revenue above that which the native rulers were able to extort.'

Many of those 'native rulers' may well have been ineligible for a modern UN good governance award, but the Company, as Shore admitted, was decidedly worse. Where the British did not choose to govern directly themselves, they installed rulers of 'princely states' who were circumstantially allied with their cause. These potentates were charged copious 'fees' in exchange for installing them on their thrones and for security from enemy states—an imperial version of the 'protection money' racket since practised by the Mafia. (The British called it, more prosaically, a policy of 'subsidiary alliances'.) The princes were allied with the Company and paid generously for the British contingents in their kingdoms that were placed there for their security. If they did not, these contingents could be turned against them.

In early nineteenth-century Hyderabad, for instance, the ruling Nizam was dragooned into signing up for British protection at the inflated costs the Company chose to charge (the commander, for instance, received an exorbitant £5,000 a month). All the payments to the British were debited to his treasury, which in turn was made to borrow, at a 24 per cent interest rate, from a bank established in 1814 by an associate of the governor-general. Before he knew it, the nizam owed millions to the bank and rueful voices had coined the catchphrase, 'Poor Nizzy pays for all'. A similar arrangement laid low the Nawab of Arcot further south, whose 'debts' to the Company so exceeded his capacity to pay that he had to cede the British most of his territories as a form of repayment.

Having acquired rights to collect revenue early on in the Company's overlordship, the British proceeded to squeeze the Indian peasant dry. On the one hand they had very few officials who were deployed into the countryside to collect revenue. On the other hand, they couldn't trust these agents entirely, and increasingly a code of written rules began to govern the collection of revenue. Where local leaders had once understood local conditions, making due allowances for droughts and crop failures or even straitened family circumstances and such exigencies as deaths and weddings, now British revenue collectors ruled with a rule book that allowed no breathing space for negotiation or understanding local problems at a given time. 'The aim of the new system was to secure the Company's collection of revenue without the need to negotiate with India's local elites... The idea was to replace face-to-face conversation with written rules. The rules insisted land-holders paid a fixed amount of money each month with rigorous punc-tuality, and did not disturb the peace... But the system undermined the negotiation and face-to-face conversation which had been so essential to the politics of eighteenth century India. As a result, it brought dis-possession and the collapse of a once-rich region's wealth.'

The British ran three major types of revenue systems: zamindari, mostly in eastern India and a third of the Madras Presidency; raiyatwari or ryotwari in much of the south and parts of the north; and mahalwari in western India. The British introduced the permanent settlement of the land revenue in 1793 as part of the zamindari system. Under this scheme, the Indian cultivators were charged not on the traditional basis of a share of crops produced but by a percentage of the rent paid on their land. This system meant that if the farmer's crop failed, he would still not be exempt from paying taxes. On occasion, the tax demanded by the British, based on the potential rather than actual value of the land, exceeded the entire revenue from it. In the ryotwari and mahal-wari areas, the revenue demand was not permanently settled, but rather periodically revised and enhanced, with even more onerous results. To compound matters, the revenue had to be paid to the colo-nial state everywhere in cash, rather than kind (whether directly by the peasants or through zamindari intermediaries) and there was a revenue or rent offensive everywhere until the 1880s, after which even larger amounts were extracted from the peasantry from the 1880s to 1930 by the mechanism of debt. William Digby calculated that 'the ryots [peas-ant cultivators] in the Districts outside the permanent settlement get only one half as much to eat in the year as their grandfathers did, and only one-third as much as their great-grandfathers did. Yet, in spite of such facts, the land tax is exacted with the greatest stringency and must be paid to the Government in coin before the crops are garnered!'

Bishop Heber acknowledged in 1826, 'No native prince demands the rent which we do'. The English-educated Romesh Chunder Dutt, an early Indian voice of economic nationalism, acknowledging that some earlier Muslim rulers had also levied swingeing taxes, pointed out that 'the difference was this, that what the Mahomedan rulers claimed they could never fully realize; what the British rulers claimed they realized with vigour'. The land tax imposed in India averaged between 80–90 per cent of the rental. Within thirty years, land revenue collected just in Bengal went up from £817,553 to £2,680,000. The extortion might have been partly excused if the taxes were being returned to the cultivators in the form of public goods or services, but the taxes were sent off to the British government in London. The 'permanent settlement' proved repressive for the Indian economy and all but destroyed Indian agriculture. Taxation and the general conditions of life under the East India Company were so unpleasant and onerous that, as mentioned above, as many as could fled their traditional homes for refuge in domains beyond the Company's remit, whereas the migration of Indian peasants from the 'native states' to British India was unheard of through most of the nineteenth century.

The Company did not care about the superstitions, the social systems or the indignities that Indians practised upon each other so long as they paid their taxes to the Company. Taxes were officially levied for the express purposes of improving the towns, building bridges and canals, reservoirs and fortifications, but (as Burke pointed out in Parliament) the work was soon forgotten and the taxes continued to be levied. A committee of the House of Commons declared 'that the whole revenue system resolved itself, on the part of the public officers, into habitual extortion and injustice', whilst 'what was left to the ryot [peasant] was little more than what he was enabled to procure by evasion and concealment'.

The ryotwari and mahalwari systems of taxation had the additional feature of abolishing all private property which had belonged both to the affluent as well as the inferior cultivating classes, thereby abolishing century-old traditions and ties that linked people to the land. As we have seen, Pitt's India Act was passed in 1784 and formalized British authority to collect revenue from India. In Bengal, the British ignored the hereditary rights of the zamindars and sold their estates by auction to enhance the Company's revenues.

As long as the East India Company was in charge, its profits skyrocketed to the point that its dividend payouts were legendary, making its soaring stock the most sought-after by British investors. When its mis-

SJ035091

management and oppression culminated in the Revolt of 1857, called by many Indian historians the First War of Independence but trivialized by the British themselves as the 'Sepoy Mutiny', the Crown took over the administration of this 'Jewel in the Crown' of Her Britannic Majesty's vast empire. But it paid the Company for the privilege, adding the handsome purchase price to the public debt of India, to be redeemed (both principal and generous rates of interest) by taxing the victims, the Indian people.

And the objective remained the same—the greater good of Britain. The drain of resources from India remained explicitly part of British policy. The Marquess of Salisbury, using a colourful metaphor as Secretary of State for India in the 1860s and 1870s, said: 'As India is to be bled, the lancet should be directed to those parts where the blood is congested... [rather than] to those which are already feeble for the want of it.' The 'blood', of course, was money, and its 'congestion' offered greater sources of revenue than the 'feeble areas'. (Salisbury went on to become prime minister.)

Cecil Rhodes openly avowed that imperialism was an essential solution to the cries for bread among the unemployed working-class of England, since it was the responsibility of colonial statesmen to acquire lands to settle the surplus population and create markets for goods from British factories. Swami Vivekananda, the Indian sage, reformer and thinker, saw the British as a caste akin to the Vaisyas, governed by the logic of commerce and purely pecuniary considerations, who understood the price of everything they found in India but the value of nothing. The Bengali novelist Bankim Chandra Chatterjee wrote of the English 'who could not control their greed' and from whose vocabulary 'the word morality had disappeared'.

By the end of the nineteenth century, India was Britain's biggest source of revenue, the world's biggest purchaser of British exports and the source of highly paid employment for British civil servants and soldiers all at India's own expense. Indians literally paid for their own oppression.

Taxation remained onerous. Agricultural taxes amounted at a minimum to half the gross produce and often more, leaving the cultivator less food than he needed to support himself and his family; British estimates conceded that taxation was two or three times higher than it had ever been under non-British rule, and unarguably higher than in any other country in the world. Each of the British 'presidencies' remitted vast sums of 'savings' to England, as of course did English civil servants, merchants and soldiers employed in India. (After a mere twenty-four years of service, punctuated by and including four years of 'home leave' furloughs, the British civil servant was entitled to retire at home on a generous pension paid for by Indian taxpayers: Ramsay MacDonald estimated in the late 1920s that some 7,500 Englishmen were receiving some twenty million pounds annually from India as pension.)

While British revenues soared, the national debt of India multiplied exponentially. Half of India's revenues went out of India, mainly to England. Indian taxes paid not only for the British Indian Army in India, which was ostensibly maintaining India's security, but also for a wide variety of foreign colonial expeditions in furtherance of the greater glory of the British empire, from Burma to Mesopotamia. In 1922, for instance, 64 per cent of the total revenue of the Government of India was devoted to paying for British Indian troops despatched abroad. No other army in the world, as Durant observed at the time, consumed so large a proportion of public revenues.[2]

It is striking how brazenly funds were siphoned off from India. Even accounting tables were subject to completely euphemistic entries to mask extraction: thus while trade figures showed a significant surplus, the subtraction of vast amounts under the headings 'Home Charges' and 'Other Invisibles' [sic] gave India a huge net deficit. Paul Baran calculated that 8 per cent of India's GNP was transferred to Britain each year. No wonder the nineteenth-century Indian nationalist Dadabhai Naoroji found evidence even in the published accounts of the British empire to evolve his 'drain theory' of extraction and indict the colonialists for creating poverty in India through what he diplomatically termed their 'un-British' practices. Naoroji argued that India had exported an average of £13,000,000 worth of goods to Britain each year from 1835 to 1872 with no corresponding

---

[2] This dubious distinction has now been inherited by the Pakistan Army, which today consumes a greater proportion of national resources than any army in the world.

return of money; in fact, payments to people residing in Britain, whether profits to Company shareholders, dividends to railway investors or pensions to retired officials, made up a loss of £30 million a year. What little investment came from Britain served only imperial interests. India was 'depleted', 'exhausted' and 'bled' by this drain of resources, which made it vulnerable to famine, poverty and suffering. The extensive and detailed calculations of William Digby, the British writer, pointed to the diminishing prosperity of the Indian people and the systematic expropriation of India's wealth by Britain— including the telling fact that the salary of the Secretary of State for India in 1901, paid for by Indian taxes, was equivalent to the average annual income of 90,000 Indians.

Angus Maddison concluded clearly: 'There can be no denial that there was a substantial outflow which lasted for 190 years. If these funds had been invested in India they could have made a significant contribution to raising income levels.' Official transfers and private remittances to the UK from Indian earnings were compounded by excessively high salaries for British officials. It did not help, of course, that the British Raj was a regime of expatriates, whose financial interests lay in England. In the past, and had an Indian administration been in power, income from government service would have been saved and spent locally; instead it all went to foreigners, who in turn sent it abroad, where their real interests lay. In most societies, the income of the overlords is an important source of economic development since it puts purchasing power into the hands of people who can spend it for the local good and indirectly promote local industry. But the lavish salaries and allowances of the Government of India were being paid to people with commitments in England and a taste for foreign goods in India. This increased imports of British consumer items and deeply damaged the local industries that had previously catered to the Indian aristocracy—luxury goods makers, handicraftsmen, fine silk and muslin weavers, who found limited or no taste for their offerings among the burra sahibs (and especially their prissy English memsahibs).

In 1901, William Digby calculated the net amount extracted by the economic drain in the nineteenth century, with remarkable (and inevitably, bitterly contested) precision, at £4,187,922,732. While that would amount, in today's money, to about a ninth of Minhaz Merchant's calculations, it only accounted for the nineteenth century. Worse was to follow in the twentieth.

* * *

A small digression is in place here. That India contributed such a significant amount to Britain's imperial expansion can be seen from the frequency with which troops were dispatched overseas for wars which had nothing to do with India and everything to do with protecting or expanding British interests. And all this was accomplished by Indian funds, especially land revenue wrested from the labour of the wretched peasantry or collected from various princely states through 'subsidiary alliances'.

A list of Indian Army deployments overseas by the British in the nineteenth century and the first decade of the twentieth is instructive: China (1860, 1900–01), Ethiopia (1867–68), Malaya (1875), Malta (1878), Egypt (1882), Sudan (1885–86, 1896), Burma (1885), East Africa (1896, 1897, 1898), Somaliland (1890, 1903–04), South Africa (1899, but white troops only) and Tibet (1903). Some significant numbers worth mentioning include: 5,787 Indian troops contributed to the Chinese War of 1856–57 that ended in the Treaty of Tientsin (1857) and control of Canton; 11,000 troops sent in 1860 to China, whose campaign ended in the capture and control of Peking; 12,000 troops to release British captives from Abyssinia (Ethiopia); 9,444 troops and over 1,479,000 rupees contributed in the suppression of rebellion in Egypt in 1882 and 1896; and 1,219 soldiers dispatched to quell mutiny in East Africa. Britain used the British Indian Army to complete its conquest of the Indian subcontinent in the Kandyan War of 1818 in Ceylon (Sri Lanka); and the Burmese War of 1824–26, in which six of every seven soldiers of the British Indian Army fell as casualties to sickness or war. As late as World War II, among the 'few of the few' who bravely defended England against German invasion in the Battle of Britain were Indian fighter pilots, including a doughty Sikh who named his Hurricane fighter 'Amritsar'.

The British had a standing army of 325,000 men by the late nineteenth century, two thirds of which was paid for by Indian taxes. Every British soldier posted to India had to be paid, equipped and fed and eventually pensioned by the Government of India, not of Britain. There were significant disparities in the rank, pay, promotion, pensions, amenities and rations between European and Indian soldiers. Biscuits, rice, flour, raisins, wine, pork and beef, authorized to the European soldier, came from Indian production.

In addition to soldiers, India's labour and commercial skills helped cement imperial rule in many of the British colonies abroad. Indian labour was used to foster plantation agriculture in Malaya, southeast Africa and the Pacific, build the railways in Uganda, and make Burma the rice bowl of Southeast Asia. Indian retailers and merchants developed commercial infrastructure with lower overheads than their European counterparts. Indians also administered, in junior positions of course, the colonies in China and Africa. In the nineteenth century, large numbers of them were forced to migrate as convicts or indentured labourers to faraway British colonies, as we shall see in Chapter 5.

But India was denied any of the rewards or benefits of imperialism. The sacrifice that Indian troops made for the advancement of British interests, the results of which linger even today, was acknowledged neither in compensation to them nor the families they left behind, nor by any significant accretion to the well-being of India. (And this does not even take into account the huge contributions made by India and Indian soldiers in the two World Wars, which I will discuss later.)[3]

In the era of Company rule, the British disregard for treaties, solemn commitments, and even the payment of sums they had demanded in exchange for peace, became legendary: Hyder Ali, a warrior-prince whom they had attacked without provocation, considered them to be 'the most faithless and usurping of mankind'. William Howitt deplored 'how little human life and human welfare, even to this day, weigh in the scale against dominion and avarice. We hear nothing of the horrors and

[3] India's immense contributions to World War I are discussed in detail in Chapter 2. The figures for World War II are also instructive. At the beginning of the war (in 1939), the Indian Army stood at 194,373 men; it was raised to 2,065,554 men by 1945, serving both in India and overseas. The air force employed another 29,201 soldiers and the Royal Indian Navy had 30,478. (Bhatia, 1977, pp. 234–235.) Indian Army battle casualties were high, amounting to 149,225 between 1 Sept 1939 and 28 Feb 1945. Material assistance was also significant. One ironic detail, given Britain's attempts to strangle India's steel industry: India shipped 7,000 tonnes of steel sheet rolls to the UK after British steel shipments were lost at sea.

violence we have perpetrated, from the first invasion of Bengal, to those of Nepaul and Burmah; we have only eulogies on the empire achieved: "See what a splendid empire we have won!"'

The assumption of responsibility by the Crown also witnessed the dawn of a new language of colonial justification—the pretence that Britain would govern for the welfare of the Indian people. When an Englishman wants something, George Bernard Shaw observed, he never publicly admits to his wanting it; instead, his want is expressed as 'a burning conviction that it is his moral and religious duty to conquer those who possess the thing he wants'. Will Durant was scathing about this pretence: 'Hypocrisy was added to brutality, while the robbery went on.'

And went on it did. The British liked to joke, with self-disparaging understatement, that they had stumbled into a vacuum and acquired their empire in India 'in a fit of absence of mind', in the oft-quoted words of the Cambridge imperial historian John Seeley. (Seeley, in his *Expansion of England*, had claimed disingenuously that the 'conquest of India was not in its proper sense a conquest at all'.) But the reality was starker and more unpleasant: large-scale economic exploitation was not just deliberate; it was only possible under an umbrella of effective political and economic control. The Company's expansion may well have flowed from a series of tactical decisions made in response to events and in a desire to seize opportunities that presented themselves to the beady eyes of Company officials, rather than from some imperial master plan. But they followed a remorseless logic; as Clive said to justify the expansion of his British empire in India, 'To stop is dangerous; to recede ruin.' As we have seen, kingdom after kingdom was annexed by the simple expedient of offering its ruler a choice between annihilation in war and a comfortable life in subjugation. When war was waged, the costs were paid by taxes and tributes exacted from Indians. Indians paid, in other words, for the privilege of being conquered by the British.

William Howitt wrote indignantly in 1839: 'The mode by which the East India Company has possessed itself of Hindostan [is] the most revolting and unchristian that can possibly be conceived... The system which, for more than a century, was steadily at work to strip the native princes of their dominions, and that too under the most sacred pleas of right and expediency, is a system of torture more exquisite than regal or spiritual tyranny ever before discovered.'

But as Ferdinand Mount—a descendant of a famous Company general himself—recently explained, it was all the simple logic of capitalism: 'The British empire in India was the creation of merchants and it was still at heart a commercial enterprise, which had to operate at profit and respond to the ups and downs of the market. Behind the epaulettes and the jingle of harness, the levees and the balls at Government House, lay the hard calculus of the City of London.'

In his *Poverty and Un-British Rule in India*, Dadabhai Naoroji—who in 1892 became the first Indian elected to the British House of Commons, there to argue the case for India in the 'mother of parliaments' (and also to support Irish Home Rule) by appealing futilely to the better nature of the English—laid out the following indictment based entirely on the words of the British themselves:

> Mr. Montgomery Martin, after examining…the condition of some provinces of Bengal and Behar, said in 1835 in his *Eastern India*: 'It is impossible to avoid remarking two facts as peculiarly striking, first the richness of the country surveyed, and second, the poverty of its inhabitants… The annual drain of £3,000,000 on British India has amounted in thirty years, at compound interest, to the enormous sum of £723,900,000. So constant and accumulating a drain, even in England, would soon impoverish her. How severe then must be its effects on India when the wage of a labourer is from two pence to three pence a day….

> Mill's *History of India* (Vol. VI, p. 671; 'India Reform Tract' II, p. 3) says: 'It is an exhausting drain upon the resources of the country, the issue of which is replaced by no reflex; it is an extraction of the life blood from the veins of national industry which no subsequent introduction of nourishment is furnished to restore.'

> Sir George Wingate has said (1859): 'Taxes spent in the country from which they are raised are totally different in their effect from taxes raised in one country and spent in another. In the former case the taxes collected from the population…are again returned to the industrious classes… But the case is wholly different when the taxes are not spent in the country from which they are raised… They constitute [an] absolute loss and extinction of the whole amount withdrawn from the taxed country… [The money] might as well be thrown into the sea. Such is the nature of the tribute we have so long exacted from India.'

Lord Lawrence, Lord Cromer, Sir Auckland Colvin, Sir David Barbour, and others have declared the extreme poverty of India...

Mr. F. J. Shore's opinion: 'the halcyon days of India are over; she has been drained of a large proportion of the wealth she once possessed, and her energies have been cramped by a sordid system of misrule to which the interests of millions have been sacrificed for the benefit of the few... The gradual impoverishment of the people and country, under the mode of rule established by the British Government, has hastened their fall.'

The Destruction of Shipping and Shipbuilding

It was bad enough that the theft was so blatant that even Englishmen of the time acknowledged it. Worse, Indian industry was destroyed, as was Indian trade, shipping and shipbuilding. Before the British East India Company arrived, Bengal, Masulipatnam, Surat, and the Malabar ports of Calicut and Quilon had a thriving shipbuilding industry and Indian shipping plied the Arabian Sea and the Bay of Bengal. The Marathas even ran a substantial fleet in the sixteenth century; the navy of Shivaji Bhonsle defended the west coast against the Portuguese threat. Further south, the seafaring prowess of the Muslim Kunjali Maraicars prompted the Zamorin rulers of Calicut in the mid-sixteenth century to decree that every fisher family in his kingdom should bring up one son as a Muslim, to man the all-Muslim navy. The Bengal fleet in the early seventeenth century included 4,000 to 5,000 ships at 400 to 500 tonnes each, built in Bengal and employed there; these numbers increased till the mid-eighteenth century, given the huge popularity of the goods and products they carried. This thriving shipping and ship-building culture would be drastically curbed by the British.

To reduce competition after 1757, the Company and the British ships that they contracted were given a monopoly on trade routes, including those formerly used by the Indian merchants. Duties were imposed on Indian merchant ships moving to and from Indian ports, not just foreign ones. This strangled the native shipping industry to the point of irrelevance in everything but some minor coastal shipping of low-value 'native' goods to local consumers.

The self-serving nature of British shipping policy was made apparent during the Napoleonic Wars, which led to a severe shortage of British merchant vessels. (The war of 1803 destroyed 173,000 tons of British shipping, forcing the government in London to employ 112,890 tonnes of foreign vessels to conduct British commerce.) Expediently, Indian shipping was now deemed to be British and Indian sailors were reclassified as British sailors, allowing them access to British trade routes under the Navigation Acts. But as soon as the Napoleonic Wars ended, the Navigation Acts were again amended to exclude Indian shipping and the industry once again declined.

The story was repeated in the early twentieth century, when V. O. Chidambaram Pillai in Madras was allowed to set up a shipping company in the run-up to World War I. His success set the alarm bells ringing, however, and when regulations alone did not destroy his business, he was quickly jailed for his nationalist views, breaking his spirit as well as the back of his enterprise. The nascent Indian shipping line was driven out of business. The experience of Indian shipping confirms that British authorities cynically and deliberately exploited Indian industries in their time of need and otherwise suppressed them.

Indian shipbuilding (which had long thrived in a land with such a long coastline) offers a more complex but equally instructive story. After an initial period of stagnation and decline after the advent of the East India Company to power, Indian shipbuilding revived in Bengal in the last quarter of the eighteenth century. This was thanks to British entrepreneurs, who realized the advantages of constructing their vessels in Calcutta itself, using Indian workers. By 1800, Governor-General Wellesley reported that the British Indian port of Calcutta had 10,000 tonnes of cargo shipping built in India. Between 1801 and 1839 a further 327 ships were built in Bengal, all British-owned.

The reasoning for this commercial British-led activity in India was purely professional and based on sound economic calculations. Indian workmanship and the country's long shipbuilding tradition were highly valued by British shipwrights, who found themselves adopting many Indian techniques of naval architecture in constructing their own vessels. The Indian vessels, a contemporary British observer wrote, 'united elegance and utility and are models of patience [sic] and fine workmanship.' Indian workers were considered expert in all shipbuilding materials—wood, iron and brass (high-tensile brass was indispensable to the building of wooden ships, since it was used for ship fittings, source-water pumps, shaft liners and even nails). And their work proved remarkably durable: the average lifespan of a Bengal-built ship exceeded twenty years, whereas English-built vessels never lasted more than eleven or twelve, and often had to be rebuilt or repaired at Indian ports. (Part of the reason for this may have lain in the quality of the hardwood Indians used in shipbuilding, mainly teak and sal, as opposed to the British oak and pine.)

This meant that not only was the production cost of vessels built in India lower than that in Britain, but depreciation took longer, adding to the value proposition for British entrepreneurs. As a result of their lower costs, they were also able to charge lower rates for freight than companies using ships made in England. So attractive was it for British entrepreneurs to build ships in India that by the second decade of the nineteenth century, there was rising unemployment in the shipbuilding industry at home—shipwrights, caulkers, sawyers and joiners in their hundreds were reported to be unemployed in London.

British-based businesses simply could not compete, and so they petitioned Parliament for a ban on Indian shipbuilding. The first legislative act in their favour came in 1813 with a law that prohibited ships below 350 tonnes from sailing between the Indian colonies and the United Kingdom. That took some 40 per cent of Bengal-built ships out of the lucrative India-England trade. A further Act in 1814 denied Indian-built ships the privilege of being deemed 'British-registered vessels' to trade with the United States and the European continent. Though they could still, in theory, trade with China, that sector had become unprofitable, since the previous practice had been to sail from Calcutta with Indian goods to China, load up on tea there for London, and then return to Calcutta with British goods; with the London sector banned to them, these ships could only sail from Calcutta to China and back, but there was no market for Chinese goods in India (Indians were not yet tea-drinkers) and the ships, denied access to London, often had to return empty.

Meanwhile Indian sailors, for good measure, were also deemed non-British and companies were discouraged from recruiting them for voyages to England, where they were likely to be exposed to licentious behaviour by the locals that would 'divest them of the respect and awe they had entertained in India for the European character'. (Morality and racism could always be used to dress up naked commercial inter-ests.) Though, given the lack of available British seamen in Indian ports, these sailors could be allowed to crew the larger vessels upon issuance of a certificate from the governor that no British substitutes were avail-able, the law required the ship-owner to hire a British crew for the return journey from England, significantly driving up the journey's costs—both because he, in effect, had to pay for two crews and because the British sailors charged much higher wages.

The advantages for British companies of building ships in India and operating them from there, in other words, began to disappear as a result of policies of deliberate legislative discrimination. India's once-thriving shipbuilding industry collapsed, and by 1850 was essentially extinct. This had nothing to do, as some have suggested, with changing technology that India could allegedly not keep up with: the collapse began well before steamships had begun to overtake sailing vessels, and in any case Bengal had proved adept at building steam vessels too, before the new laws and the resultant reduction in market opportuni-ties made such activity unremunerative. As William Digby was to observe, the Mistress of the Seas of the Western world had killed the Mistress of the Seas of the East.

Other commercial enterprises were no exception to the practice of discrimination. One form of colonial discrimination that was almost ubiquitous and extremely effective was the use of currency to separate British businesses from Indian ones, and regulate the opportunities available to each. The division of businesses into 'sterling' (companies operating out of London) and 'rupee' (companies that operated out of India) created a commercial gulf that could not easily be bridged. Only the British could invest in sterling companies, while rupee companies were open to both British and Indian investment. Sterling companies tended to focus on utilities, tea and jute; this meant that there were significant barriers to entry for Indians in these markets, which the British reserved for themselves. Moreover, all sterling companies were required to have a British managing agent to oversee them before London-based investors would commit capital. Indian investors were simply kept out. Thus, of 385 joint stock companies in the tea industry in India as late as 1914, 376 were based in Calcutta; and all were owned by the British. Scholars have established that in 1915, 100 per cent of the jute mills in India were in British hands; by 1929 this was down to 78 per cent, still enshrining British dominance.

British India occupied a unique position in the imperial trade and payments system. From 1910 to 1947, the Indian economy underwent a series of monetary and exchange rate experimentations. These included, amongst others, a transition from gold bullion to a sterling exchange standard; a controversial fixed-exchange rate system to manage the deliberate depreciation of the rupee; a gradual improvement in a weakly functioning formal banking system; and finally, the establishment of the Reserve Bank of India (1934/35) with limited authority. Buffeted by global and imperial forces of demand and supply, India suffered severe price volatility of some 20–30 per cent a year. The British used the fixed exchange rate regimes as it suited them, basically to accommodate British current-account deficits and other domestic exigencies, with scant regard for their Indian subjects. Such policies exacerbated India's financial instability, adding to the miseries endured by Indians under the Raj.

The manipulation of currency, throughout a feature of the colonial enterprise, reached its worst during the Great Depression of 1929–30, when Indian farmers (like those in the North American prairies) grew their grain but discovered no one could afford to buy it. Agricultural prices collapsed, but British tax demands did not; and cruelly, the British decided to restrict India's money supply, fearing that the devaluation of Indian currency would cause losses to the British from a corresponding decline in the sterling value of their assets in India. So Britain insisted that the Indian rupee stay fixed at 1 shilling sixpence, and obliged the Indian government to take notes and coins out of circulation to keep the exchange rate high. The total amount of cash in circulation in the Indian economy fell from some 5 billion rupees in 1929 to 4 billion in 1930 and as low as 3 billion in 1938. Indians starved but their currency stayed high, and the value of British assets in India was protected.

At other times, the steady depreciation of the rupee was a deliberate part of British policy to strengthen the purchasing power of the pound sterling and weaken the economic clout of those who earned only in local currency. A currency which had once been among the strongest in the world in the seventeenth century was reduced to a fraction of its former value by the end of the nineteenth. Even Miss Prism in Oscar Wilde's 1895 play *The Importance of Being Earnest* could not fail to take note, instructing her impressionable ward Cecily to 'read your Political Economy in my absence. The chapter on the Fall of the Rupee you may omit. It is somewhat too sensational. Even these metallic problems have their melodramatic side.'

Stealing From Indian Steel

The story of the Indian steel industry demonstrates how the exploitation continued into the late colonial period, which has sometimes been represented by apologists for Empire as a more enlightened episode of colonial rule. Oppression and discrimination had merely become more sophisticated.

The British were unalterably opposed to India developing its own steel industry. India had, of course, been a pioneer of steel; as early as the sixth century, crucible-formed steel, which came to be known as 'wootz' (a corruption of the Kannada word 'ukku', mistranscribed in English as 'wook' and mangled into 'wootz') steel was made in the country, and Indian steel acquired global renown as the world's finest. (The establishment by Arabs of a steel industry based on Indian practices in the twelfth century gave the world the famous Damascus steel.) Indian-made swords were legendary. Indeed, in the early days of British colonial expansion into India, Indian swords were so far superior to European ones that English troopers in battle would often dismount and swap their own swords for the equipment of the vanquished foe. The British learned as much of the technology as possible and then shut down India's metallurgical industries by the end of the eighteenth century. Attempts to revive it met with resistance and then with racist derision.

When Jamsetji Tata tried to set up India's first modern steel mill in the face of implacable British hostility at the turn of the century (he began petitioning the British for permission in 1883, and raised money from Indian investors; after repeated denials and delays it finally began production in 1912 under his son Dorabji), a senior imperial official sneered that he would personally eat every ounce of steel an Indian was capable of producing. It's a pity he didn't live to see the descendants of Jamsetji Tata taking over what remained of British Steel, through Tata's acquisition of Corus in 2006: it might have given him a bad case of indigestion.

When the Tatas went ahead anyway, inspiring other Indians, the British devised effective ways to curb their growth. The two biggest consumers of steel in India, the government and the railways (both controlled by the British) insisted on British Standard Specification Steel (BSSS), which was of much higher quality than the Non-British Standard Specification Steel (NBSSS) used by most of the rest of the world. The requirement for BSSS was originally designed to exclude cheaper continental steel from the colonial Indian market, but it also served to hamper Indian steelmakers. Domestic producers of steel in India, such as Tata, were forced to meet these higher standards or be excluded from contracts with the government and railways.

By focusing on producing BSSS, as required by law, Indian firms could not simultaneously produce the cheaper NBSSS that was used throughout most of the non-British world. The high cost base of India's domestic production as a result of BSSS production rendered Indian steel uncompetitive in the wider international market, both during the Great Depression and the late 1930s recovery. Other developing countries in a comparable situation to India in the 1930s developed their steel industries using NBSSS without major problems.

They could, of course, export BSSS steel to Britain, which the British steel industry would not welcome. So restrictions were placed by Britain on Indian steel imports. The British demonstrated brilliantly that they could have their steel cake and eat it too.

India was, in other words, forced to make and use steel that was surplus to its requirements, restricted in its ability to find overseas markets for it, and curbed in every attempt at expansion. Indian companies such as Tata Steel thus had few opportunities to grow within the British economic ecosystem.

As we know, some apologists for British rule argue that the condemnation of Britain for its destruction of Indian industry and economic growth is unjustified. Britain, they claim, did not deindustrialize India; India's share of world GDP merely went down because India 'missed the bus' for industrialization, failing to catch up on the technological innovations that transformed the West. India had a significant world share of GDP when the world was highly agrarian. As the world changed, they argue, other countries overtook India because of scientific and industrial progress that India was unable to make.

That is a highly disputable proposition. As I have demonstrated, deindustrialization was a deliberate British policy, not an accident. British industry flourished and Indian industry did not because of systematic destruction abetted by tariffs and regulatory measures that stacked the decks in favour of British industry conquering the Indian market, rather than the other way around. The economic exploitation of India was integral to the colonial enterprise. And the vast sums of Indian revenues and loot flowing to England, even if they were somewhat less than the billions of pounds Digby estimated, provided the capital for British industry and made possible the financing of the Industrial Revolution.

Left to itself, why wouldn't existing Indian industry have modernized, as industry in other non-colonized countries did? None of those criticizing India's lack of technological innovation can explain why a country that was at the forefront of innovation and industrial progress in other eras suddenly lost its ability to innovate in the eighteenth and nineteenth centuries. I have touched upon the skills of Indian steelmakers and shipbuilders, but under other rulers and regimes that fostered innovation, Indians excelled at mathematics, physics, medicine, mining, metallurgy and even rocketry (under Tipu Sultan and Hyder Ali).

True, there could only have been scientific and technological innovation if a forward-looking Indian ruler had endowed the country with educational and scientific institutions where such research would have taken place. The British, however, failed to create such institutions; the foremost Indian research institution under the British empire, the Indian Institute of Science, was endowed by the legendary Jamsetji Tata, not by any British philanthropist, let alone by the colonial government. And if competition with an industrializing Europe was a challenge, why wouldn't a free India have exploited the situation to its own advantage, levying its own tariffs when protection was needed, giving its own subsidies and developing its own existing global markets?

It is preposterous to suggest that India's inability to industrialize while the Western world did so was an Indian failure, the result of some sort of native deficiency, rather than the deliberate result of systematically planned policies by those who ruled India, the British. If India's GDP went down because it 'missed the bus' of industrialization, it was because the British threw Indians under the wheels.

THE LOOTING OF INDIA

There is an ironic footnote to the issue of Britain's economic exploitation of India, in these days of Scottish nationalism and febrile speculation about the future of the Union. It is often forgotten what cemented the Union in the first place: the loaves and fishes available to Scots from participation in the colonial exploits of the East India Company. Before Union with England, Scotland had attempted, but been singularly unsuccessful at, colonization, mainly in Central America and the Caribbean. Once Union came, India came with it, along with myriad opportunities. A disproportionate number of Scots were employed in the colonial enterprise, as soldiers, sailors, merchants, agents and employees. Though Scots constituted barely 9 per cent of Britain's people, they accounted for 25 per cent of those employed by the British in India. Their earnings in India pulled Scotland out of poverty and helped make it prosperous. The humming factories of Dundee, the thriving shipyards, and the remittances home from Scots working in India, all stood testimony to the profitable connection. Sir Walter Scott wrote of India as 'the corn-chest for Scotland'. With India gone, no wonder the Scottish bonds with England are loosening...

2

DID THE BRITISH GIVE INDIA POLITICAL UNITY?

The British like to point out, in moments of self-justifying exculpation, that they deserve credit for the political unity of India—that the very idea of 'India' as one entity (now three, but one during the British Raj) instead of multiple warring principalities and statelets, is the unchallengeable contribution of British imperial rule.

It is difficult to refute that proposition except with a provable hypothesis: that throughout the history of the subcontinent, there has existed an impulsion for unity. This was manifest in the several kingdoms throughout Indian history that sought to extend their reach across all of the subcontinent: the Maurya (322 BCE–185 BCE), Gupta (at its peak, 320–550 CE), and Mughal (1526–1857 CE) empires, and to a lesser extent, the Vijayanagara kingdom in the Deccan (at its peak 1136–1565 CE) and the Maratha confederacy (1674–1818 CE). Every period of disorder throughout Indian history has been followed by a centralizing impulse, and had the British not been the first to take advantage of India's disorder with superior weaponry, it is entirely possible that an Indian ruler would have accomplished what the British did, and consolidated his rule over most of the subcontinent.

The same impulse is also manifest in Indians' vision of their own nation, as in the ancient epics the *Mahabharata* and the *Ramayana*, which reflect an 'idea of India' that twentieth-century nationalists would have recognized. The epics have acted as strong, yet sophisticated, threads of

Indian culture that have woven together tribes, languages, and peoples across the subcontinent, uniting them in their celebration of the same larger-than-life heroes and heroines, whose stories were told in dozens of translations and variations, but always in the same spirit and meaning. The landscape the Pandavas saw in the *Mahabharata* (composed approximately in the period 400 BCE to 400 CE) was a pan-Indian landscape, for instance, as their travels throughout it demonstrated, and through their tale, Indians speaking hundreds of languages and thousands of dialects in all the places named in the epic, enjoyed a civilizational unity. Lord Rama's journey through India and his epic battle against the demonking of Lanka reflect the same national idea.

After all, India has enjoyed cultural and geographical unity throughout the ages, going back at least to Emperor Ashoka in the third century BCE. The vision of Indian unity was physically embodied by the Hindu sage Adi Shankara, who travelled from Kerala in the extreme south to Kashmir in the extreme north and from Dwarka in the west to Puri in the east, as far back as the seventh century after Christ, establishing temples in each of these places that endure to this day. Diana Eck's writings on India's 'sacred geography' extensively delineate ancient ideas of a political unity mediated through ideas of sacredness. As Eck explains: 'Considering its long history, India has had but a few hours of political and administrative unity. Its unity as a nation, however, has been firmly constituted by the sacred geography it has held in common and revered: its mountains, forests, rivers, hilltop shrines… linked with the tracks of pilgrimage.'

Nor was this oneness a purely 'Hindu' idea. The rest of the world saw India as one: Arabs, for instance, regarded the entire subcontinent as 'al-Hind' and all Indians as 'Hindi', whether they hailed from Punjab, Bengal or Kerala. The great nationalist Maulana Azad once remarked upon how, at the Haj, all Indians were considered to be from one land, and regarded themselves as such. Surely such impulses, fulfilled in those distant times by emperors and sages, would, with modern transport, communications and far-sighted leaders, have translated themselves into political unity?

Starting from these incontrovertible facts, it is possible to construct an alternative scenario to British colonialism in the late eighteenth and early nineteenth centuries, with the Marathas extending their conquests across the country, while finding it politically convenient to mask their power under a titular Mughal emperor, a process that had already begun. Though the Marathas would have ruled the country under the nominal overlordship of a weak Mughal monarch (as the British themselves were briefly to do), this would have led to an inevitable transition to constitutional rule, just as England transitioned (with the seventeenth-century Glorious Revolution and the subsequent strengthening of the House of Commons) from an absolute monarchy to a constitutional monarchy. This could have happened in India just as it did in several other countries in the non-colonized world, across Europe and in the handful of Asian countries that were not colonized, notably China, Japan and Thailand. The process would not have been painless; there may well have been revolutions and military struggles; there would have been disruption and conflict; but India's resources would have stayed in India and its future would have been resolved by its own people. The onset of British colonialism interrupted this natural evolution and did not allow it to flower. But to suggest that Indian political unity would not have happened without the British is absurd and unsupported by the evidence.

Counterfactuals are, of course, impossible to prove. One cannot assert, for instance, with any degree of certitude, events that did not in fact occur, nor name that centralizing figure who might have been India's Bismarck, Mazzini, Atatürk or Garibaldi in the absence of the British. But historical events find their own dramatis personae, and it is unreasonable to suggest that what happened everywhere else would not have happened in India. From such an initially hybrid system could have emerged a modern constitutional monarchy and political institutions built upon the Mughal administrative system, as modified by the Marathas. But these are hypotheticals. The British came, and no such non-colonial India emerged.

Counterfactuals are theoretical but facts are what they are. The facts point clearly to the dismantling of existing political institutions in India by the British, the fomenting of communal division and systematic political discrimination with a view to maintaining and extending British domination.

When the British eventually left in 1947, they left India as a functioning democracy, and many Britons would take credit for having instilled in their Indian subjects the spirit of democracy and the rule of law, even if Indians were denied its substance by the British. This claim is worth examining closely.

The Destruction of Political Institutions

It is arguable that the democratic values of the British imperialists were more highly developed than those of other colonists. Some scholars have recently demonstrated, with impressive statistics (based on analyses of the aggregate correlates of political regimes), that a large number of former British colonies are democracies, and, indeed, that having once been a British colony is the variable most highly correlated with democracy. Myron Weiner has pointed out that, except for countries in the Americas, 'every country with a population of at least 1 million (and almost all the smaller countries as well) that has emerged from colonial rule and has had a continuous democratic experience is a former British colony'. (There have also been former British colonies whose democratic experience has not been continuous, but featured bouts of military dictatorship, including both Pakistan and Bangladesh.) So it would seem that however much they failed to live up to their own ideas—however strongly they denied to Indians, as they had to Americans before 1776, 'the rights of Englishmen'—the British did instil sufficient doses of the ethos of democracy into their former colonies that it outlived their tutelage.

But the actual history of British rule does not suggest this was either policy or practice.

In the years after 1757, the British astutely fomented cleavages among the Indian princes, and steadily consolidated their dominion through a policy of 'divide and rule' that came to be dubbed, after 1858, '*divide et impera*'. At this time it was a purely political ploy, and the divisions the Company sought to encourage were entirely based on greed and the desire for self-advancement rather than religion or social group. One aristocratic cousin was pitched against another for the Company's support; often it was merely a question of who could pay more to the British. Loyalties were purchasable, sometimes more than once. Thus in 1757, as we have seen, Clive installed Mir Jafar on the throne of Bengal for a handsome sum, as a reward for having betrayed the previous nawab, Siraj-ud-Daula, at Plassey; Clive's successors deposed Mir Jafar and put Mir Kasim in his place for somewhat less (for the money went to them, after all, and not to Clive); three years later, they restored Mir Jafar, since he now paid them two and a half times more than Mir Kasim did; and two years after that, they took money from Najim-ud-Daula to depose Mir Jafar yet again. That sort of 'bribe, suborn and rule' system was comprehensible in terms of the crass motives that animated the East India Company in India. But it would be a forerunner of a more insidious divide-and-rule policy from the late nineteenth century, which instigated Indian against Indian on the basis of divisions that would do far more lasting damage.

The early crude practices of installing and defenestrating the rulers behind whose nominal authority the East India Company would rule, revealed little respect for the existing political institutions of India nor for the need to develop them to face the challenges of a new era. But the weakening of India's political institutions went deeper. As part of the 'Permanent Settlement', the British enfeebled village communities, since they made direct arrangements with individual local potentates in order to increase revenue collections. They also centralized judicial and executive powers, functions previously dispensed by village communities in their jurisdiction. Reports written by observers of the Company described the village communities as self-governing republics and functioning economic units, linked to the wider precolonial global market, that had governed themselves even as powers at the centre came and went. Under the British this ceased to be true.

It is important to remember that these villages did not exist in some kind of rustic agrarian isolation but were active and functioning political and economic units as well. 'In India,' wrote an eminent English civil servant, 'the village system was the one organism that survived the long years of anarchy and invasion, and it was in full vigour when we conquered India. Those who care to read up the subject can see it in Sir Henry Sumner Maine's *Indian Village Communities*.' But instead of building self-government from the village level up, as the British could have done had they been sincere, the Company destroyed what existed, and the Crown, when it eventually took charge of the country, devolved smidgens of government authority, from the top, to unelected provincial and central 'legislative' councils whose members represented a tiny educated elite, had no accountability to the masses, passed no meaningful legislation, exercised no real power and satisfied themselves they had been consulted by the government even if they took no actual decisions.

Part of the problem was that the Indian social structures were unfamiliar to the British, whose own villages survived in a largely feudalistic relationship to their landlords. Empire was in many ways the vehicle for the extension of British social structures to the colonies they conquered. The socio-political constructs that the British made in their Empire were primarily reflections of the traditional, individualistic, unequal and still class-ridden society that existed in England. The architects of Empire, responding to what they knew, sought to recreate the rural arcadia of Tory England, where local government since the sixteenth century had been controlled by those with high social prestige and ruled by an established squirearchy. Instead of the autonomous village governments the British dismantled in India, English villages were in the hands of the traditional lords, the grandees being supplemented by gentry attached to them. The English tried to find similar structures in the traditional societies of their colonies, and when they could not, they invented an approximation of them. Thus was born the 'indirect rule' system of government that characterized much of the Empire, with power devolved to an entire hierarchy of greater and lesser imitation 'gentlemen', many given British-invented titles like 'Rai Bahadur' or even knighted (and, in a couple of cases, ennobled) for their pains. This was both less expensive for the Empire and, as with the English system at home, it was run by complicit amateurs, so there was no need to create a professional class of Indians who would wield, and then seek to exercise, political authority.

This British practice, previously unknown in India, caused long-lasting damage. The historian Jon Wilson has argued that India had a dynamic economic and political order—'a society of little societies'—where constant negotiation between the rulers and the ruled was the norm. India's villages were not self-reliant republics that lived in blissful isolation. They were networked and connected, and it was the destruction of Indian industry that forced people to retreat and focus on farming, creating both a more agrarian society and the problem of peasant dispossession. By the early 1800s, India had been reduced from a land of artisans, traders, warriors and merchants, functioning in thriving and complex commercial networks, into an agrarian society of peasants and moneylenders. Extensive scholarship has shown how the British created the phenomenon of landlessness, turned self-reliant cultivators into tenants, employees and bondsmen, transformed social relations and as a result undermined agrarian growth and development. The impact of such policies endures to the present day and has had a distorting effect on India's evolution: Banerjee and Iyer, for instance, demonstrate how British colonial policy choices led to sustained differences in economic outcomes: 'Areas in which proprietary rights in land were historically given to landlords have significantly lower agricultural investments and productivity in the post-independence period than areas in which these rights were given to the cultivators.' There are no victimless colonial actions: everything the British did echoes down the ages.

Underlying the British imperial expansion in India was a congeries of motivations and assumptions—crass commercial cupidity, as we have demonstrated, and the need to consolidate political power in order to safeguard profits, but also the racist European notion, expressed most bluntly during the Iberian conquest of the New World, that 'heathen' Indian nations were unworthy of the status of sovereign legal entities. In the Americas, hostility to European traders and resistance to the Christian gospel were considered adequate causes for 'just' war, justifying territorial conquest and the enslavement of the losers. While such a proposition was not explicitly advanced in India, the British broadly shared the same sets of beliefs as their European confrères in the West.

Initially the game of thrones was played one step removed, as it were, with nawabs propped up by the Company as the official rulers. This was because the Company's official status, as of 1764, was as revenue administrators of three major Mughal provinces in eastern India, an authority granted, as we have seen, by a *firman* from the chastened and weak-kneed Mughal emperor, who issued an edict to this effect. Robert Clive explained his role to the board of directors of the East India Company in a letter dated 27 January 1764: 'We may be regarded as the spring which, concealed under the shadow of the Nabob's name, secretly gives motion to this vast machine of government without offering violence to the original constitution. The increase of our own, and diminution of his, power are effected without encroachment on his prerogative. The Nabob holds in his hands, as he always did, the whole civil administration, the distribution of justice, the disposal of offices, and all those sovereign rights which constitute the essence of his dignity, and form the most convenient barrier between us and the jealousy of the other European settlements.'

Arguably, however, the reality of British paramountcy over India had already become clear thanks to the numerous military victories of the East India Company over Indian princes, and the unequal treaties that reified their subjugation. William Bolts, a Dutch trader who had worked for a few years for the East India Company, wrote in 1772 that the Company was nothing more than a despotic oligarchy of merchants who had usurped the status of sovereigns. The Nawab of Bengal was little more than a 'stipendiary servant' and the Mughal emperor, a pensioner and a 'mere instrument of their power'. The fig leaf of revenue administration was, according to Bolts, a 'mere fiction' invented to legitimize the acquisition of these newly acquired territorial possessions 'for the private purposes of the Company and their servants'. The British historian Edward Thompson argues that after 1819, when Lord Lake defeated the Marathas, 'only stupidity or hypocrisy, or an excess of tactfulness, could pretend that the East India Company was not the paramount power or that any of the [Indian] Princes were equal to its status'.

Presiding over all of this was the governor-general of India, an executive appointed by the East India Company but, in effect, the monarch of all he surveyed. William Dalrymple quotes one contemporary observer as saying: 'Of all human conditions, perhaps the most brilliant and at the same time the most anomalous, is that of the Governor-General of British India. A private English gentleman, and the servant of a joint-stock company, during the brief period of his government he is the deputed sovereign of the greatest empire in the world; the ruler of a hundred million men; while dependent kings and princes bow down to him with a deferential awe and submission. There is nothing in history analogous to this position...'

The ad hoc nature of the expansion of British power brought with it its own deinstitutionalization of India's governance. Between 1746 and 1763 the Company fought three 'Carnatic Wars', which combined a quest for local dominance with a British conflict for supremacy against the French, mirroring the parallel wars in Europe at the same time. In many of its conquests and campaigns the Company did not hesitate to outsource its military efforts to mercenaries and armed bands of various sorts. Scholars see the East India Company as an example of a military patronage state, which distributed its patronage to itinerant bands of warriors without regard to any formal or institutional structures. The Company paid soldiers in exchange for their service and others for essential procurements, offering various benefits to ensure their support. Violence, to use today's language, was contracted to non-state actors. Such methods accentuated the informal, non-institutionalized nature of the British conquest of India, stunting the prospect of the normal development of political institutions in the country.

This resort to free-floating mercenary warrior elements served India ill. Lord Cornwallis, for instance, did not have the resources to provide irregular mounted units with regular rations, so he ordered them to find their own means of subsistence. This led to pillage and extortion as the troops advanced, only adding to the suffering and deprivation of the indigenous population; but then the well-being of the inhabitants had never been a priority for the Company. The freelance warriors and mercenaries associated with the Company enjoyed the license to loot everything they could lay their hands on: hardly a British contribution to good governance in India.

This method of expansion was not to last, however, thanks to the Company's unquestioned military superiority, especially once 'the other European settlements' Clive had referred to had all been routed or taught their place, and the Company—though still a trading corporation—soon had few compunctions about deposing native princes and absorbing their kingdoms. The Crown, when it assumed responsibility for the Raj, through Queen Victoria's Proclamation of 1858, largely preferred to leave the traditional rulers of India in place, with their authority subordinate to the British. (They exercised their power through an official parked at the princely court with the nominally modest title of 'the Resident', another case of British understatement masking the uglier reality of brute power.)

Where the British during their gradual takeover of India did not annex the territory of a subjugated ruler, they made him sign an unequal treaty. This mixture of devices by which the British ruled India was, as I have pointed out throughout this chapter, far from conducive to the development of Indian political institutions, and nor did it engender respect for the nominal authority in whose name power was supposedly exercised.

It is also pertinent to nail the canard that whatever the deficiencies of the Company, its rule was no worse than the supposedly rapacious princes whom the British supplanted. This is simply false. Much of the British conquest and expansion before 1857 took place against either benign, or not particularly oppressive, native rulers. The Maratha Peshwas, the Mysore rulers and the chess-playing Nawab of Oudh, to name three, were not accused of misgovernance: they were merely too powerful for colonial comfort or too rich to avoid attracting British avarice. (Indeed there were outstanding examples of good governance in India at the time, notably the Travancore kingdom, which in 1819 became the first government in the world to decree universal, compulsory and free primary education for both boys and girls.) The British charges against the rulers they overthrew were largely specious: a 1907 study concluded that 'we discover that there is little basis for all this pessimism of the past beyond the eagerness to exalt, however dishonestly, the superiority of European methods'. Where British charges of misrule had any validity, they were principally against rulers the Company had installed in the first place or, in the twentieth century, princes they had removed from their cultural context and educated at Eton and Harrow, leaving them aliens in their own land.

This is not to suggest that precolonial India was universally well-ruled—as we know, it was going through a period of disintegration, collapsing Mughal authority, and in many places, conditions bordering on anarchy—but is merely intended to reject the notion that British rapacity would have been seen as an improvement by most Indians of that time. In large parts of India during the period of British colonial expansion, fairly decent governments, broadly accepted by the people, were removed and replaced by British rulers whose motives and methods were, on the whole, much more reprehensible than those they had overthrown.

The Crown Takes Over Its Jewel

While the case against the misgovernance of Company rule in India is irrefutable—having been made, among others, by Edmund Burke in his celebrated impeachment of Warren Hastings, by Macaulay in his denunciations of the greed of the nabobs, and by Clive himself through his act of suicide—the assumption of power by the British Crown of its imperial 'jewel' changes the argument somewhat. With Queen Victoria's Proclamation in 1858, the British offered a different narrative for their rule of India: that they would govern in pursuit of 'that prosperity and that social advancement which can only be secured by internal peace and good government...' The Queen added her 'earnest desire to stimulate the peaceful industry of India, to promote works of public utility and improvement, and to administer the government for the benefit of all our subjects resident therein. In their prosperity will be our strength, in their contentment our security, and in their gratitude our best reward'.

This was a stirring manifesto of the 'we are ruling you for your own good' school, far removed, at least in declared intent, from the naked rapacity of the East India Company. With the coronation of 1877, the British monarchy was reinvented by Benjamin Disraeli as an imperial instrument—the queen became an empress, with India the newest and most glittering possession, and her domains stretched across the world to an unprecedented extent. Equally important to the imperial project was the perception of grandeur that accompanied it. The British in India spent a great deal on extravagant display, but the gaudy glitter also had an imperial purpose: it was intended by the British, suggests Jan Morris, 'partly to amaze the indigenes, partly to fortify themselves. In a country of princes, they deliberately used the mystique of monarchy as an instrument of dominion.'

In pursuance of this 'schlock and awe' strategy, three gigantic durbars were held to mark imperial occasions—the crowning of Queen Victoria as the Empress of India was commemorated with the grand pageantry of an imperial durbar presided over by Viceroy Lord Lytton in 1887; the accession of Edward VII by an even grander durbar held by Lord Curzon on New Year's Day 1903; and the final imperial durbar of the Raj, in 1911, to welcome King George V and Queen Mary to the new capital, Delhi.

At the peak of its pomp, the British empire in India conceived and built an immense and hugely impressive new imperial capital at New Delhi. The French statesman Georges Clemenceau was sceptical, see-

47

ing it as the latest in a long line of imperial follies; it is said that he laughed when he saw half-built New Delhi in 1920 amid the rubble of seven previous cities in the same area, and observed: '*Ça sera la plus magnifique de toutes ces ruines.*' (This will be the most magnificent of all these ruins.) Years later, the management theorist C. Northcote Parkinson would cite the building of New Delhi among many examples in formulating his 'second law', that institutions build their grandest monuments just before they crumble into irrelevance.

Morris describes in lavish detail the imperial durbar conducted by Lord Curzon in Delhi, where, amid elephants and trumpets, bejewelled maharajas paying tribute and a public assembled from all four corners of the subcontinent to view the imperial panoply, 'theatre became life'. Appropriately enough, Curzon had the durbar filmed, using the-then novel technology of the moving image. (Though Mahatma Gandhi, in his autobiography, noted that many of the maharajas privately deplored the lengths to which they had to go, the elaborate costumes and finery they had to wear, in order to impress the British sufficiently to hold on to their thrones and their privileges.)[4]

Curzon, who conducted the grandest of the three durbars just two years after a ruinous famine, was the epitome of imperial majesty as Viceroy. What Jan Morris called Curzon's 'taste for lordliness,' and Niall Ferguson dubs his 'Toryentalism', was integral to his viceroyalty, which he conducted in a manner and with a paternalism befitting a scion of the old British aristocracy (his family was descended from Norman stock). Curzon's public life had long been haunted by four lines of Balliol doggerel targeting him in his student days at Oxford, which were unfailingly cited by the popular press whenever he received a new appointment: 'My name is George Nathaniel Curzon / I am a most superior person / My hair is black, my face is sleek / I dine at Blenheim every week'.[5] If this undergraduate humour had immortal-

---

[4] It was not just the maharajas who had to suffer: every Indian schoolchild must lament the influence of the British dress code on Indians—especially the tie as a permanent noose around the necks of millions of schoolchildren, in India's sweltering heat, even today.

[5] I have consulted British newspapers of the 1890s to satisfy myself of the accuracy of this version. It has since been improved in the retelling, and some readers might be more familiar with the altered update of the verse: 'My

ized him, so would his viceroyalty, which was to eclipse every other accomplishment in his ultimately disappointing political career. Curzon had nurtured the ambition to be Viceroy since childhood, and he brought to it a vision of imperial grandeur that he sought both in substance and style to fulfil.

The style that Curzon brought to its apogee reflected what the British writer David Cannadine dubbed 'Ornamentalism'. Curzon was, to Cannadine, a 'ceremonial impresario'. Cannadine devoted an entire book to the proposition that the British empire was about 'antiquity and anachronism, tradition and honour, order and subordination; about glory and chivalry, horses and elephants, knights and peers, processions and ceremony, plumed hats and ermine robes; about chiefs and emirs, sultans and nawabs, viceroys and proconsuls; about thrones and crowns, dominion and hierarchy, ostentation and ornamentalism'. It continued in this vein right until the final surrender, when the ceremonial costumes of the last Viceroy, Lord Louis Mountbatten, seemed to be in inverse proportion to his dwindling hold on political power.

This pageantry involved the British not merely exalting the principle of hierarchy in ensuring reverence for their own queen, but extending it to India, honouring 'native princes', ennobling others and promoting the invention of ersatz aristocratic tradition so as to legitimize their rule. Thus the British created a court culture that the princes had to follow, and a hierarchy that sought to show the Crown as successors of the Mughal emperor. The elaborately-graded gun salutes, from nine guns to nineteen (and in only five cases, twenty-one)[6], depending on the importance, and cooperativeness, of the ruler in question; the regulation of who was and was not a 'Highness', and of what kind (the Nizam of Hyderabad went from being His Highness to His Exalted Highness during World War I, mainly because of his vast donation of money to the war

---

name is George Nathaniel Curzon/I am a most superior person./My cheek is pink, my hair is sleek/I dine at Blenheim every week.'

[6] Up to World War I, only Hyderabad, Baroda and Mysore enjoyed 21-gun salutes; Gwalior and Jammu & Kashmir were added to the list in 1917 and 1921 in appreciation of their soldiers' services to the British in the Great War. Other monarchs were allowed 21-gun salutes within their own domains, but only 19 outside, and so on: the protocol was fastidiously elaborate.

effort); the careful lexicon whereby the 'native chiefs' (not 'kings'), came from 'ruling', not 'royal', families, and their territories were 'princely states' not 'kingdoms'—all these were part of an elaborate system of monarchical illusion-building. The India Office in London even had a room with two identical doors for entry, in case two Indian potentates of equivalent rank had to be received at the same time, so that neither had to precede the other. And so it went…

For all the elaborate protocol and ostentation, as David Gilmour points out, the British had very little respect for the Indian aristocracy they were indulging. Curzon himself sneered at 'the category of half-Anglicised, half-denationalised, European women-hunting, pseudo-sporting, and very often in the end spirit-drinking young native chiefs'. But he realized that Britain alone was to blame for the invention of the Indian royals as an imperial category. In 1888, one imperial official in Central India reported that in his zone of responsibility the result of 'an English training for princely youths' so far was 'sodomites 2, idiots 1, sots 1…[and a] gentleman …prevented by chronic gonorrhoea from paying his respects on the Queen's birthday'. Curzon himself complained in 1900 of the 'frivolous and sometimes vicious spendthrifts and idlers' who made up the bejewelled ranks of the Indian princes. The Rana of Dholpur, he wrote to Queen Victoria, was 'fast sinking into an inebriate and a sot', the Maharaja of Patiala was 'little better than a jockey', the Maharaja Holkar was 'half-mad' and 'addicted to horrible vices', and the Raja of Kapurthala was only happy philandering in Paris. Of course, there were enlightened and benevolent Indian princes, and even visionary ones—Baroda, Travancore and Mysore, to name three, enjoyed stellar reputations as exemplary rulers concerned about the well-being of their subjects—but stories of dissolute rajas were far more frequent than tales of good governance.

The Un-Indian Civil Service

If the panoply and external trimmings of the Crown's takeover of India were grand enough, the queen went farther in respect of the substance of her rule. In her celebrated 1858 Proclamation, she expressed her wish that 'our subjects, of whatever race or creed, be freely and impartially admitted to office in our service, the duties of which they may be qualified by their education, ability and integrity duly to discharge'.

DID THE BRITISH GIVE INDIA POLITICAL UNITY?

But what was the reality? In Will Durant's words, it was one of 'political exclusion and social scorn'. In 1857, F. J. Shore, the colonial administrator in Bengal whom I have quoted earlier, testifying before the House of Commons, confessed that 'the Indians have been excluded from every honour, dignity or office which the lowest Englishman could be prevailed upon to accept'. Decades later, Indian graduates from the finest universities of India, Europe and America found that, for the most part, only the lowest places in government service were open to them; according to Durant, just 4 per cent of the 'covenanted' positions in the Indian (initially the 'Imperial') Civil Service, the top cadre, were filled by Indians in as late as 1930.

As critics have pointed out, it is not as if the best and brightest staffed the posts available to Britons in India. Lord Asquith declared in 1909 that 'if high places were given to Hindus half as unfit as the Englishmen who then occupied them in India, it would be regarded as a public scandal'. Mediocrities ruled the roost, and they were paid far more than Indians, since they had to endure the 'hardships' of the Indian heat—despite the warmth of the sun offering a welcome respite, for most, from the cold and fog of grey, benighted Blighty. (As Rudyard Kipling memorably put it in his novel, *The Light That Failed*, describing a return to London: 'A thin grey fog hung over the city, and the streets were very cold; for summer was in England.') They were also, as a rule, singularly smug and self-satisfied and insufferably patronizing in their attitudes to Indians (when they were not simply contemptuous). Jawaharlal Nehru put it sharply: the Indian Civil Service, he said, was 'neither Indian, nor civil, nor a service'.

The British ruled nineteenth-century India with unshakeable self-confidence, buttressed by protocol, alcohol and a lot of gall. Stalin found it 'ridiculous' that 'a few hundred Englishmen should dominate India'. He was not arithmetically accurate, but in principle he was right: it was remarkable that the British Raj was run by so few people. There were only 31,000 Britons in India in 1805 (of whom 22,000 were in the army and 2,000 in civil government). The number increased substantially after 1857, but still, as of 1890, 6,000 British officials ruled 250 million Indians, with some 70,000 European soldiers and a larger number of Indians in uniform. In 1911, there were 164,000 Britons living in India (of whom 66,000 were in the army and police and just 4,000 in civil government). By 1931, this had gone up to just 168,000 (including 60,000 in the army and police and still only 4,000 in civil government) to run a country approaching 300 million people. It was an extraordinary combination of racial self-assurance, superior military technology, the mystique of modernity and the trappings of enlightenment progressivism—as well as, it must be said clearly, the cravenness, cupidity, opportunism and lack of organized resistance on the part of the vanquished—that sustained the Empire, along with the judicious application of brute force when necessary. The British in India were never more than 0.05 per cent of the population. The Empire, in Hobsbawm's evocative words, was 'so easily won, so narrowly based, so absurdly easily ruled thanks to the devotion of a few and the passivity of the many.'

In Clive's time, the Company presided over a 'dual' system: the Company exercised power but propped up a puppet nawab. Warren Hastings ended the pretence and overthrew the nawab: direct administration was now under the control of the Company. Cornwallis, in 1785, created a professional cadre of Company servants who were to govern the country for the Company, reserving all high-level posts for the British, and placing Englishmen in charge of each district with the blunt title of 'Collector', since collecting revenue was their raison d'etre. The Collector usually exercised the dual function of magistrate in his district.[7] The British thus ran government, tax collection, and administered what passed for justice. Indians were excluded from all of these functions.

With these tasks to be performed, a civil service came into being, nominated by the Company's bigwigs from influential young people of

[7] The British ran a complex administrative system with multiple variants. In essence, and at its peak, British India, under the Governor-General (later Viceroy), was divided into a number of presidencies and provinces, each headed by a Governor, Lieutenant Governor or Commissioner, depending upon its size and importance. Each province or presidency comprised a number of divisions, each headed by a Divisional Commissioner. These divisions were in turn subdivided into districts, which were the basic administrative units; each district was headed by a Collector and District Magistrate or Deputy Commissioner (in most cases these were all the same person, usually a young Englishman in his mid to late twenties).

their acquaintance, and trained after 1806 in Haileybury College, near London, to serve the Company. After 1833, competitive examinations were introduced, though directors' nominees could still be recruited on a nod and a wink. After 1853, selection was entirely examination-based, and thrown open to all white Britons. Demand for the Imperial Civil Service was high, since the work was ridiculously well-compensated, and the Company's servants exercised genuine political power in India, which they could not hope to do in any equivalent job they might get in Britain. The tests did not seek to establish any knowledge of India or any sensitivity to its peoples; they sought to identify proper English gentlemen, and emphasized classical learning and good literary skills. After 1860, Indians were allowed to take the examinations too. But the Indian Civil Service remained, in ethos, British. One viceroy, Lord Mayo, declared, 'we are all British gentlemen engaged in the magnificent work of governing an inferior race'. Few shared Victoria's 'romantic feelings for brown skins'. In David Gilmour's telling, they had no illusions about preparing Indians for self-government; their view of Indians was at best paternalist, at worst contemptuous (well into the twentieth century, they spoke and wrote of the need to treat Indians as 'children', incapable of ruling themselves). Several generations of some families served in India, some over three centuries, without ever establishing roots there: they sent their own children 'home' to school and 'endured' years of separation from loved ones. It was not, of course, all self-sacrifice and hard work: ICS men earned the highest salaries of any officials in the world, with, as we have seen, generous furloughs and a guaranteed pension, and some at least found it 'quite impossible' to spend their income. The English political reformer John Bright, unsurprisingly, called the Empire a 'gigantic system of outdoor relief for the aristocracy of Great Britain'.

The attitudes the ICS men brought to bear to their work in India had greatly deteriorated by the end of the nineteenth century from curiosity and concern to complacency and cant. 'The whole attitude of Government to the people it governs is vitiated,' wrote H. Fielding-Hall, after thirty years of service in the ICS. 'There is a want of knowledge and understanding. In place of it are fixed opinions based usually on prejudice or on faulty observation, or on circumstances which have changed, and they are never corrected. Young secretaries read up back circulars, and repeat their errors indefinitely…"following precedent".'

The British Labour politician Keir Hardie described British rule in India as 'a huge military despotism tempered somewhat by a civil bureaucracy'. That bureaucracy was all-pervasive, overpaid, obtusely process-ridden, remarkably inefficient and largely indifferent to the well-being of the people for whose governance it had, after all, been created. Lord Lytton, in a lighter mood, described British governance in India as 'a despotism of office-boxes tempered by an occasional loss of keys'. This bureaucratic despotism went back to the early years of Company rule in the late eighteenth century, when Lord Cornwallis had announced that 'all rights had been reduced to writing'. As John Stuart Mill, who luxuriated in the title of 'Examiner of Indian Correspondence' for the East India Company, put it, the 'great success of our Indian administration' was that it was 'carried on in writing'. But this was in fact the great flaw of the British system. Indian rulers had in the past negotiated with their local subjects because they had to live with them. Now the Company kept a distance from its subjects and only cared for one thing—a network that delivered cash to directors in faraway London as quickly and efficiently as possible. In reality, as Jon Wilson points out, the extraordinary flow of paper that Mill celebrated 'constructed a world of letters, ledgers and account books that had its own pristine order but could not comprehend or rule the forces which shaped rural society…the new maze of paperwork blocked the creation of the public, reciprocal relationship between the state and local lords which political authority and economic prosperity had relied on before'.

It also meant that decisions were increasingly made in offices, behind closed doors, by foreigners with no connection to those whose fates they were deciding. The public display of the rulers' authority was replaced by the private circulation of incomprehensible paper. Decisions were being made by people who were out of the view of those impacted by the decisions. As the public places where Indians could hold their rulers to account were out of bounds, so the scope for intrigue and corruption expanded. Indians were anxious that decisions were being made over which they had no say. Clerks were bribed to find out what was being written in the all-important files. The Raja of Nadia was so concerned about what was happening behind closed doors that he paid a Bengali clerk in the Collector's office to tell him what was written in the letters exchanged between the district capital and Calcutta.

The old accessible Indian rulers were replaced by new officious British bureaucrats who were good at manipulating the paperwork created by the new rules but had little interest in the well-being of their subjects nor the capacity to establish their authority other than by reference to their rules. When these were violated, they could only take recourse in the forcible imposition of law and order. 'The new system was not designed to create a stable political order in the Indian countryside,' says Wilson. 'Its aim was to defend the integrity of the East India Company from accusations in Britain of venality and vice. It began life as an effort to manage metropolitan moral anguish, not to handle the complaints of Indians about what Company officers were doing in India.' The neat registers kept in the Company's offices 'allowed British officials to imagine they had created an effective, unitary structure of rule; they fostered a delusion of power'.

This was the tradition that the Company passed on to the Crown, which continued it without change. Much of the British bureaucracy, as Lytton implied, was excessively formalistic; perhaps the obsession with procedure and paperwork resulted from a sneaking hope that anything resulting from the filling of forms in quadruplicate could not possibly be an injustice. (Or written on stamp paper, a British invention, that imparted a sense of authority to a document and gave the British a feeling of control.) Creating rule book after rule book concealed the fragile nature of the hold they had on the society they ruled. Regulations were framed and were meant to be applied across the board without reference to context and without any sensitivity to the circumstances of the individuals being regulated. Decisions were based on rules rather than facts, 'often merely disconnecting officers from the political circumstances that called upon them to make decisions in the first place'.

The British system of rule in India was, by any standards, remarkable. A twenty-four-year-old district officer found himself in charge of 4,000 square miles and a million people. The duties which the district officer had to perform were enumerated in a contemporary account as follows: 'Collector of the Land Revenue. Registrar of the landed property in the District. Judge between landlord and tenant. Ministerial officer of the Courts of Justice. Treasurer and Accountant of the District. Administrator of the District Excise. Ex officio President of the Local Rates Committee. Referee for all questions of compensation for lands taken up for public purposes. Agent for the Government in all local suits to which it is a party. Referee in local public works. Manager of estates of minors. Magistrate, Police Magistrate and Criminal Judge. Head of Police. Ex officio President of Municipalities...' All these tasks were performed by a young man, in a foreign country, with little knowledge of the local language or conditions, following uniform rules of procedure laid down by the distant government, but convinced of his innate superiority over those he had been assigned to rule and his God-given right to dispense authority in all these functions. Authority, but not welfare; there was no 'development work' listed for any British official in a district.

If all this were not enough, the young man was subject to the tyranny of the 'Warrant of Precedence' and the rigidities of protocol in a hierarchy-conscious society, learned the desperate importance of being able to play whist as an antidote to loneliness, and in, due course, to humour the incessant social obligations of higher office (a lieutenant-governor hosted, on a single day, a boathouse lunch, a thé dansant and a garden party, and a dinner at the club). The diversions were plentiful. Wedded inexcusably to its own pleasures, the British bureaucracy retreated to mountain redoubts in the hills for months on end to escape the searing heat of the plains, there to while away their time in entertainments, dances and social fripperies while the objects of their rule, the Indian people, were exploited ruthlessly below.

In the summer capital of Simla, with its population of 'grass widows' enjoying the cooler air while their husbands toiled in the hot plains, the 'main occupations' were 'gambling, drinking, and breaking the 7th Commandment'.

And yet there is no doubt about the heroic efforts of many individual civilians, who dug canals, founded colleges, administered justice and even, in some cases, advocated Indian self-rule. Their names became part of the geography of the subcontinent: towns called Abbottabad, Lyallpur and Cox's Bazar, Corbett Park, Cotton Hill, the Mcnabbwah Canal. As a rare left-winger in the ICS, John Maynard, explained, 'ugly pallid bilious men' were able to 'do great things in the very midst of their querulous discontents and unideal aspirations'.

But their lifestyles, for the most part, separated them from the masses they sought to rule. The British in India created little islands of Englishness, planting ferns and roses and giving their cottages nostalgia-suffused names like Grasmere Lodge (in Ooty) and Willowdale (in Darjeeling). By the early nineteenth century, the British had established themselves as a ruling caste, but at the top of the heap: they did not intermarry or inter-dine with the 'lower' castes, in other words, the Indians; they lived in bungalows in their own areas, known as cantonments and 'civil lines', separated from the 'Black Towns' where the locals lived; they kept to their clubs, to which Indians were not admitted; their loyalties remained wedded to their faraway homeland; their children were shipped off to the British public-school system and did not mingle with the 'natives'; their clothes and purchases came from Britain, as did their books and ideas. At the end of their careers in India, for the most part, they returned 'home'. As the English writer Henry Nevinson observed in the first decade of the twentieth century: 'A handful of people from a distant country maintain a predominance unmitigated by social intercourse, marriage, or permanent residence'. 'India,' wrote another sympathetic Englishman in 1907, 'is, in fact, now administered by successive relays of English carpet-baggers, men who go out with carpet-bags and return with chests, having ordinarily as little real sympathy with the natives as they have any deep knowledge of their habits and customs.'

The Indian Civil Service, peculiarly, insisted that all ICS men remain bachelors until after the age of thirty. This made them ripe for capture by the 'fishing-fleet', as the boatloads of Englishwomen who came over to India to trawl for husbands in the mid- and late-nineteenth century were known. These ladies were usually the rejects of the British upper and upper-middle classes, women who were too smart or too plain to find a 'good husband' and were in their late teens or early twenties. Once you were deemed too old for the English marriage-market, it was either the boat to India or a spinster's life as governess at home— and tales of the comforts of British life in the colonies certainly made the boat a more attractive option. ICS officers (and other civilians, for that matter), forbidden to consort with local women, bored, lonely and frustrated by thirty, were ripe for the picking. At English clubs and tennis matches, elegant balls and tiger shoots, the women of the 'fishing-fleet' allowed themselves to be reeled in by eligible civilians. Insulated from India by their upbringing and new social circumstances, waited upon by a flotilla of servants and ignorant of contact with any other Indian, and susceptible to the prejudices of white Victorian England, these women were often the most guilty of racism and disdain for the country. They were responsible for turning British society prim and proper and rather priggish in its attitudes to relations with Indians.

That was the life of the ICS men. Then, after twenty-five or more years in the subcontinent, as we have seen, they would retire to Cheltenham or South Kensington, to English suburbs that became known as 'Asia Minor' or 'the Anglo-Indian Quarter', surrounded by reminders and relics of the land they had ruled. One civilian settled in Teddington on the Thames and named his last home 'Quetta', for the capital of Baluchistan. Another, William Strachey, set his watch to Calcutta time even in England, 'eating breakfast at tea-time and living most of his life by candlelight'. It is a poignant image. But the candle-light has dimmed: the places named for the British have mostly been renamed. Lyallpur, in Pakistan, has been renamed Faisalabad, for a Saudi king. The old ruling caste no longer takes precedence.

Indians in Imperial Service

The very element that indicts this system in the eyes of an Indian—its foreignness and its disconnection from the Indian people for whose benefit it was supposed to govern—was, however, seen as a virtue in English eyes. The promised admission of Indians to the ICS was resisted at every level of the British government, and it had to be prised from the British grasp like the last gold nugget from the fist of a dead prospector. Even a moderate civil servant like H. Fielding-Hall (who, after retirement, wrote books about India that were suffused with sympathy for Indians though leavened by imperial attitudes), had this to say in objecting to the admission of Indians into the covenanted civil services: 'the Government of India is not Indian, it is English. It is essentially English, the more so and the more necessarily so because it is in India... England has made herself responsible for India, and she cannot shirk or divide this responsibility'. He added: 'Government must do its work in its own way, and that is the English way. No Indian can tell what this is.'

The result was that there were more statues to Queen Victoria on Indian territory than Indians in the higher reaches of the civil service. There was always, of course, the excuse of a substantive, as opposed to merely racialist, argument: 'It would be impossible to place Indian civilians in places where co-operation with military or military police-officers would be essential'. But the essence of the problem emerged soon enough. The whites in India would never accept an Indian in a position of real authority. Fielding-Hall insisted in 1913: 'That an Indian should rule Europeans, and that it should be to an Indian they looked for the maintenance of peace and order and for the administration of justice, criminal and civil, is unthinkable. The stability of the administration is due to its being English, and any threat to that stability would not be borne.'

In substantiation of his case, Fielding-Hall recounted the experience of an early Indian in the ICS, a 'Mr Chetty', who after an English education at Wren's and Oxford, ranked high in the civil services examination and was posted to a district in India. But there the club—the centre of all social life for officialdom and other English civilians—refused to admit him as a member. This was more than a personal privation: it was an absolute handicap in his career, since so much official work, and so many professional relationships, were dealt with and processed over a drink at the club. Fielding-Hall, who did not disapprove of the racial discrimination practised by his fellow Englishmen, blamed it on the unwise policy of recruiting Indians for jobs only the English should do. He muses about ICS officers like Chetty: 'Socially he belongs to no world. He has left his own and cannot enter the other. And you cannot divorce social life from official life. They are not two things, but one.' He adds: 'In the end Chetty shot himself. It was a sad end for a man gifted and likeable. And although such an end was unusual, the causes which led to it are universal. I have known several civilians who were Indians, and... I think they were all unhappy.'

This reads chillingly to any modern mind, but Fielding-Hall was by no means the worst of his tribe: reading him, you realize he was more broad-minded and humane than most of his peers. Racial discrimination was pervasive in the ICS. While Indians were theoretically entitled to senior positions in the Indian Civil Service, and Satyendranath Tagore (elder brother of the great Nobel Prize-winning poet Rabindranath Tagore) broke into its elite ranks as early as 1863, most applicants were turned down and only a handful succeeded him for decades afterwards. Satyendranath Tagore and the ones who came after him suffered the most appalling racial discrimination and personal humiliation in their careers. After thirty years' ICS service, in a series of insignificant posts, Satyendranath, who was a brilliant linguist, lyricist and social reformer, could only retire as a judge in the provincial Maharashtrian town of Satara.

Lord Lytton, writing confidentially as viceroy in 1878 to his superiors in London, was frank about the betrayal of 'educated Indians whose development the Government encourages without being able to satisfy the aspiration of its existing members; every such Indian, once admitted to Government employment in posts previously reserved to the Covenanted [i.e. the senior civil] Service, is entitled to expect and claim appointment in the fair course of promotion to the highest posts in that service. We all know that these claims and expectations *never can or will be fulfilled*. [emphasis in original] We have had to choose between prohibiting them and cheating them, and we have chosen the least straight-forward course.'

The cheating continued in awful ways for several decades more. Another of the very early Indian entrants into the ICS, the second after Satyendranath Tagore, Surendra Nath Banerjea, was initially barred from the service he had entered in 1869, on allegations of misrepresenting his age. He appealed this successfully and was posted to a minor position in Sylhet, but not forgiven, and was dismissed from the service altogether in 1874 for a minor infraction (an inadvertent procedural irregularity in requesting accommodation in the civil lines equal to that given to Britons, that might not have earned an English officer even a reprimand). He went on to become a distinguished academician, journalist, editor, orator (one English journalist hailed him as the finest orator he had heard in English since Gladstone) and twice president of the Indian National Congress, but it is noteworthy that an individual of intellectual and administrative ability far in excess of most of his contemporaries should have been seen by the British not as a talent to be made use of in the government's interest, but as an element to be eliminated by dismissal from its employment. (After nearly four decades of struggle, though, Banerjea, who memorably had urged his countrymen to 'agitate, agitate, agitate—you have yet to learn the great art of grumbling', accepted a knighthood. Perhaps, as disappointed nationalists argued, he had changed but by then, to some degree, so had the British. The path carved and hacked against such impossible odds by the first two ICS Indians was now trodden somewhat more easily by larger numbers of their countrymen.)

Similarly, Aurobindo Ghosh—then named Ackroyd Ghosh—after studying at Manchester, St Paul's School, and Cambridge University, also ranked second out of several thousand candidates in the examinations for the Indian Civil Service but unlike Banerjea, was not selected because he was deemed to have failed the riding test. (This may well have spared him the experience of being dismissed later on like his illustrious predecessor, since his temperament would have sat ill with British overlords. He went on to achieve worldwide renown and immortality as Sri Aurobindo, founder of a global spiritual movement that still flourishes in Pondicherry.)

It was only when World War I drove thousands of young British men to officer duty in the trenches rather than service in the Empire that the British grudgingly realized the need to recruit more Indians, and the numbers of Indians in the ICS slowly inched upwards in the last three decades of the Raj.

But till then, Indians may have had positions, but no real authority. A rare Cambridge-educated Indian judge appointed on the bench of the Allahabad High Court in 1887, Justice Syed Mahmud, suffered daily discrimination and prejudice, especially from Chief Justice Sir John Edge, who Mahmud felt treated him like a conquered subject rather than a judicial equal. As a young man freshly returned from England enthusiastic about Empire, Mahmud had dreamed of a day when 'the English people are known to us more as friends and fellow subjects, than as rulers and foreign conquerors'. That was not to be. On the verge of being dismissed, Mahmud—the second son of the famous reformer Sir Syed Ahmed Khan, whose support was so crucial for the British among Indian Muslims—resigned in 1892, unable to reconcile his faith in British law with his exclusion from the high table at the institutions administering it, turned to drink and depression, and died a broken man at the age of just fifty-three.

His father, Sir Syed Ahmed Khan, the founder of the Anglo-Mohammedan College and a famed advocate of British rule in India, wrote at the time of his son's forced resignation as a judge of the Allahabad High Court:

If an Indian in such a position tries to preserve his self-respect which is concomitant to nobility and uprightness, the relations between him and his European colleagues get embittered. On the other hand, if utterly regardless of self-respect, he makes himself quite subservient to the wishes of his European colleague, who because he belongs to a conquering race, *naturally* believes in his superiority, he is able to pull on pretty well. But this can never be expected from a man who wishes to remain true to his conscience, and in whose veins runs the blood of his (noble) ancestors. It is no secret that there is as much difference between the Englishman's treatment of his own countryman and that of others as there is between *black* and *white* [emphasis in original].

Black and white, night and day: the differences were rubbed in at every level. I have touched upon how well compensated British bureaucrats in India were, but what made things worse was how imbalanced their salaries were when compared with their local counterparts. In the first decades of the twentieth century, J. T. Sunderland observed that the difference in salaries and emoluments was so great that 8,000 British officers earned £13,930,554, while 130,000 Indians in government service were collectively paid a total of £3,284,163. The Indians were shown their place in their ranks, authority, positions assigned, lack of career advancement—and every month when their salary slips arrived.

The long-term consequences of this included the failure to build up human capital in India, as Dadabhai Naoroji argued in 1880: 'With the material wealth go also the wisdom and experience of the country. Europeans occupy almost all the higher places in every department of Government directly or indirectly under its control. While in India they acquire India's money, experience, and wisdom; and when they go, they carry both away with them, leaving India so much poorer in material and moral wealth. Thus India is left without, and cannot have those elders in wisdom and experience who in every country are the natural guides of the rising generations in their national and social conduct, and of the destinies of their country; and a sad, sad loss this is!'

Imperial Racism: Only Disconnect

But this was deliberate policy. William Makepeace Thackeray spoke of the need to suppress 'haughtiness', 'deep thought' and 'independence' of spirit in India: 'they are directly adverse to our powers and interest.

We do not want generals, statesmen and legislators. We want industrious husbandmen'. The result, of course, was racist discrimination in every sphere. As a tract put out by the 'Indian National Party' in London in 1915 argued: 'It is not the Roman System of thoroughly Latinizing and assimilating the subject races that is tried by England, but the system of exploitation and degradation of a race by another for the material benefits of the latter.'

This racism infected every aspect of the Empire, and not just its civil service. Racism, of course, was central to the imperial project: it was widespread, flagrant and profoundly insulting, and it worsened as British power grew. It is instructive to note the initial attitudes of whites in India when they were not yet in a dominant position. William Dalrymple has described well how the rule of the East India Company, in the first two centuries from 1600 to 1800, was characterized by a remarkable level of interaction between the colonized and the colonizer. This included not just business ties and political and financial relations, but friendships, love affairs, and, quite frequently, marriage. During the eighteenth century, Dalrymple writes, 'it was almost as common for Westerners to take on the customs and even the religions of India as the reverse. Contrary to stereotype, a surprising number of company men responded to India by slowly shedding their Britishness like an unwanted skin and adopting Indian dress and taking on the ways of the Mughal governing class they came to replace'. Salman Rushdie has called this 'chutnification'; Dalrymple dubs the practitioners of this approach 'White Mughals'.

Between 1780 and 1785, Dalrymple says, 'the wills of company officials show that one in three were leaving everything to Indian wives, often accompanied by moving declarations of love asking their close friends to care for their "well beloved" Indian partners, or as one put it, "the excellent and respectable Mother of my two children for whom I feel unbounded love and affection and esteem". Family portraits from the period are remarkable for the ease with which two races and religions cohabit, with British men dressed in turbans and kurta pajamas, while their Indian wives sit in the European manner on European furniture. One official, the Boston-born Sir David Ochterlony, who every evening used to take all thirteen of his Indian consorts around Delhi, each on the back of her own elephant, went so far as to build a Mughal garden tomb for himself and his chief wife, where the central dome was topped by a cross and flanked by a forest of minarets. A note from Ochterlony gives a measure of the surprisingly multi-religious tone of this period. "Lady Ochterlony," he reported to Calcutta, "has applied for leave to make the Hadge to Mecca.'"

The contrast with the later half of British rule, with the assertion of incontestable British political and military dominance and the arrival of the 'fishing fleet', as well as the fear and rage that multiplied after the Revolt (or 'Mutiny') of 1857, is striking. Sir John Malcolm, later Governor of Bombay, wrote in 1832, 'our Eastern empire... has been acquired, and must be maintained, by the sword'. Not only was there no pretence of ruling with the consent of the governed ('a passive allegiance', Malcolm added, 'is all [Indians] will ever give to their foreign masters'); there was, in essence, almost complete apartheid, a profound belief in racial differences, 'and little friendship or marriage across strictly policed racial and religious boundaries.'

This became apparent again as late as 1942 during the disastrous British retreat from Malaya, Singapore and Burma. As Mahatma Gandhi wrote in his newspaper column in August 1942: 'Hundreds, if not thousands, on their way from Burma perished without food or drink, and the wretched discrimination stared even these miserable people in the face. One route for whites, another for blacks! Provision of food and shelter for the whites, none for the blacks! India is being ground down into the dust and humiliated even before the Japanese advent.' Bitterness at racial discrimination even in defeat played no small part in Gandhi's decision to launch the 'Quit India' movement that month, calling for Britain's departure from India.

Much of imperial literature portrayed the British empire as a 'family', the Queen as the benign mother figure presiding like a humourless matriarch over her far-flung progeny, the Indians as simple children in need of strict discipline, and the imperial space itself as a sort of elaborate Victorian drawing-room in which civilized manners could be imparted to the unruly heathen brood. This very metaphor pops up in the quarrel between Ronny and Mrs Moore in E. M. Forster's *A Passage to India*, when Ronny argues that 'India isn't a drawing-room' while his mother sees the domestic virtues of courtesy and kindness as leading the British empire into becoming 'a different institution'.

DID THE BRITISH GIVE INDIA POLITICAL UNITY?

The inversion of values so essential to the imperial project is evident in a story like Rudyard Kipling's 'Naboth', the tale of an Indian hawker or street-vendor who takes advantage of a colonial Englishman's kindness to gradually appropriate more and more of the latter's land and build himself a hut there. In the end, of course, the Englishman throws out the Indian (from what is, after all, Indian soil!) and the story ends with the lone narrator's triumphalism over the ungrateful Indian: 'Naboth is gone now, and his hut is ploughed into its native mud with sweetmeats instead of salt for a sign that the place is accursed. I have built a summer house to overlook the end of the garden, and it is as a fort on my frontier where I guard my Empire.'

Though he turned down several invitations to become Britain's Poet Laureate, Rudyard Kipling (1865–1936) was for much of his adult life the unofficial Poet Laureate of Empire. His roots as the quintessential writer of imperialism ran deep: Kipling, the cub reporter for seven years with newspapers in Lahore and Lucknow, was eighteen when Lord Ripon unsuccessfully attempted to allow Indian judges to try Europeans, and the controversy (in which he, of course, sympathized with his racist fellow settlers) shaped his attitude to the need for 'dominion' over 'lesser breeds without the Law'. Kipling wrote articles designed to show the inability of Indians to govern themselves, prefiguring Kipling the later imperial prophet declaiming thunderous anapests about the white man's burden. In both incarnations, Kipling the arch-imperialist, in the admission of a sympathetic biographer, wrote of Indians 'sometimes with a rare understanding, sometimes with crusty, stereotyped contempt'. What matters in Kipling's work is not Indians, not even the physical and social details of India that he knowingly throws into his narratives, but the vastness and passion animating his vision and rendering of Empire itself. Scholars have come to see Kipling's writings as 'part of the defining discourse of colonialism' which both 'reinscribe cultural hegemony and the cultural schizophrenia that constructed the division between the Englishman as demi-God and as human failure, as colonizer and semi-native'.

The British saw themselves as a civilizing force, the 'brave island-fortress/of the storm-vexed sea' in the line of the poet Sir Lewis Morris, written on the occasion of Queen Victoria's Diamond Jubilee. Macaulay, for all his sins, was more alive to the contradictions of the imperial mission: 'Be the father and the oppressor of the people,' he wrote, 'be just and unjust, moderate and rapacious.' Not every Englishman in India can be accused of having any great notions of serving such warped ideas of Empire. Many, like the teacher Cyril Fielding in Forster's *A Passage to India*, saw themselves as merely being in India because they needed the job—petty men in the service of a great cause they did not personally think about, a cause they saw propagated in the form of bibles, bayonets and brandy.

The British aristocracy, of course, saw themselves as transcending every possible distinction held by Indians of whatever lineage. 'The Aga Khan,' the College of Heralds in London once noted, 'is held by his followers to be a direct descendant of God. English Dukes take precedence.'

Rudyard Kipling was emblematic of a late nineteenth-century paradox: imperialists saw their mission not only in terms of the lands they subjugated and ruled, but as part of a vital task of stiffening the backbone of an increasingly soft metropole. The wild frontier was a place for the hardy Englishman to test his mettle, demonstrate his toughness, and celebrate the virtues of manliness, fidelity to a band of brothers, and loyalty to Queen and country. *Kim* begins with the English protagonist atop the Zam-Zammah cannon that symbolized authority and control over the Punjab, having knocked Hindus and Muslims off the gun before him. 'Who hold Zam-Zammah, that "fire-breathing dragon", hold the Punjab, for the great green-bronze piece is always first of the conqueror's loot. There was some justification for Kim…since the English held Punjab and Kim was English'.

According to this line of thinking, the imperial enterprise required men of courage, capable of violence, prepared for action and ready at all times to prevail against the unwashed hordes, qualities reaffirmed in the works of Kipling (such as *Stalky & Co.*, where British schoolboys triumph through savagery) and other 'masculinist' writers of Empire. This literary reaffirmation is all the more ironic, since it celebrates qualities that are proudly deployed in pursuit of a civilizing mission. The Empire's heroes were, in other words, men who used barbarity to pacify the supposedly barbarous.

As Lieutenant Herbert Edwardes wrote in 1846 of his mission in India: 'There is something noble in putting the hand of civilization upon the mane of a nation like the Punjab...and looking down brute passions.' It is striking that the Punjab in this metaphor is like an untamed beast on whose 'mane' the civilizing British hand must be firmly placed. Lord Curzon told an audience at Oxford University in 1907 that it was on the uncivilized outskirts of Empire that were found 'the ennobling and invigorating stimulus for our youth, saving them alike from the corroding ease and the morbid excitements of Western civilization'. Impelled by such ideas, imperialists during the second half of the nineteenth century developed and expressed a strong preference for the noble savage (the primitive, wild, martial but 'manly' tribesman and his ilk) over the educated 'wog' (the effete, culturally-hybrid Westernized Oriental gentlemen later to be derided as Macaulayputras). In Kipling's racially repugnant *Kim*, the latter is typified in the character of Hurree Chunder Mookerjee, the 'baboo' ethnographer in the employ of the British authorities, who, with his mangled English and forlorn hopes of being elected to the British Royal Society, is mocked for aspiring to be that which he never can be—a member of the colonizing class rather than merely one of its subjects.

Even E. M. Forster, the English novelist whose *A Passage to India* received the most uncritical reception from Indian nationalists in his time (the India League chief, Krishna Menon, even arranged its publication by Allen Lane) echoed the idea of Empire, most notably in his depiction of the impossibility of friendship between an Englishman and an Indian in the famous closing lines to his novel:

'Why can't we be friends now?' said the other, holding him affectionately. 'It's what I want. It's what you want.' But the horses didn't want it—they swerved apart: the earth didn't want it, sending up rocks through which riders must pass single file; the temple, the tank, the jail, the palace, the birds, the carrion, the Guest House, that came into view as they emerged from the gap and saw Mau beneath: they didn't want it, they said in their hundred voices, 'No, not yet,' and the sky said 'No, not there.'

Forster's Indian protagonist, a middle-class doctor with a traditional Muslim family, was not the social or intellectual equal of his Englishman, Fielding, and perhaps true friendship between them would have been impossible even in a non-imperial India. But Forster, whose book omits all mention of the Indian nationalist movement, and who caricatures his only major Hindu character, seemingly cannot conceive of either the kind of Indian (like Surendra Nath Banerjea) who had won entry into the ICS or the kind (like Jawaharlal Nehru) whose critiques of Empire were challenging the foundations of the Raj. It is a stultifying limited vision, which never arises above the mystery and the muddle that this well-intentioned Englishman saw India as. 'Only connect', says the memorable epigraph in Forster's *Howards End*: as an Indian reader, one can only wish that he, and the British in India, had.

British Governance, the Swadeshi Movement and the Advent of Mahatma Gandhi

Britain's motives may have been entirely selfish, as I demonstrate in Chapter 1, but on the positive side, its imperialism brought in law and order amid what looked perilously like anarchy, settled the perennial conflicts amongst warring groups and principalities, and permitted a less violent form of political competition than might otherwise have occurred in India. 'Imperialism,' Robert Kaplan suggests, 'confers a loose and accepted form of sovereignty, occupying a middle ground between anarchy and full state control'. 'Accepted' is a contestable term, of course, but acquiescence is also a form of acceptance, and many Indians, in the end, accepted British sovereignty, if only because they had no choice.

The Government of India Act, 1858, transformed the post of governor-general (soon re-designated as the viceroy), who would be directly responsible for the administration of India, along with provincial governors. The governors-general or viceroys were provided with councils, in which members were nominated. In 1861, new legislation allowed Indians to be added by nomination to the legislative councils of the governor-general and the provincial governors. Indians had to wait till the Indian Councils Act of 1892 (which amended the Act of 1861) and the subsequent Minto–Morley Reforms of 1909, both well after the 1885 founding of the Indian National Congress by Allan Octavian Hume and William Wedderburn, together with a number of prominent Anglophone Indians to benefit from the increased participation of Indians in the councils both at the centre and the provinces.

However, the Acts of 1892 and 1909 were at best cosmetic alterations to the established system and marginally affected how these

Indian councils were constituted and functioned. They increased the council membership through indirect election (in other words, selection by the British) but in reality, these councils had no powers worth the name. They had the right to raise issues in the councils but not to make any decisions; they could express the voice of the Indian public (or at least its élite, English-educated sections) but had no authority to pass laws or budgets. That power still lay with the governor-general, who could reject any resolutions passed by the council or impose upon the council the need to discuss and pass a resolution if he deemed it necessary for India.

The secretary of state for India who gave his name to the 1909 reforms, John Morley, had even opposed increasing membership of Indians to the Indian councils and argued that in his view the British government of India was run with all the consent and representation of the Indian people it needed. '[If] this chapter of reform led directly or necessarily to the establishment of a parliamentary system in India, I for one will have nothing at all to do with it', he declared. Indeed, such a thought could not have been farther from the minds of the reformers; every 'reform' that the British government brought into India's governance, up to the Government of India Act of 1935, protected the absolute authority of the governor-general and the Parliament of Britain. The Indian councils at the centre and provincial levels were always bodies with no real authority on any significant matter, and budgets, defence and law and order remained firmly in British hands. The objective was a gradual increase in representative government, not the establishment of full-fledged democracy.

In the book *Recovering Liberties*, the late Professor C. A. Bayly made an impressive case for the argument that Britain helped liberalism take root in India by institutionalizing it through schools and colleges, newspapers, and colonial law courts, and thereby converted an entire generation of Indians to a way of thinking about their own future that led to today's Indian democracy. The problem is that this liberalism was practised within severe limits. The Indian National Congress was established in 1885 as a voice of moderate, constitutionalist Indian opinion by a Scotsman, Allan Octavian Hume, and a group of well-educated, establishmentarian Indians. Far from welcoming such a development, as a truly liberal regime seeking to instil democracy in its charges ought to have done, the British reacted to it with varying degrees of hostility and contempt.

The English journalist Henry Nevinson wrote in 1908:

> For twenty-two years, 'it [the Congress] was a model of order and constitu-tional propriety. It passed excellent resolutions, it demanded the redress of acknowledged grievances, in trustful loyalty it arranged deputations to the representatives of the Crown. By the Anglo-Indians [the British in India][8] its constitutional propriety was called cowardice, its resolutions remained unnoticed, its grievances un-redressed, and the representative of the Crown refused to receive its deputation...[Indians realized] that it was useless addressing pious resolutions to the official wastepaper basket.

It was this attitude, more than anything else, that was to transform the Indian nationalist movement into becoming more militant. British attempts to suppress political activities that merely involved the exer-cise of free speech showed up the insincerity, or at least the poverty, of any claims of liberalism. For instance, Nevinson, who attended an Indian political meeting on the beach in Madras at the dawn of the century, recorded his impressions:

> The chairman...summarized the history of the last year of suspicion, repression, deportation, imprisonment, flogging of boys and students for political causes, and the Seditious Meetings Act. It was all done without passion or exaggeration, and he ended with a simple resolution calling on the Government to repeal the deportation statute as contrary to the rights which England had secured for herself under the Habeas Corpus. Four speakers supported the resolution, and all spoke with the same quiet rea-sonableness, so different from our conception of the Oriental mind... Only Anglo-Indians [i.e. the English in India] could have called the speeches seditious. To a common type of Anglo-Indian mind, any criticism of the Government, any claim to further freedom, is sedition. But though this was avowedly a meeting of Extremists, the claim in the speeches was

---

[8] The British used the term 'Anglo-Indian' to refer to British people living and working in India, and 'Eurasian' to refer to those of mixed parentage, usu-ally the children of lower-ranking Europeans and 'other ranks' who could not afford to snare one of the women from the 'fishing fleet' and ended up cohabiting with, and in a few cases marrying, Indian women. Today, the descendants of these Eurasians are known as 'Anglo-Indians', a term that causes confusion to readers of colonial documents, where the term only refers to the English in India.

for the simple human rights that other peoples enjoy the right to a voice in their own affairs, and in the spending of their own money.

Since such approaches never worked, the national movement soon began to take a different approach, that of mass political agitation against Curzon's 1905 Partition of Bengal, in order to make an effective impact upon the British. Outraged Bengali youths campaigned in towns and villages for the people to show their opposition to the colonial division of their homeland, preaching *swadeshi* (reliance on Indian-made goods) and urging a boycott of British goods. Shops that continued the sale of foreign goods were surrounded by youths who implored customers, often by prostrating themselves in supplication before prospective purchasers, never by intimidation, for the sake of their country, to depart without purchasing. This form of picketing was never violent, but it was not what the British were used to. As British merchants in Bengal complained of a dramatic downturn in their sales and the conversion of regular profits into unaccustomed losses, the agitation triumphed: the British reversed the Partition.

It was with complete awareness of the success of this short-lived burst of mass politics that a thin, bespectacled lawyer wearing coarse home-spun, Mohandas Karamchand Gandhi, returned to India in 1915 from a long sojourn in South Africa. There, his 'experiments with truth' and his morally-charged leadership of the Indian diaspora had earned him the sobriquet of Mahatma ('Great Soul'). Starting off as a not particularly gifted lawyer engaged by an Indian in South Africa to plead a routine case, Gandhi had developed into a formidable figure. Appalled by the racial discrimination to which his countrymen were subject in South Africa, Gandhi had embarked upon a series of legal and political actions designed to protest and overturn the iniquities the British and the Boers imposed upon Indians. After his attempts to petition the authorities for justice (and to curry favour with them by organizing a volunteer ambulance brigade of Indians) had proved ineffective, Gandhi developed a unique method of resistance through civil disobedience.

Gandhi's talent for organization (he founded the Natal Indian Congress) was matched by an equally rigorous penchant for self-examination and philosophical enquiry. Instead of embracing the bourgeois comforts that his status in the Indian community of South Africa might have entitled him to, Gandhi retreated to a communal farm he established outside Durban, read Henry David Thoreau, and corresponded with the likes of John Ruskin and Leo Tolstoy, all the while seeking to arrive at an understanding of 'truth' in both personal life and public affairs. The journey from petition politics to *satyagraha* (holding on to truth or, more commonly, if not entirely accurately, non-violent resistance) was neither short nor easy, but having made it and then returned to his native land, the Mahatma brought to the incipient nationalist movement of India an extraordinary reputation as both saint and strategist.

His singular insight was that self-government would never be achieved by the resolutions passed by a self-regarding and unelected elite pursuing the politics of the drawing room. To him, self-government had to involve the empowerment of the masses, the toiling multitudes of India in whose name the upper classes were clamouring for Home Rule. This position did not go over well with India's political class, which consisted in those days largely of aristocrats and lawyers, men of means who discoursed in English and demanded the rights of Englishmen. Nor did Gandhi's insistence that the masses be mobilized not by the methods of 'princes and potentates' (his phrase) but by moral values derived from ancient tradition and embodied in *swadeshi* and *satyagraha*.

To put his principles into practice, the Mahatma lived a simple life of near-absolute poverty in an ashram and travelled across the land in third-class railway compartments, campaigning against untouchability, poor sanitation and child marriage, and preaching an eclectic set of virtues from sexual abstinence to the weaving of khadi (homespun cloth) and the beneficial effects of frequent enemas. That he was an eccentric seemed beyond doubt; that he had touched a chord amongst the masses was equally apparent; that he was a potent political force soon became clear.

Gandhi's ascent, enabled by the Raj's failure to live up to the principles and values it professed, proved a repudiation of British liberalism, and not, as Bayly suggests, its vindication.

* * *

Even in the twentieth century, when the British moved grudgingly and fitfully towards what Secretary of State for India Lord Montagu had termed 'responsible self-government', there was no serious intent to develop credible political institutions in India. There had been wide-spread expectations that, in response to India's, and specifically Mahatma Gandhi's, support for Britain in World War I, not to mention the sacrifices of Indian troops, India would, at the end of the conflict, be granted Dominion status (connoting autonomous self-government within the Empire, as enjoyed by Australia, Canada and the rest of the 'White Commonwealth'). In 1917, Lord Montagu had placed before the British Cabinet a proposed declaration pledging 'the gradual development of free institutions in India with a view to ultimate self-government'. The former viceroy and later foreign secretary, Lord Curzon, thought this went too far, and suggested an alternative phrasing straight out of Sir Humphrey Appleby in *Yes, Minister*—that the government would work towards 'increasing association of Indians in every branch of the administration and the gradual development of self-governing institutions with a view to the progressive realization of responsible government in India as an integral part of the British empire'. The Cabinet approved this convoluted and insincere formula in place of Montagu's original wording and promptly reneged on the intent it had signalled.

Self-government under the 'Montagu–Chelmsford Reforms' ushered in to fulfil this declaration turned out to involve a system where Indians would serve as window-dressing for British imperial power. Representatives—elected by a franchise so restricted and selective that only one in 250 Indians had the right to vote—would exercise control over 'harmless' subjects the British did not care about, like education and health, while real power, including taxation, law and order and the authority to nullify any vote by the Indian legislators, would rest with the British governor of the provinces. The governor, and at the centre the viceroy, retained the right to reject any vote of the elected legislators and enact any laws the elected representatives refused to pass. Far from leading to 'the progressive realization of responsible government in India', this was regressive indeed, and it was unanimously rejected by Indian public opinion and by the Mahatma, who felt a deep sense of personal betrayal.

The Non-Cooperation movement ensued, and though it was suspended by Gandhi after a shocking incident of violence by Indian nationalists, the turn away from compromise with British colonialism had become irreversible. By 1930, the Indian National Congress had decided to go beyond its modest goals of 1918. It issued a Declaration of Independence on 26 January 1930:

> The British government in India has not only deprived the Indian people of their freedom but has based itself on the exploitation of the masses, and has ruined India economically, politically, culturally and spiritually… Therefore…India must sever the British connection and attain *Purna Swaraj* or complete independence.

The Great War and the Great Betrayal

The background to this sense of betrayal is important to understand. Eight years before Gandhi's return to India, and well before the War, Henry Nevinson had already spelled out in 1908 the reasons why Indians were dissatisfied with the Raj:

> Unrest in India was occasioned by…the contemptuous disregard of Indian feeling in the Partition of Bengal and Lord Curzon's University speech upon Indian mendacity; the exclusion of fully qualified Indians from public positions, in contradiction to Queen Victoria's Proclamation of 1858; several notorious cases of injustice in the law courts, where English criminals were involved; numerous instances of petty persecution for political opinions; the well-known measures for the suppression of personal liberty and freedom of speech; the espionage of police and postal officials; and the increasing insolence of the vulgar among Anglo-Indians, as shown in ordinary behaviour and in the newspapers which represent their views.

To this was added the extraordinary Indian support for the war effort and its humiliating British recompense.

As many as 74,187 Indian soldiers died during World War I and a far higher number were wounded. Their stories, and their heroism, were largely omitted from British popular histories of the war, or relegated to the footnotes.

India contributed a number of divisions and brigades to the European, Mediterranean, Mesopotamian, North African and East African theatres of war. In men, animals, rations, supplies and money given to Britain its assistance exceeded that of any other nation. In historical texts, it often appears formally that the Government of India 'offered' such help to the British and that His Majesty's Government 'graciously accepted' the offer to pay unfairly large amounts of money, including a lump sum of £100 million as a special contribution to HMG's expenses towards a European war. This elides the fact, of course, that the 'Government of India' consisted of Englishmen accountable to His Majesty's Government in Britain.

The number of soldiers and support staff sent on overseas service from India during World War I was huge: among them 588,717 went to Mesopotamia, 116,159 to Egypt, 131,496 to France, 46,936 to East Africa, 4,428 to Gallipoli, 4,938 to Salonica, 20,243 to Aden and 29,457 to the Persian Gulf. Of these Indians, 29,762 were killed, 59,296 were wounded, 3,289 went missing, presumed dead, and 3,289 were taken prisoner. Of the total of 1,215,318 soldiers sent abroad there were 101,439 casualties.

The British raised men and money from India, as well as large supplies of food, cash and ammunition, collected both by British taxation of Indians and from the nominally autonomous princely states. In addition, £3.5 million was paid by India as the 'war gratuities' of British officers and men of the normal garrisons of India. A further sum of £13.1 million was paid from Indian revenues towards the war effort. It was estimated at the time that the value of India's contribution in cash and kind amounted to £146.2 million, worth some £50 billion in today's money. (Some estimates place the value of India's contribution much higher.)

In Europe, Indian soldiers were among the first victims who suffered the horrors of the trenches. They were killed in droves before the war was into its second year and bore the brunt of many a German offensive. Indian infantrymen stopped the German advance at Ypres in the autumn of 1914, soon after the war broke out, while the British were still recruiting and training their own forces. Hundreds were killed in a gallant but futile engagement at Neuve Chapelle. More than a thousand of them died at Gallipoli, thanks to Churchill's folly in ordering an ill-conceived and badly-planned assault reminiscent of the Charge of the Light Brigade in the Crimean War. Nearly 700,000 Indian sepoys fought in Mesopotamia against the Ottoman empire, Germany's ally, many of them Indian Muslims taking up arms against their co-religionists in defence of the British empire.

Letters sent by Indian soldiers in France and Belgium to their family members in their home villages speak an evocative language of cultural dislocation and tragedy. 'The shells are pouring like rain in the monsoon', declared one. 'The corpses cover the country like sheaves of harvested corn', wrote another.

These men were undoubtedly heroes: pitchforked into battle in unfamiliar lands, in harsh and cold climatic conditions they were neither used to nor prepared for, fighting an enemy of whom they had no knowledge, risking their lives every day for little more than pride. Yet they were destined to remain largely unknown once the war was over: neglected by the British, for whom they fought, and ignored by their own country, from which they came. Part of the reason is that they were not fighting for India. None of the soldiers was a conscript: soldiering was their profession. They served the very British empire that was oppressing their own people back home.

In return for India's extraordinary support, the British had insincerely promised to deliver progressive self-rule to India at the end of the war. Perhaps, had they kept that pledge, the sacrifices of India's World War I soldiers might have been seen in their homeland as a contribution to India's freedom.

But the British broke their word. As we have seen, Mahatma Gandhi, who had returned to his homeland for good from South Africa in January 1915, supported the war, as he had supported the British in the Boer War. He hoped, he wrote, 'that India, by this very act, would become the most favourite partner [of the British], and racial distinctions would become a thing of the past'. Sir Rabindranath Tagore was somewhat more sardonic about nationalism: 'We, the famished, ragged ragamuffins of the East are to win freedom for all humanity!' he wrote, during the War. 'We have no word for "Nation" in our language.' India was wracked by high taxation to support the war and the high inflation accompanying it, while the disruption of trade caused by the conflict led to widespread economic losses—all this while the country was also reeling from a raging influenza epidemic that took millions of lives. But nationalists widely understood from Montagu's 1917 declaration that at the end of the war India would receive the Dominion status hitherto reserved for the 'White Commonwealth'.

It was not to be. When the war ended in triumph for Britain, India was denied its promised reward. Instead of self-government, the British offered the fraudulent Montagu–Chelmsford Reforms in 1918 that left all power in British hands and attempted to fob off the Indians with minimal authority over inconsequential issues. If Indians were disappointed, so were Britons with a sense of fair play. British MP Dr Vickerman Rutherford declared:

> Never in the history of the world was such a hoax perpetrated upon a great people as England perpetrated upon India, when in return for India's invaluable service during the War, we gave to the Indian nation such a discreditable, disgraceful, undemocratic, tyrannical constitution.

Instead of offering more democracy, Britain went farther in the opposite direction. It passed the repressive Rowlatt Act in 1919, reimposing upon India all the wartime restrictions on freedom of speech and assembly that had been lifted with the Armistice. The Act vested the viceroy's government with extraordinary powers to quell 'sedition' against the Empire by silencing and censoring the press, detaining political activists without trial, and arresting without a warrant any individuals suspected of treason against the Empire. The Act granted the authorities the power to arrest Indians on mere suspicion, and to try them in secrecy without a right to counsel or a right of appeal. It was a return to the practices of the Spanish Inquisition animated by the presumption of guilt and with no rights for the accused against a people who thought they had just earned the right to control their own political destiny.

Public protests against this draconian legislation were quelled ruthlessly. The worst incident was the Jallianwala Bagh massacre of hundreds of unarmed innocents in April 1919, which is discussed more fully in chapters 3 and 4. The fact that Brigadier General Reginald Dyer, who showed exceptional brutality and racism in Amritsar, was hailed as a hero by the British, who raised a handsome purse to reward him for his deed, marked the final rupture between British imperialism and its Indian subjects. Sir Rabindranath Tagore returned his knighthood to the British in protest against 'the helplessness of our position as British subjects in India'. Tagore's early ambivalence about the costs and benefits of British rule was replaced after Amritsar by what he termed a 'graceless disillusionment' at the 'misfortune of being governed by a foreign race'. He did not want a 'badge of honour' in 'the incongruous context of humiliation'.

With British betrayal providing such a sour ending to the narrative of a war in which India had given its all and been spurned in return, Indian nationalists felt that self-governance could never be obtained by legal means from perfidious Albion, but would have to be wrested from the unwilling grasp of the British through a struggle for freedom.

DEMOCRACY, THE PRESS, THE PARLIAMENTARY SYSTEM AND THE RULE OF LAW

A good part of the British case for having created India's political unity and democracy lies in the evolution of three of democracy's building-blocks during the colonial era: a free press, an incipient parliamentary system and the rule of law. This trifecta, which India retains and has continued to develop in its own ways, existed in the colonial era, but with significant distortions, and is therefore worth examining.

At the high noon of early twenty-first-century imperial hubris, with America poised to invade Iraq, Russia in retreat, the Taliban in disarray and Bin Laden in hiding, and the currents of globalization flowing strongly (and seemingly irresistibly) around the world, the controversial Scottish historian Niall Ferguson published *Empire: How Britain Made the World*, which saw in the past all the virtues he wished to celebrate in the present. The British, Ferguson wrote, combined commerce, conquest, and some 'evangelical imperialism' in an early form of globalization—or, in a particularly infelicitous word, 'Anglobalization'—and in so doing Britain bequeathed to a large part of the world nine of its most distinctive and admirable features, the very ones that had made Britain great: the English language, English forms of land tenure, Scottish and English banking, the common law, Protestantism, team sports, the 'night watch-man' state, representative assemblies, and the idea of liberty. The last of these, he tells us, is 'the most distinctive feature of the Empire' since 'whenever the British were behaving despotically, there was always a liberal critique of that behaviour from within British society'.

We shall return to the broader elements of Ferguson's analysis (and that of other apologists for Empire like Lawrence James) in Chapter 7, but it is the claims to liberal democracy that detain us now. Ferguson is uncompromising: 'India, the world's largest democracy, owes more than it is fashionable to acknowledge to British rule. Its elite schools, its universities, its civil service, its army, its press and its parliamentary system all still have discernibly British models... Without the influence of British imperial rule,' he adds, 'it is hard to believe that the institutions of parliamentary democracy would have been adopted by the majority of states in the world, as they are today'.

As befits an economic historian, Ferguson contends, in a later thesis that ventures beyond India, that Empire 'not only underwrites the free international exchange of commodities, labour and capital but also creates and upholds the conditions without which markets cannot function—peace and order, the rule of law, non-corrupt administration, stable fiscal and monetary policies as well as provides public goods, such as transport infrastructure, hospitals and schools, which would not otherwise exist'. The liberalism of Empire means that those who become its subjects gain greatly from their subjection and this, to Ferguson, proves that Empire benefits the colonized as well as the imperial centre. British rule in India is one of Ferguson's exhibits for this thesis, and in this (as in the previous and the next) chapter we shall examine the actual record of Britain in advancing the much-vaunted elements of liberal democracy so often cited by Raj apologists.

The (Partly) Free Press

Apologists for Britain, and many critics, tend to give the Empire credit for introducing the concept of the free press to India, starting the first newspapers and promoting a consciousness of the rights a free citizen was entitled to enjoy. It is certainly true that Indian nationalism and the independence movement could not have spread across the country without the active involvement of the free press.

Although the first printing press was introduced to the subcontinent by the Portuguese in 1550, it only printed books, as indeed did the first

British printing press, established in Bombay in 1664. It took more than a century for the first newspaper to be printed in India when, in 1780, James Augustus Hicky published his *Bengal Gazette,* or *Calcutta General Advertiser.* But the East India Company soon looked askance at his inconvenient views and, after two years of mounting exasperation, seized his press in 1782.

This did not, however, dissuade others less contentious in manner than Hicky, and soon a raft of British newspapers began printing in India: the first four in the Company capital of Calcutta—*The Calcutta Gazette* in 1784, *The Bengal Journal* and *The Oriental Magazine of Calcutta* in 1785, and *The Calcutta Chronicle* in 1786—and then two in the other principal British trading centres, *The Madras Courier* in 1788 and *The Bombay Herald* in 1789. These newspapers all reflected the interests of the small European community, particularly commercial interests, and provided useful, if not always accurate, information about the arrivals and departures of ships and developments in the governance of the colony. They did establish a newspaper culture in British India, however, and though none of the initial newspapers survived, it was soon apparent that the press was here to stay.

Alarmed by their proliferation, and concerned that the Company's critics and enemies (including conceivably the French) could use the press to the Company's disadvantage, Lord Wellesley introduced the Censorship of the Press Act, 1799, which brought all newspapers in India under the scrutiny of the Government of India prior to publication. This Act was later extended in 1807 to cover all kinds of publications—newspapers, magazines, books and pamphlets. Some of the more obstreperous publications were closed down; the editors of *Indian World, Bengal Gazette* and *Calcutta Journal* were even arrested and deported to England for their intemperate criticism of Company officials and policies. It was not a propitious beginning for the idea of a free press in India.

The draconian restrictions were eased soon enough, as the Company established its stranglehold over India and the threats to it from European rivals disappeared. The growing independence of the press in the mother country also began to be reflected in India. While many of the early newspapers faded away—sometimes with the death or departure of their publishers, sometimes because they were not commercially viable given their small readership base, and sometimes because the editors and staff simply ran out of enthusiasm for their task and adequate replacements could not be found—others not only survived but established a considerable following. The *Times of India*, established in Bombay in 1838, and the Calcutta *Statesman* (which began life in 1875, but incorporated the *Friend of India* which was founded in 1818) soon established themselves as reliable pillars of the establishment, solidly committed to British imperial interests but able to criticize the policies and actions of the government in a responsible manner. As the British expanded across northern India, *The Pioneer* established itself in Lucknow as the third in a colonial triumvirate of newspapers whose views could be taken as broadly representative of the British community in India.

It must, therefore, be acknowledged that it was the British who first established newspapers in India, which had been unknown before colonial rule, and it is to their credit that they allowed Indians to emulate them in doing so both in English, catering to the tiny English-educated elite (and its aspirational imitators) and in Indian vernacular languages. The *Bombay Samachar*, in Gujarati, was founded in 1822 (it is still running, and proudly calls itself the oldest newspaper in Asia still in print) and a few decades later, two Bengali-owned newspapers followed suit in Calcutta, *The Bengalee* in 1879 (later purchased, and edited for thirty-seven years, by Surendra Nath Banerjea after he left the ICS) and the formidable *Amrita Bazar Patrika* in 1868 (which, after being founded as a Bengali-language publication, then became a bilingual weekly for a time, before turning into an English-language newspaper in 1878 to advocate nationalist interests. The *Amrita Bazar Patrika* became a formidable pro-Congress voice and survived till the late twentieth century, before closing in 1986).

Other English-language, Indian-owned newspapers addressed themselves to Indian readers but in the awareness that their views would be paid attention to by the colonial authorities; this made them increasingly influential in the freedom movement. Arguably the most notable of these was *The Hindu* in Madras, established as a weekly in 1878 and converted into a daily from 1889, which the British came to regard for a long time as the voice of responsible Indian opinion. (*The Hindu*'s first issue counted a grand total of eighty copies, printed with 'one rupee and eight annas' of borrowed money by a group of four law students and two teachers).

In the early twentieth century, Indian nationalists began to establish newspapers explicitly to advocate their cause: the best of these were the *Bombay Chronicle*, founded by former Congress president Sir Pherozeshah Mehta in 1910, *Hindustan Times*, which was started by the Congress-supporting Birla business family in 1924, and Jawaharlal Nehru's own *National Herald*, which started publication in 1938. The Muslim League followed suit, when its political fortunes picked up during the war years, Muhammad Ali Jinnah establishing *Dawn* in Karachi and Delhi in 1941.

By 1875, it was estimated that there were 475 newspapers in India, the vast majority owned and edited by Indians. They catered to the literate minority—less than 10 per cent of the population at that time—but their influence extended well beyond this segment, since the news and views they published were repeated and spread by word of mouth. The nascent library movement in India also helped, as did public reading-rooms, and each copy sold enjoyed at least a dozen readers. Though the newspapers were printed and published in the big cities, editions made their way, sometimes three days later, to the rural areas and 'mofussil [district, non-metropolitan] towns', where they were eagerly awaited and avidly read. There is no doubt that the press contributed significantly to the development and growth of nationalist feelings in India, inculcated the idea of a broader public consciousness, exposed many of the failings of the colonial administration and played an influential part in fomenting opposition to many aspects of British rule.

Inevitably, the British authorities began to be alarmed: Lord Lytton brought in a Vernacular Press Act in 1878 to regulate the Indian-language papers, and his government kept a jaundiced eye on the English-language ones. (It was the introduction of this Act that prompted the *Amrita Bazar Patrika* to convert itself into an English-language newspaper overnight, to avoid coming under the new law's purview.) Still, outright censorship and repression would not have gone down well with the British public at home, and the authorities had to tread warily. While on certain occasions of grave danger to Britain, especially at times of war, and during periods of elevated nationalist resistance, the press was directly curtailed to protect imperial interests—the Rowlatt

Acts come to mind—a wide range of criticism of British administration was permitted most of the time. Indeed, the Indian vernacular press was allowed to get away with crude invective: for instance, in 1889, a Bengali newspaper, *Halishaher Patrika*, colourfully described the British Lieutenant Governor Sir George Campbell as 'the baboon Campbell with a hairy body… His eyes flash forth in anger and his tail is all in flames'. But had its anti-colonialism taken on a more explicitly political tone, for instance in questioning the very premises of British rule at all or calling for its overthrow, the authorities would not have been quite as tolerant.

One of the most notable accomplishments of the Indian nationalist media, during a period of relative freedom, ironically has implications that haunt the subcontinent even today. In 1891, a journalist from the *Amrita Bazar Patrika* managed to rummage through the wastepaper basket at the office of Viceroy Lord Lansdowne. There he found the fragments of a torn-up letter, which with great enterprise he managed to piece together. The letter contained explosive news, revealing as it did in considerable detail the viceroy's plans to annex the Hindu maharaja-ruled Muslim-majority state of Jammu & Kashmir. To the consternation of the British authorities, *Amrita Bazar Patrika* published the letter on its front page. The cat was out of the bag: the newspaper reached the maharaja of Kashmir, who promptly protested, set sail for London and vehemently lobbied the authorities there to honour their predecessors' guarantees of his state's 'independent' status. The maharaja was successful, and Indian nationalists congratulated the *Patrika* on having thwarted the colonialists' imperial designs. Had this exposé not taken place, Kashmir would not have remained a 'princely state', free to choose the country, and the terms, of its accession upon Independence in 1947; it would have been a province of British India, subject to being carved up by a careless British pen during Partition. The contours of the 'Kashmir problem' would have looked very different today.

Nonetheless, the Lansdowne-*Patrika* episode was an exception: for much of the time, the Indian media operated under severe constraints. The revised Press Act of 1910 was designed to limit the influence of editors on public opinion; it became a key instrument of British control of the Indian press. Under its provisions an established press or newspaper had to provide a security deposit of up to five thousand rupees (a considerable sum in those days); a new publication would have to pay up to two thousand. If the newspaper printed something of which the government disapproved, the money could be forfeit, the press closed down, and its proprietors and editors prosecuted. The Congress leader Annie Besant, for instance, had refused to pay a security on a paper she published advocating Home Rule, and was arrested for failing to do so and thereby violating the Act.

It is noteworthy that only Indian publications were vulnerable to forfeiting the substantial bond they had posted with the authorities if they failed their undertaking not to publish inflammatory or abusive articles; the racism of the British-owned press was never subject to similar strictures. The British colonial governments in the provinces enjoyed the right to search any newspaper's premises and confiscate any material they found 'seditious'. The Indian press, in other words, was fettered rather than free, but that it existed, and could serve as a rallying point for public opinion, is to the credit of both the British authorities and the Indians who worked in the media.

Indian papers—especially the vernacular ones which tended to be less retrained in their abuse of the colonial masters—were fined, suppressed, and shut down; their editors were frequently imprisoned, and several times given twenty-three months of hard labour for a piece of invective; and under the Press Act, their stock of type, without which they could not print, was liable to confiscation. But such threats were never focused on the pro-imperialist British papers in India. In no Indian newspaper, wrote the fair-minded British observer, Henry Nevinson, in 1908, 'have I seen more deliberate attempts to stir up race hatred and incite to violence than in Anglo-Indian [i.e. British settlers'] papers, which suffer nothing'. Nevinson offers as an example 'this obvious instigation to indiscriminate manslaughter by *The Asian*, an Anglo-Indian weekly in Calcutta (9 May 1908)':

> Mr Kingsford [a British magistrate in Calcutta whose court was the target of a bomb] has a great opportunity, and we hope he is a fairly decent shot at short range. We recommend to his notice a Mauser pistol, with the nickel filed off the nose of the bullets, or a Colt's automatic, which carries a heavy soft bullet and is a hard-hitting and punishing weapon. We hope Mr. Kingsford will manage to secure a big 'bag', and we envy him his opportunity. He will be more than justified in letting daylight into every

strange native approaching his house or his person, and for his own sake we trust he will learn to shoot fairly straight without taking his weapon out of his coat pocket. It saves time and gives the elevation fairly correctly at any distance up to about ten or fifteen yards. We wish the one man who has shown that he has a correct view of the necessities of the situation the very best of luck.

Nevinson adds that 'the tone of the Anglo-Indian press is almost invariably insolent and provocative. If "seditious" only means "likely to lead to violence", it is seditious too.'

The press, in other words, was free, but some newspapers (the British-owned ones) were freer than others.

The Parliamentary System in India

By the time of Independence, British India, and many other British colonies, had elections, parties, a more or less free press, and the rule of law, unlike their Spanish, Portuguese, French, Dutch, and Belgian counterparts. Democratization may have been slow, grudging and gradual, but it was also more successful in the ex-British colonies than elsewhere. The Indian nationalist struggle and its evolution through various stages—decorous liberals seeking legislative rights, 'extremists' clamouring for swaraj, Gandhi and his followers advocating non-violent struggle, the Congress, the Muslim League and other parties contending for votes even with limited franchise: all these pre-Independence experiences served as a kind of socialization process into democracy and helped to ease the country's transition to independence.

It is remarkable that when the Indian nationalists, victorious in their freedom struggle, sat down to write a Constitution for independent India, they created a political system based entirely on British parliamentary democracy. Was this simply because they had seen it from afar and been denied access to it themselves, and so wanted a replica of Westminster in India, or might it be that the British, through the power of example, actually convinced Indians that theirs was a system worth emulating?

A digression here: Personally, I am far from convinced that the British system is suited to India. The parliamentary democracy we have adopted involves the British perversity of electing a legislature to form an executive: this has created a unique breed of legislator, largely unqualified to legislate, who has sought election only in order to wield (or influence) executive power. It has produced governments obliged to focus more on politics than on policy or performance. It has distorted the voting preferences of an electorate that knows which individuals it wants but not necessarily which policies. It has spawned parties that are shifting alliances of individual interests rather than the vehicles of coherent sets of ideas. It has forced governments to concentrate less on governing than on staying in office, and obliged them to cater to the lowest common denominator of their coalitions. It is time for a change.

Pluralist democracy is India's greatest strength, but its current manner of operation is the source of its major weaknesses. India's many challenges require political arrangements that permit decisive action, whereas they increasingly promote drift and indecision. India must have a system of government whose leaders can focus on governance rather than on staying in power. The parliamentary system has not merely outlived any good it could do; it was from the start unsuited to Indian conditions and is primarily responsible for many of the nation's principal political ills. This is why I have repeatedly advocated a presidential system for India not just for the federal government in New Delhi, but a system of directly elected chief executives at the levels of villages, towns, states and the centre, elected for fixed terms and accountable to the voters every five years, rather than to the caprices of legislatures and the shifting majorities of municipal councils or village panchayats (councils).

The parliamentary system devised in Britain—a small island nation with electorates initially of a few thousand voters per MP, and even today fewer than 100,000 voters per constituency—assumes a number of conditions which simply do not exist in India. It requires the existence of clearly defined political parties, each with a coherent set of policies and preferences that distinguish it from the next, whereas in India a party is all too often a label of convenience which a politician adopts and discards as frequently as a Bollywood film star changes costume. The principal parties, whether 'national' or otherwise, are fuzzily vague about their beliefs: every party's 'ideology' is one variant or another of centrist populism, derived to a greater or lesser degree from the Nehruvian socialism of the Congress. But we cannot blame the British for saddling us with this system, though it is their 'Mother of Parliaments' our forefathers sought to emulate. First of all, the British had no intention of imparting democracy to Indians; second, Indians freely chose the parliamentary system themselves in a Constituent Assembly.

Like the American revolutionaries of two centuries ago, Indian nationalists had fought for 'the rights of Englishmen', which they thought the replication of the Houses of Parliament would both epitomize and guarantee. When former British Prime Minister Clement Attlee, as a member of a British constitutional commission, suggested the US presidential system as a model to Indian leaders, he recalled, 'they rejected it with great emphasis. I had the feeling that they thought I was offering them margarine instead of butter.' Many of our veteran parliamentarians—several of whom had been educated in England and watched British parliamentary traditions with admiration—revelled in their adherence to British parliamentary convention and complimented themselves on the authenticity of their ways. Indian MPs still thump their desks in approbation, rather than applauding by clapping their hands. When bills are put to a vote, an affirmative call is still 'aye', rather than 'yes'. Even our Communists have embraced the system with great delight: an Anglophile Marxist MP, Professor Hiren Mukherjee, used to assert proudly that British Prime Minister Anthony Eden had felt more at home during Question Hour in the Indian Parliament than in the Australian.

But six decades of Independence have wrought significant change, as exposure to British practices has faded and India's natural boisterousness has reasserted itself. Some of the state assemblies in our federal system have already witnessed scenes of furniture overthrown, microphones ripped out and slippers flung by unruly legislators, not to mention fisticuffs and garments torn in scuffles among politicians. Pepper spray has been unleashed by a protesting Member of Parliament in the well of the national legislature. We can scarcely blame the British for that either.

* * *

And yet the argument that Britain left us with self-governing institutions and the trappings of democracy fails to hold water in the face of the reality of colonial repression. Let me cite one individual who actually lived through the colonial experience, Jawaharlal Nehru, who wrote in a 1936 letter to an Englishman, Lord Lothian, that British rule is 'based on an extreme form of widespread violence and the only sanction is fear. It suppresses the usual liberties which are supposed to be essential to the growth of a people; it crushes the adventurous, the brave, the sensitive, and encourages the timid, the opportunist and time-serving, the sneak and the bully. It surrounds itself with a vast army of spies and informers and agents provocateurs. Is this the atmosphere in which the more desirable virtues grow or democratic institutions flourish?' Nehru went on to speak of 'the crushing of human dignity and decency, the injuries to the soul as well as the body' which 'degrades those who use it as well as those who suffer from it'. These were hardly ways of instilling or promoting respect for democracy and its principles in India. This injury to India's soul—the very basis of a nation's self-respect—is what is always overlooked by apologists for colonialism.

'Rule of Law': The Boot and the Spleen

A corollary of the argument that Britain gave India political unity and democracy is that it established the 'rule of law' in the country. This was, in many ways, central to the British self-conception of imperial purpose. We have noted earlier other aspects of what the British saw as their 'mission' in India. Bringing British law to the natives was arguably one of the most important constituent elements of this mission; Kipling would wax eloquent on the noble duty to bring law to those without it. The British both laid down the law and derived legitimacy, in their own eyes and in those of the world, from doing so. It was, of course, through 'the law' that British authority was exercised; but where a system of laws pre-existed the British legal system, as was the case in India, British law had to be imposed upon an older and more complex civilization with its own legal culture, and here the Kiplingesque arguments began to fray at the edges. In India the British were forced to use coercion and cruelty to get their way; often they had to resort to the dissolution of prior practices and traditional systems, as well as, in the process, to reshape civil society. In the circumstances, as a British scholar has noted, 'the law that was erected can hardly be said to have served the interests of colonial subjects.'

Pride of place to the legacy of British imperialism in India is often given to the Empire giving India its penal code, drafted by Macaulay with the avowed purpose of 'legislating for a conquered race, to whom the blessings of our constitution cannot as yet be safely extended'. Macaulay sat for three years behind high walls, completely disconnected from the people he was ostensibly working for, and created a code of criminal law that was 'a body of jurisprudence written for everyone and no one, which had no relationship to previous Indian laws or any other form of government at all'. Even the British were uncertain about his effort, and Macaulay's penal code sat un-enacted for twenty-four years after he finished it in 1837. Finally enacted in 1861, it is still largely in force in India today, in all its Victorian glory. In addition, the British introduced their ideas of trial by jury, freedom of expression and due process of law. These are incontestable legal values, except in their actual manner of working, for in its application during the colonial era, the rule of law was not exactly impartial.

Justice, in British India, was far from blind: it was highly attentive to the skin colour of the defendant. Crimes committed by whites against Indians attracted minimal punishment; an Englishmen who shot dead his Indian servant got six months' jail time and a modest fine (then about 100 rupees), while an Indian convicted of attempted rape against an Englishwoman was sentenced to twenty years rigorous imprisonment. Only a handful of Englishman were convicted of murder in India in the first 150 years of British rule. The death of an Indian at British hands was always an accident, and that of a Briton because of an Indian's actions always a capital crime. Indian judges also suffered racial discrimination, as we have seen with the case of Justice Syed Mahmud. When Lord Ripon—the only humane, non-racist viceroy sent to India in the nineteenth century—attempted to allow Indian judges to try British defendants and to play a stronger role in municipal matters (through the 'Ilbert Bill'), the backlash was severe. His aides protested that it would hardly 'subvert the British Empire to allow the Bengali Baboo to discuss his own schools and drains', but neither courts nor municipalities were acceptable terrain for Indian participation as far as the British were concerned. Ripon was boycotted by British expatriates and the racist outcry resulted in the collapse of the Ilbert Bill and Ripon's premature removal from office.

A certain type of case popped up frequently in the British colonial courts. Many Indians suffered from enlarged spleens as a result of malaria (or other diseases); when a British master kicked a native servant in the stomach—a not uncommon form of conduct in those days—the Indian's enlarged spleen would rupture, causing his death. The jurisprudential question was: did the fatal kick amount to murder or criminal misconduct? When Robert Augustus Fuller fatally assaulted his servant in these circumstances in 1875—Fuller claimed he struck him on the face, but three witnesses testified that he had kicked him in the stomach—he was found guilty only of 'voluntarily causing hurt', and was sentenced to fifteen days' imprisonment or a fine of thirty rupees to be paid to the widow. (According to the coroner, the servant's spleen was so enlarged that even 'moderate' violence would have ruptured it.)

'In the middle of the hot night,' wrote Captain Stanley de Vere Julius in his 1903 *Notes on Striking Natives*, 'the fan stops, and a man in the barrack-room, roused to desperation by heat and sleeplessness, rushes forth, careless of the consequences, and kicks the fan-puller in the wrong spot, his spleen. Do you blame him? Yes and No. It depends partly on whether he stopped to put his boots on.' *Punch* wrote an entire ode to 'The Stout British Boot' as the favoured instrument of keeping the natives in order. It ended: 'Let us sing, let us shout for the leather-shod foot, / And inscribe on our Banners, "The Stout British Boot".'

The disinclination of British judges in India to find any Englishman guilty of murdering any Indian was curiously mirrored in a recorded decline in murder charges in Victorian London. Martin Wiener proposed an 'export' model: the murder rate had dropped in Britain, he suggested, because 'the most aggressive citizens were busily wreaking havoc overseas'. It helped, of course, that fatal kicking in London was handled as 'wilful murder,' whereas in India it would only be charged as 'causing hurt' or 'committing a rash and negligent act'—provided the victim was an Indian.

There was, it is true, a threat of terrorism from Indian nationalists in the early years of the twentieth century that may have influenced judges in deciding cases of white violence against natives. But most of the Indian deaths at European hands involved servants or other menials rather than swadeshi bomb-throwers, and their cases were unrelated to political terrorism. Still, circumstances could always be stretched to extenuate the murderous conduct of an Englishman. When an Indian boy was shot dead by Lieutenants Thompson and Neave in Bangalore and Indian villagers forcibly confiscated Neave's gun, it was two of the villagers who were sentenced to six months' imprisonment for the crime of misappropriating the white man's weapon, whereas the murderers went unpunished. Indeed the case was filed as an incident of 'Natives Against Europeans'.

Sentences handed down by British judges were never equal for Indians and Europeans: in Calcutta, it was estimated that Indian prisoners' sentences exceeded those for Europeans by a factor of ten for the same crimes. Indian defendants were more than twice as likely as European ones to face murder or attempted murder charges for violent crimes. Statistically, European assaults on Indians were far more frequent than those by Indians on Europeans, yet almost all of the latter were charged as murder whereas most European misdeeds were deemed to be either accidental or in self-defence, and were in any case downgraded from murder to assault. In one case in which a British judge found evidence that a crime was 'clearly' murder, the British killer was found insane and hence not responsible for his actions.

Not all the British were equally comfortable with this form of justice. In 1902, when three troopers of the 9th Lancers beat to death an Indian man in Sialkot for refusing to bring them a woman for the night, regimental authorities made no effort to investigate and they tried to get away by painting the victim as a drunkard. But the incident outraged a sizeable number of Britons living in India. Even the viceroy, Lord Curzon, who was no lover of Indians, was horrified enough to declare: 'I will not be a party to any scandalous hushings up of bad cases of which there is too much in this country, or to the theory that a white man may kick or batter a black man to death with impunity because he is only a d[amne]d nigger.' Curzon could not increase the punishment, but he had the entire British regiment involved transferred to Aden. Still, he was forced to watch stonily at a parade in Delhi a few weeks later, as the English sections of the crowd cheered the same regiment wildly as it marched past. If Curzon, of all people, was moved to make a statement sympathetic to Indians, one can imagine the scale of the problem.

One scholar, Jordanna Bailkin, points out that there were a few (though very few) exceptions to this norm of race-conscious justice. In three rare cases, Britons were executed for killing Indians: John Rudd in Bengal (1861), four sailors named Wilson, Apostle, Nicholas, and Peters in Bombay (1867), and George Nairns in Bengal (1880). But in two hundred years of British rule, and thousands of cases in which Indians died at the hands of their colonial masters, these three cases were the only exceptions. Generally speaking, British civilian judges and up-country magistrates were reluctant to punish Europeans, whereas military courts and urban High Courts were willing to impose relatively more serious punishments for attacks on Indians. In the view of an ICS officer, who served thirty years in the late nineteenth century, 'there is a great and dangerous gap between the people and the Courts, and there is no way of bridging it.'

The moderate nationalist *Prabhat* magazine, in its issue of December 1925, writing after the exoneration and acquittal of an Englishman for kicking an Indian to death, lamented:

> The answer to why Indians are dissatisfied with the [*sic*] British rule is to be found in such incidents. Such painful disregard of Indian life cannot but produce a deep impression upon the heart of every Indian, and no wonder that, despite Mahatma Gandhi's insistent advice regarding non-violence, revolutionary conspiracies are heard of in the misguided India. So long as this relation exists between the boot and the spleen, India will be the most untouchable and degraded country in the world.

The imperial system of law was created by a foreign race and imposed upon a conquered people who had never been consulted in its creation. It was, pure and simple, an instrument of colonial control. As Henry Nevinson also pointed out, the rule of law, such as it was, functioned in a system in which Indians were 'compelled to live permanently under a system of official surveillance which reads their private letters, detains their telegrams, and hires men to watch their actions'.

This, then, was the rule of law the British taught us. We have much to unlearn.

* * *

There were other problems. The colonial 'rule of law' generally worked in favour of white settlers, elites and men. Racial discrimination was legal: as we have seen, in addition to private clubs that were open only to whites, many British hotels and other establishments sported signs saying 'Indians and dogs not allowed'. (It was the experience of being expelled from one of them, Watson's Hotel in Bombay, that led Jamsetji Tata to build one of the world's finest and most opulent hotels of its time, the Taj Mahal, which was open to Indians.)

Women were treated with Victorian paternalism and not a little misogyny. Institutionally, for instance, women on the Malabar coast who benefited from matrilineal law and enjoyed vast property and social rights, not to speak of bodily autonomy, were pushed to accept patriarchal shackles as the 'correct' and 'moral' way of living and subject themselves to husbands and sons, physically, socially, and economically. (Southern Indian women, whose breasts were traditionally uncovered, found themselves obliged to undergo the indignity of conforming to Victorian standards of morality; soon the right to cover one's breasts became a marker of upper-caste respectability and efforts were made to deny this privilege to lower-caste women, leading to such missionary-inspired colonial curiosities as the Breast Cloth Agitation from 1813 to 1859 in Travancore and the Madras Presidency.) India's rape law, enshrined in the colonial-era Indian Penal Code, placed the burden of the victim to establish her 'good character' and prove that a rape had occurred, which left her open to discredit by opposing counsel. Many rapes were never reported as a result of the humiliation to which this system subjected the victims.

Since the rule of law was intended to perpetuate the British hold over India, it was designed as an instrument of imperial rule. Political dissidence was legally repressed through various acts. The penal code contained forty-nine articles on crimes relating to dissent against the state (and only eleven on crimes involving death).

The racism of the colonial state was also reflected in its penal code. The Criminal Tribes Legislation, 1911, gave authority to the British to restrict movement, search and even detain people from specific groups, because their members were deemed to be chronically engaging in 'criminal' activity. This was bad sociology and worse law, but it stayed on the books till after Independence. Worse, its effects were inhumane. The scholar Sanjay Nigam's work has shown how the British invention of the notion of 'criminal tribes', and their passing legislation to confirm this categorization, led to the collection of intrusive records of personal details, restrictions on the movement of members of these tribes, forcible relocation of people belonging to 'criminal tribes' to rural settlements or reformatory camps, and the deliberate separation of children from their parents.

Of course, the court system, the penal code, the respect for jurisprudence and the value system of justice—even if they were not applied fairly to Indians in the colonial era—are all worthy legacies, and Indians are glad to have them. But in the process Britain has saddled us with an adversarial legal system, excessively bogged down in procedural formalities, which is far removed from India's traditional systems of justice. There is no doubt that traditional systems like the *khap panchayats* (caste or village councils) of the north had severe limitations of their own and were often used to uphold an iniquitous social order, but as Rwanda has shown with its *gacaca* courts, traditional systems can be adapted to meet modern norms of justice without the excessive procedural delays, formalism and expense of the Western system. The colonial legacy has meant a system of interminable trials and long-pending cases, leaving India with an unenviable world record for judicial backlog that exceeds by far every other country in the world. (There are still cases pending, in some of India's lower courts, which were filed in the days of the British Raj.)

Non-Interference or Manipulation?

Part of the argument for the benevolence of British colonialism is that the British were, beyond a point, largely non-intrusive rulers with no desire to interfere in the local affairs of the Indian population, who believed that India's traditions and customs, 'however "abhorrent" and "primitive" they might be', must be respected. As the Queen's Proclamation of 1858 plainly put it:

> We declare it Our royal will and pleasure that…none be molested or disquieted, by reason of their religious faith or observances, but that all shall alike enjoy the equal and impartial protection of the law; and We do strictly charge and enjoin all those who may be in authority under Us that they abstain from all interference with the religious belief or worship of any of Our subjects on pain of Our highest displeasure.

Since the British were not motivated by either the crusading Christianity of the Spanish or the cultural zeal of the French, but merely by pecuniary greed, they were not unduly anxious to transform Indian society or shape it in their image. It is true enough that British racism was accentuated by convictions of Christian superiority: as William Wilberforce, Britain's most famous evangelical Christian, put it: 'Our religion is sublime, pure, and beneficent. Theirs is mean, licentious, and cruel.'

For many Britons, imperialism was principally justified as a moral crusade to liberate Indians from 'ignorance, idolatry and vice'. But they were curiously reluctant to act on it. Whereas the Portuguese rapidly Christianized Goa, for instance, the British did not import their first Bishop till 1813. 'The first, and often the only, purpose of British power in India,' writes Jon Wilson, 'was to defend the fact of Britain's presence on Indian ground.' For most of the imperialists, India was a career, not a crusade. Changing India was not the object; making money out of India was. As Angus Maddison observes, 'there were no major changes in village society, in the caste system, the position of untouchables, the joint family system, or in production techniques in agriculture'. He was not entirely right: in fact, as we shall see, the caste system became more rigid under the British than it had been in precolonial India. Yet the British also claim credit for ending the barbarous practices of *sati* (or *suttee*, the self-immolation of widows on their husbands' funeral pyres, made even more grotesque by the fact that many of the victims were young girls married off to much older men) and *thuggee* (ritual robbery and murder carried out in the name of Goddess Kali by a bunch of criminals who gave the English language their collective epithet, the Thugs). The fact is that the British interfered with social customs only when it suited them to do so. The gap between liberal principles of universalism and the actual colonial practice of justice and governance was vast. I address some of the more misguided claims of British social reforms later in the book; what I would like to say here is that the British would interfere with local practices when they were minded to, and desist otherwise, claiming great virtue in either course of conduct.

In the process, while codifying the legal system and instituting an Indian Penal Code, the British have saddled India with colonial-era prejudices which they have long abandoned at home but which remain entrenched in India, causing untold misery to millions. A number of raging controversies in India in 2016, though seemingly unrelated, have brought into sharp focus the one element they have in common—they all relate to criminal offences codified in colonial-era British legislation that India has proved unable or unwilling to outgrow.

Among other things (and these are just a few examples), the Indian Penal Code, drafted by British imperial rulers in the mid-nineteenth century, criminalizes homosexuality under Section 377; creates a crime of 'sedition' under which students shouting slogans have been arrested; and applies a double standard to the commission of adultery.

The draconian concept of 'sedition' was enacted as an offence in 1870 to suppress any criticism of British policies. Under Section 124A of the Indian Penal Code, any person who uses 'words, signs or visible representation to excite disaffection against the Government' can be charged with sedition and potentially sentenced to life. This was explicitly justified by its proponents at the time on the grounds of restricting free speech in a subject state: one Briton spoke candidly in 1870 of needing a law to curb 'seditious offences not involving an absolute breach of the peace'. In other words, no free speech for Indians.

When the law was tightened further in 1898, to make it harsher than it was in England, the British lieutenant governor of Bengal admitted: 'It is clear that a sedition law which is adequate for a people ruled by a government of its own nationality and faith may be inadequate, or in some respects unsuited, for a country under foreign rule.'

Sedition was therefore explicitly intended as an instrument to terrorize Indian nationalists: Mahatma Gandhi was amongst its prominent victims. Seeing it applied in democratic India shocked many Indians. The arrest in February 2016 of students at New Delhi's Jawaharlal Nehru University (JNU) on charges of sedition, for raising 'anti-Indian' slogans in the course of protests against the execution of the accomplice of a convicted terrorist, and the filing of a legal case against Amnesty International in August 2016 on the same charges, would not have been possible without the loose, colonially-motivated wording of the law.

Agreeing with the outrage against colonial era provisions in the law, as a Member of Parliament, I introduced bills in the Lower House, seeking to amend these laws. I argued that the existence of these provisions on the statute books had made our penal code liable to misuse by the authorities in ways that infringed upon the constitutional right of Indians. My bill would allow an individual to be charged with sedition only when his words or actions directly result in the use of violence or incitement to violence or constitutes an offence which is punishable with imprisonment for life under the Indian Penal Code—like culpable homicide, murder, or rape. Mere words or signs criticizing the measures or administrative actions of the government will not constitute sedition. My objective is to promote the freedom of speech and the right to express dissent against the government, while ensuring safeguards against the use of words to incite violence—options that were not available to Indians under British rule.

Similarly, Section 377 of the Indian Penal Code, enacted in 1860, criminalizes 'carnal intercourse against the order of nature'—a term so archaic that it would invite derision in most modern societies. There had never been a taboo against homosexuality in Indian culture and social practice—until the British Victorians introduced one. Section 377, in so far as it criminalizes consensual sexual acts of adults in private, violates the fundamental rights guaranteed under Article 21 (life and liberty, including privacy and dignity), Article 14 (equality before law) and Article 15 (prohibition of discrimination) of the Constitution of free India.

My amendment to Section 377 would have decriminalized sex between consenting adults of any gender or orientation. Conservative MPs from the ruling BJP party, however, voted against its introduction in Parliament, prompting LGBT activists to move the Supreme Court, which has agreed to hear a 'curative review' petition against its earlier judgement upholding the law. The judicial route may, indeed, offer a more effective way to overturn this iniquitous section of the penal code. Fifty-eight Indians have been arrested under Section 377 in just two years (2014 and 2015) for actions performed in the privacy of their homes. That's fifty-eight Indians too many.

The irony is that in India there has always been place for people of different gender identities and sexual orientations. Indian history and mythology reveal no example of prejudice against sexual difference. On the contrary, in the great epic the *Mahabharata*, the gender-changing Shikhandi killed Bhishma. The concept of the *Ardhanareeshwara* imagined God as half man and half woman, prompting the movie-star chief minister of Andhra Pradesh in the 1980s, N. T. Rama Rao, to dress up as Ardhanareeshwara and surprise his followers—an unusual, even eccentric, act that was still seen as very much in keeping with Indian traditions. Transgender people were recognized as a *napunsakh* gender in Vedic and Puranic literature and were given due importance in India throughout history (and even in the Islamic courts during the Mughal era). The Jain texts recognized a broader concept of gender identity by speaking about the idea of a psychological sex being different from that of a physical one. Unfortunately, the British-drafted Indian Penal Code criminalized aspects of human behaviour and human reality that in India had not previously been regarded as criminal or requiring legal sanction. Section 377 of the Indian Penal Code and the Criminal Tribes Act of 1871 target the transgender community as well as the homosexual community. They violate the Indian ethos and the traditions of perhaps at least 2,000 years of Indian cultural practice, mythology, history, the Puranas, and Indian ways of living. Instead of India's traditional tolerance and 'live and let live', the British saddled the country with a colonial-era interpretation of what was good and right for Indians. It is ironic to see the self-appointed defenders of Bharatiya Sanskriti (traditional 'Vedic' India) on the Treasury Benches now defending the worst prejudices of British Victorian morality.

The Indian Penal Code is no easier on straight women than on gays. Section 497, criminalizing adultery, punishes extramarital relationships involving married women but not married men. A husband can prosecute his wife for adultery, and a man having sexual relations with his wife, but a woman cannot sue her husband for having an extramarital relationship, provided his partner is not underage or married. This double standard, exposed in a series of recent cases, again reflects Victorian values rather than twenty-first century ideas of morality. Ironically, in all three cases, the British have revised their own laws, so none of the offences they criminalized in India are illegal in Britain. One of the worst legacies of colonialism is that its ill effects outlasted the Empire.

I do not mean to blame the British alone for the persistence of these injustices. But the British enshrined these laws that have proved so difficult to amend. Strikingly, no less an eminence than India's head of state, President Pranab Mukherjee, chose the 155th anniversary of the

Indian Penal Code to underscore the need for its thorough revision. Our criminal law, he declared, was largely 'enacted by the British to meet their colonial needs'. It needed to be revised to reflect our 'contemporary social consciousness' so that it could be a 'faithful mirror of a civilization underlining the fundamental values on which it rests'. That Indians have not done this so far is, of course, hardly Britain's fault, but by placing iniquitous laws on the books, Britain has left behind an oppressive legacy. It is time for twenty-first-century India to get the government out of the bedroom, where the British were unembarrassed to intrude. It is also past time to realize that the range of political opinion permissible in a lively and contentious democracy cannot be reconciled with the existence of a pernicious colonial sedition law.

4

DIVIDE ET IMPERA

If British claims to creating viable political institutions in India, a democratic spirit, an efficient bureaucracy and the rule of law all seem hollow after the analysis in the previous chapter, it is their overarching assertion of having bequeathed India its political unity that underpins these claims. But while the events outlined above were occurring, another anti-democratic British project was coming to fruition that would discredit any credible view that the political unity of India was an objective of British colonialism.

The sight of Hindu and Muslim soldiers rebelling together in 1857 and fighting side by side, willing to rally under the command of each other and pledge joint allegiance to the enfeebled Mughal monarch, had alarmed the British, who did not take long to conclude that dividing the two groups and pitting them against one another was the most effective way to ensure the unchallenged continuance of Empire. As early as 1859, the then British governor of Bombay, Lord Elphinstone, advised London that '*Divide et impera* was the old Roman maxim, and it should be ours'. (He was not quite right: the term was coined not by the Romans, but by Philip II of Macedonia, though some Roman conquerors followed its precepts.) A few decades later, Sir John Strachey opined that 'the existence of hostile creeds among the Indian people' was essential for 'our political position in India'.

Caste, Race and Classification

The British had a particular talent for creating and exaggerating particularist identities and drawing ethnically-based administrative lines in all their colonies. Scholars have theorized that this practice may have stemmed from the British horror of diluting their own, idealized English identity, to which their colonial subjects were not allowed to aspire. In this respect they were quite unlike the French, whose policy of cultural assimilation went so far that little African and Asian children could be found dutifully reciting '*nos ancêtres les Gaulois* (Our ancestors the Gauls)' in their schoolrooms in Senegal or Vietnam. Indians were always subjects, never citizens; throughout the days of Empire, no Indian could have presumed to say 'I am British' the way a French African was encouraged to say '*Je suis français*'.

This tendency to separate was apparent in British attitudes from the start. Indeed, it had been evidenced in the only already-white country the British colonized, Ireland; instead of assimilating the Irish into the British race, they were subjugated by their new overlords, intermarriage was forbidden (as was even learning the Irish language or adopting Irish modes of dress) and most Irish people were segregated 'beyond the Pale'. If the British could do that to a people who looked like them, they were inclined to do much worse to the darker-skinned peoples they conquered in India. While we have examined some aspects of this phenomenon in previous chapters, I would like to examine how they classified Indians into various immutable categories, especially those of caste and religion.

Let us start by giving the British the benefit of the doubt and assuming that they might have been inclined to suspect that Indians, too, must be like them, and would like nothing more than to shield themselves behind their own identities. But the British effort to understand ethnic, religious, sectarian and caste differences among their subjects inevitably became an exercise in defining, dividing and perpetuating these differences. Thus colonial administrators regularly wrote reports and conducted censuses that classified their subjects in ever-more bewilderingly narrow terms, based on their language, religion, sect, caste, sub-caste, ethnicity and skin colour. In the process of such categorization and classification, not only were ideas of community reified, but also entire new communities were created by people who had not consciously thought of themselves as particularly different from others around them.

The American anthropologist Nicholas Dirks explains it lucidly:

'Colonialism was made possible, and then sustained and strengthened, as much by cultural technologies of rule as it was by the more obvious and brutal modes of conquest that first established power on foreign shores... Colonialism was itself a cultural project of control. Colonial knowledge both enabled conquest and was produced by it; in certain important ways, knowledge was what colonialism was all about. Cultural forms in societies newly classified as "traditional" were reconstructed and transformed by this knowledge, which created new categories and oppositions between colonizers and colonized, European and Asian, modern and traditional, West and East... As India was anthropologized in the colonial interest, a narrative about its social formation, its political capacity, and its civilizational inheritance began increasingly to tell the story of colonial inevitability and of the permanence of British imperial rule.'

Bernard Cohn, a scholar of British colonialism in India, has argued that the British simultaneously misinterpreted and oversimplified the features they saw in Indian society, placing Indians into stereotypical boxes they defined and into which they were assigned in the name of ancient tradition: 'In the conceptual scheme which the British created to understand and to act in India, they constantly followed the same logic; they reduced vastly complex codes and their associated meanings to a few metonyms.' Laws had to be translated into terms the British could understand and apply. A complicated, often chaotic and always fluid society like India was 'redefined by the British to be a place of rules and orders; once the British had defined to their own satisfaction what they construed as Indian rules and customs, then the Indians had to conform to these constructions.'

Such an exercise might not have been possible in a pre-modern era, where identities were looser and more 'fuzzy', and the difficulties of breaching distance, and extending communications, made it difficult to create a consciousness of identity beyond the merely local. The pathbreaking writer and thinker on nationalism, Benedict Anderson, has convincingly pointed out that identities uniting large numbers of people could arise only after a certain technological level had been attained. It is not seriously disputed that the sharper articulation of identities encompassing broad communities is a relatively recent phenomenon, nor that such identities have been 'imagined' and 'invented' to a great extent, as Anderson famously postulated. The British ruled India just as this kind of identity-creation was becoming possible, thanks to modern developments in transport and communication. Whereas the Great Mughal Akbar might have used such technologies to fuse his diverse people together, the British used them to separate, classify and divide.

Some critics point out that the British can scarcely be blamed for the pre-existing divisions in Indian society, notably caste, which divided (and still divides) the majority Hindu population into mutually exclusive and often incompatible social stratifications. Fair enough, but it is also true that the British, knowingly or unknowingly, helped solidify and perpetuate the iniquities of the caste system. Since the British came from a hierarchical society with an entrenched class system, they instinctively tended to look for a similar one in India. They began by anatomizing Indian society into 'classes' that they referenced as being 'primarily religious' in nature. They then seized upon caste. But caste had not been a particularly stable social structure in the pre-British days; though there were, of course, variants across time and place, caste had broadly been a mobile form of social organization constantly shaped and reinvented by the beliefs, the politics and quite often the economic interests of the dominant men of the times. The British, however, promulgated the theory that caste hierarchy and discrimination influenced the workings of Indian society. This is arguably a very narrow definition of how Indian society actually functioned in the pre-British era, and it is thanks to colonial rule that it has now become conventional wisdom.

In his seminal book *Castes of Mind*, Dirks has explained in detail how it was, under the British, that 'caste' became a single term 'capable of expressing, organizing, and above all "systematizing" India's diverse forms of social identity, community, and organization. [A]s the result of a concrete encounter with colonial modernity during two hundred years of British domination…colonialism made caste what it is today.' Dirks is critical of the British imperial role in the reification of caste, using their colonial power to affirm caste as the measure of all social things.

In fact, caste, he says, 'was just one category among many others, one way of organizing and representing identity. Moreover, caste was not a single category or even a single logic of categorization, even for Brahmins, who were the primary beneficiaries of the caste idea. Regional, village, or residential communities, kinship groups, factional parties, chiefly contingents, political affiliations, and so on could both supersede caste as a rubric for identity and reconstitute the ways caste was organized…Under colonialism, caste was thus made out to be far more pervasive, far more totalizing, and far more uniform than it had ever been before.' This Dirks sees as a core feature of the colonial power to shape knowledge of Indian society. Quite deliberately, he suggests, caste 'became the colonial form of civil society', or, in Partha Chatterjee's terms, the colonial argument for why civil society could not grow in India; it justified the denial of political rights to Indians (who were, after all, subjects, not citizens) and explained the unavoidable necessity of colonial rule.

Scholars who have studied precolonial caste relations dismiss the idea that *varna*—the classification of all castes into four hierarchical groups, with the Brahmins on top and even kings and warriors a notch beneath them—could conceivably represent a complete picture of reality (Kshatriya kings, for example, were never in practical terms subordinate to Brahmins, whom they employed, paid, patronized, heeded or dismissed as they found appropriate at different times). Nor could such a simplistic categorization reasonably organize the social identities and relations of all Indians across the vast subcontinent; alternative identities, sub-castes, clans and other formulations also existed and flourished in different ways at different places. The idea of the four-fold caste order stretching across all of India and embracing its complex civilizational expanse was only developed, modern scholars assert with considerable evidence, under the peculiar circumstances of British colonial rule. The British either did not understand, or preferred to ignore, the basic fact that the system need not have worked as described in theory.

The British Punditocracy

In the late eighteenth century, when the East India Company was establishing its stranglehold on India and its senior officials included some with a genuine interest in understanding the country, the British began to study the *shastras*, or Sanskrit treatises covering law and much else besides, in order to develop a set of legal principles to help them adjudicate disputes in Indian civil society. Governor-General Warren Hastings hired eleven pandits (Brahmin scholars) to create what became known as the Code of Gentoo Laws or the Ordinations of the Pandits. As the British could not read or interpret the ancient Sanskrit texts, they asked their Brahmin advisers to create the code based on religious Indian texts and their knowledge of Indian customs. The resulting output was an 'Anglo-Brahminical' text that arguably violated in both letter and spirit the actual practice: in letter, because it was imprecise in regard to the originals, and in spirit, because the pandits took advantage of the assignment to favour their own caste, by interpreting and even creating sacrosanct 'customs' that in fact had no shastric authority. This served to magnify the problem of caste hierarchy in the country.

Prior to this, scholars argue, disputes in Indian civil society were settled by *jati* or *biradri* (caste or clan), i.e. a person's fate was decided within a community or clan by his own peers in accordance with their local traditions and values and without needing approval from any higher caste authority. The pandits, instead of reflecting this widespread practice, cited doctrinal justifications from long-neglected texts to enshrine their status as the only authority figures, and most of the British took them at their word. (Some had their doubts. The most learned of British Orientalists, William Jones, who in 1797 founded the Asiatic Society in Calcutta and served in the Supreme Court of Judicature, remarked, 'I can no longer bear to be at the Mercy of our pandits who deal out Hindu Law as they please, and make it at reasonable rates, when they cannot find it ready made'. But Jones died tragically young and his wisdom was not replicated in his successors.)

It was evident from a cursory look at Indian society that actual social practices did not necessarily follow the official or 'shastric' code, but the ancient texts were now cited, and given an inflexibility they did not in fact possess, essentially to restrict the autonomy of society and so control it more easily in the name of religious authority. This served the interests of British policy, which explicitly sought to 'enumerate, categorize and assess their [colonial] populations and resources' for administrative purposes. Ethnic, social, caste and racial classifications were conducted as part of an imperial strategy more effectively to impose and maintain British control over the colonized Indian population. The process also reaffirmed their initial conviction that the Brahmins, with their knowledge of the Vedas, were the most qualified and best suited as their intermediaries to rule India. The Brahmins enjoyed British patronage over other groups and began considering themselves above all other castes, whom the British, internalizing Brahmin prejudice, thought of as lower castes.

The result was a remarkable preponderance of Brahmins in positions of importance in the British Raj. Brahmins, who were no more than a tenth of the population, occupied over 90 per cent of the positions available to Indians in government service, except the most menial ones; they dominated the professions open to Indians, especially lawyering and medicine; and they entered journalism and academia, so it was their voices that were heard loudest as the voices of Indian opinion. India had arguably been a far more meritocratic society before the British Raj settled down to enshrine the Brahmins in such a position of dominance.

Nineteenth-century ideas of race also got into the mix. The American scholar Thomas Metcalfe has shown how race ideology in that era defined European civilization as being at the peak of human attainment, while the darker-skinned races were portrayed as being primitive, weak and dependent on European tutelage in order to develop. Indians internalized many of these prejudices, instilled in them by two centuries of the white man's dominance and the drumming into them of the cult of British superiority. I recall reading, as a child, the account of an early Indian visitor to England, astonished that even the shoeshine boys there were British, so completely had the mystique of English lordliness been internalized in India. The young prince, and later cricket star, Ranji, arriving in England as a student, was taken aback by 'the sight of Britishers engaging in low-caste work' (he was assured the stevedores were 'only Irishmen').

How the Census Undermined Consensus

British cartography defined spaces the better to rule them; the map became an instrument of colonial control. Even the valuable British legacy, the museum, was devised in furtherance of the imperial project because here objects, artefacts and symbols could be appropriated, named, labelled, arranged, ordered, classified and thus controlled, exactly as the people could be.

The census joined the map and the museum as tools of British imperial dominance in the nineteenth century. The British fondness for taxonomy and social classification continued to be in evidence throughout their rule, and was formalized by means of the census they undertook first in 1872 and then every ten years from 1881, converting it into an 'ethnographic census' in 1901.

The census reconfirmed the process of defining castes, allocating them certain attributes and inventing extraordinary labels for entire communities, such as 'martial races' and 'criminal tribes'. Just as 'Brahmin' became a sought-after designation enshrining social standing, the census definition of an individual's caste tended to seal the fate of any 'Shudra', by fixing his identity across the entire country. Whereas prior to British rule the Shudra had only to leave his village and try his fortunes in a different princely state in India where his caste would not have followed him, colonialism made him a Shudra for life, wherever he was. The British belief in the fighting qualities of the 'martial races' also restricted the career possibilities of those not so classified, since British army recruitment policies were usually based on caste classifications. In the old days, any individual with the height and musculature required could make a livelihood as a warrior, whatever his caste background. In British India, this was far more difficult, if not impossible, since entire regiments were constructed on the basis of caste identities.

Census-taking in British India differed significantly from the conduct of the census in Britain, since unlike in the home country, the census in India was led by British anthropologists seeking to anatomize Indian society, the better to control and govern it. As I have mentioned earlier, Indians in precolonial times lived in communities with overlapping cultural practices, minimal self-awareness and non-existent consciousness of the details of their differences from other communities, except in the most general terms. This is underscored by the scholar Sudipta Kaviraj, who observes that precolonial communities had imprecise ('fuzzy') boundaries because some collective identities are not territorially based, and because 'part of this fuzziness of social mapping would arise because traditional communities, unlike modern ones, are not enumerated'.

The census, of course, changed that, as did the more stable territorial lines drawn by the colonists on their new, and very precise, maps. In the precolonial era, community boundaries were far more blurred, and as a result these communities were not self-conscious in the way they became under colonial rule. In the absence of the 'focused and intense allegiances' of the modern era, precolonial groups were less likely to be antagonistic to each other over perceived community or communal differences. They have become so only as a consequence of their 'definition' by the British in mutually exclusive terms.

The British could find no one to tell them authoritatively where or in what number any particular community was; the census commissioners discovered that boundary lines among Hindus, Sikhs and Jains barely existed, and that several Hindu and Muslim groups in different parts of the country shared similar social and cultural practices with regard to marriage, festivals, food, and worship. This went against the colonial assumption that communities must be mutually exclusive and that a person had to belong to one community or another. The British then simply superimposed their assumptions on the Indian reality, classifying people by religion, caste or tribe on the basis of imprecise answers to the census commissioners' questions.

The British approach inevitably suffered from the prejudices and limitations of the age: thus, the ICS's Herbert Risley, census commissioner for the 1901 census and author of the compendious *The People of India*, took an anthropological and eugenicist approach, making physical measurements of Indian skulls and noses on the then-fashionable assumption that such physical qualities reflected racial stereotypes. (It was he who announced that 1901's would be an ethnographic census, and led it personally.) Backed up by extensive photographs of facial features and social practices, Risley's work helped the British use such classification both to affirm their own convictions about European biological superiority over Indians, and to construct racial, social and 'tribal' differences between different segments of India's people which served to reshape and substantiate 'the dominant paradigms of social knowledge'.

Indians questioned by Risley's team predictably asserted both their caste identities and their entitlement to special privileges over other castes, accentuating the very differences the British wanted to see and had brought to the fore. By so doing they sought benefits for their group—admission to certain military regiments, for instance, or scholarships to some educational institutions—at the expense of, or equal to, others. Such caste competition had been largely unknown in pre-British days; caste consciousness had never been made so explicit as in the late nineteenth century.

All these classifications in turn served the interests of the colonizers by providing them with a tool to create perceptions of difference between groups to prevent unity amongst them, and justifying British overlordship—which alone could be seen as transcending these differences and guiding the Indians to a higher, more civilized, plane of being, under the benign tutelage of the well-meaning Empire. The British made these divisions such an article of faith that even a writer seen as broadly sympathetic to Indians, E. M. Forster, has his Indian protagonist, Aziz, say in *A Passage to India*, 'Nothing embraces the whole of India, nothing, nothing'.

This colonial process of identity-creation in British India occurred even in the formation of linguistic identities. Both David Washbrook and David Lelyveld believe that territorially-defined linguistic populations came into being out of the British colonial project to categorize, count and classify—in order to control—Indian society. The very notion of linguistic identities, they suggest, emerged from the nineteenth-century belief in language as the cementing bond of social relations, and the implicit conviction that 'races' or 'nations' spoke a common language and lived within defined territorial locations. Incidentally, in their zeal for classification, the British even subsumed ancient, and not dishonourable, professions like *devadasis* (temple dancers) or *baijis* (court musicians), who in some respects served functions akin to the geishas of Japan, into a rough-and-ready category of 'prostitutes', thus casting them out for the first time from respectable society.

A troubling side effect of this changed pattern of social dominance was political: ideas of democracy were not extended to all strata of Indian society under British rule. An instructive indication of this has lain in the rise of the more numerous 'backward classes' to positions of political prominence in independent India, which only became possible as democracy permitted free Indians to undo some of the more pernicious rigidities of the British-buttressed Indian social order.

The result of these British policies, whether by accident or design, or both, was a process of social separation that soon manifested itself as psychological separation and conscious of difference, leading in turn, where possible, to physical separation and—when demands for self-governance arose in time—political fragmentation, as each community was encouraged to fear that its self-interest could be jeopardized by the success of others.

The Hindu-Muslim Divide

The most important of these identity differences was the religious cleavage, real or imagined, but immediately focused upon, between Hindus and Muslims.

Religion became a useful means of divide and rule: the Hindu–Muslim divide was, as the American scholar of religion Peter Gottschalk documents, defined, highlighted and fomented by the British as a deliberate strategy. Three arguments, as the eminent historian Romila Thapar has explained, were foundational to the colonial interpretation of Indian history. The first was the British division of Indian history into 'periods' labelled in accordance with the religion of the rulers: thus the 'Hindu', 'Muslim' and 'British' periods formulated by James Mill in *The History of British India* (published between 1817 and 1826). Implicit in such periodization was the assumption that India was always composed of monolithic and mutually hostile religious communities, primarily Hindu and Muslim. Another foundational argument was that India's precolonial political economy was a form of 'Oriental Despotism', which essentially held that Indian society was a static society ruled by 'despotic and oppressive rulers' who impoverished the people. This is a notion I touch upon and have dismissed earlier in this book. The third foundational argument—that Hindu society had always been divided into four main castes or varnas—is addressed separately in this chapter.

By the mid-nineteenth century, the trio of Mill, Macaulay and [Friedrich Max] Müeller, the German Indologist working in Britain, had effectively established a colonial construction of the Indian past which even Indians were taught to internalize. In their reading, Indian civilization was seen as essentially Hindu, as defined by the upper castes, and descended from the Aryan race, which it was claimed invaded around 1500 BCE from the Central Asian steppes in the north, displaced and merged with indigenous populations, evolved a settled agrarian civilization, spoke Sanskrit and composed the Vedas. The Muslims came as a first wave of invaders and conquerors, in turn supplanted by the British. This history in turn became the received wisdom for late-nineteenth century Indian nationalists, Hindu and Muslim revivalists, and even cosmopolitan movements rooted in ancient Indian spiritualism like the Theosophical Society, whose co-founder, Colonel H. S. Olcott, became a major propagator of the 'Aryan origins' theory in the nineteenth century. Olcott was the first, though, to argue that the Aryans were indigenous to India and took civilization from India to the West, an idea that is today promoted by Hindutva ideologues.

By excluding Muslims from the essential national narrative, the nineteenth-century colonial interpretation of Indian history helped give birth in the twentieth to the two-nation theory that eventually divided the country. It also legitimized, with a veneer of scholarship, the British strategic policy of 'divide and rule' in which every effort was made by the imperialists to highlight differences between Hindus and Muslims to persuade the latter that their interests were incompatible with the advancement of the former.

Once again, as with caste and linguistic differences, this had no basis in precolonial history. The scholar Gyanendra Pandey suggests that religious communalism was in large part a colonial construction. His work demonstrates how the colonialists' efforts to catalogue, classify and categorize the Indians they ruled directly led to a heightened 'horizontal caste consciousness', and also contributed to the consciousness of religious difference between Hindus and Muslims The colonial authorities often asked representatives of the two communities to self-consciously construct an 'established' custom, such as by asking them what the prevailing beliefs and practices were around cow-slaughter, which prompted both groups to give an exaggeratedly rigid version of what they believed the beliefs and practices should be! Though Pandey confirms that such identities existed in the precolonial period, he believes colonial policies led to the hardening of these communal identities.

This is entirely plausible. Stories abound of the two communities habitually working together in precolonial times on issues that benefited principally one: for instance, Hindus helping Muslims to rebuild a shrine, or Muslims doing the same when a Hindu temple had to be reconstructed. Devout Hindus were sometimes given Muslim names and were often fluent scholars in Persian; Muslims served in the army of the Maratha (Hindu) warrior king Shivaji, as did Hindu Rajputs in the forces of the fiercely proud Muslim Emperor Aurangzeb. The Vijayanagara army included Muslim horseback contingents. At the village level, many historians argue that Hindus and Muslims shared a wide spectrum of customs and beliefs, at times even jointly worshipping the same saint or holy spot. In Kerala's famous pilgrimage site of Sabarimala, after an arduous climb to the hilltop shrine of Lord Ayyappa, the devotee first encounters a shrine to his Muslim disciple, Vavar Swami. In keeping with Muslim practice, there is no idol therein, merely a symbolic stone slab, a sword (Vavar was a warrior) and a green cloth, the colour of Islam. Muslim divines manage the shrine. (In another astonishing example, astonishing since it is both anachronistic and syncretistic, a temple in South Arcot, Tamil Nadu, hosts a deity of Muttaal Raavuttan, a Muslim chieftain—complete with beard, *kum-kum* and toddy pot—who protects Draupadi in the *Mahabharata*. Note, of course, that Islam did not exist when the *Mahabharata* was composed, but in post-Islamic retellings, a Muslim chieftain has entered the plot!)

Indians of all religious communities had long lived intertwined lives, and even religious practices were rarely exclusionary: thus Muslim musicians played and sang Hindu devotional songs, Hindus thronged Sufi shrines and worshipped Muslim saints there, and Muslim artisans in Benares made the traditional masks for the Hindu Ram-Leela performances. Northern India celebrated what was called a 'Ganga-Jamuni *tehzeeb*', a syncretic culture that melded the cultural practices of both faiths. Romila Thapar has recounted how deeply devotional poetry was written by some poets who were born Muslim but worshipped Hindu deities, notably Sayyad Ibrahim, popularly known as Raskhan, whose *dohas* and *bhajans* dedicated to Lord Krishna were widely recited in the sixteenth century. The Mughal court, she points out, became the most impressive patron of the translation of many Sanskrit religious texts into Persian, including the epic *Mahabharata* (translated as the *Razmnamah*) and the *Bhagavad Gita*, with Brahmin priests collaborating on the translations with Persian scholars.

To Gyanendra Pandey, such tales, as well as parables of Hindu generals in Mughal courts, or of Hindu and Muslim ministers in the Sikh
ruler Ranjit Singh's entourage, suggests there was 'fuzziness' about
self-conscious identities and a lack of self-definition on the basis of
religion (or even of caste), within both the Hindu and Muslim populations. These stories do not suggest mutually incompatible or hostile
ideologies. Acceptance of difference, as Swami Vivekananda famously
declared at the World Parliament of Religions in Chicago, was central
to the Indian experience throughout its long civilizational history.

Nor was religion in the past necessarily the overall basis for collective action, let alone political mobilization: caste, community, *jati* and
biradari played their parts. But by encroaching on the terrain of the
various communities, thereby invalidating indigenous social relations,
the colonial state loosened the bonds that had held them together for
generations across these divides.

The facts are clear: large-scale conflicts between Hindus and
Muslims (religiously defined), only began under colonial rule; many
other kinds of social strife were labelled as religious due to the colonists' Orientalist assumption that religion was the fundamental division
in Indian society. There is a general consensus that it is questionable
whether a totalizing Hindu or Muslim identity existed in any meaningful sense in India prior to the nineteenth century.

I realize this assertion will rouse the sceptics, who will argue that
Muslims and Hindus were slaughtering each other since at least 712
CE, when the teenaged Arab warrior Muhammad bin Qasim conquered the Hindu kingdom of Sindh. Indeed, the argument that tensions existed for 1,200 years, since the advent of Islam in north India,
is often made both by Pakistanis (to justify separation) and by acolytes
of the Hindutva (Hindu nationalist) cause, who routinely assert that as
many as 60,000 Hindu temples were razed to the ground by Muslim
rulers over the centuries, and mosques built on 3,000 of those temples' foundations.

That some of this happened is indisputable: one only has to visit
Sultan Iltutmish's celebrated mosque and its surrounding architecture
at the Qutb Complex in Delhi to see the elaborate Hindu religious
carvings that still adorn the pillars. But the research carried out separately by historians Cynthia Talbot and Richard M. Eaton in two differ-

ent parts of India suggest that temple desecration was largely 'a phenomenon of the advancing frontier', occasioned by warfare and
occurring mainly in the intense frenzy of armed conflict across changing territorial lines. Eaton believes that temple destruction by Turkic
and other Muslim rulers throughout India occurred mainly in kingdoms in the process of being conquered; a royal temple symbolized the
king's power in Hindu political thought, and so destroying it signified
that king's utter humiliation. Talbot's research in Andhra Pradesh at the
time of Muslim expansion into the region confirms similar findings. In
other words, invaders' attacks on temples were politically, rather than
religiously, motivated. The portrayal of Muslims as Islamist idol-breakers, driven to destroy temples because of religious fanaticism, argue
both Eaton and Talbot, is far from the truth. Obviously raiders who
came and went like Mahmud of Ghazni, Muhammad Ghori and Nadir
Shah were bent on destruction and pillage, but the Muslims who stayed
in India attacked temples not to destroy them, but because they valued
them and understood their importance.

Such an argument is bound to prove contentious, especially given
numerous examples of iconoclasm on the part of Muslim warriors. But
there are far more numerous examples of harmony and co-existence.
The best example of Indian religious coexistence in the precolonial
era, of identities being so creatively held that they could accommodate
easily to each other, comes from today's state of Kerala, dubbed by the
British the Malabar Coast. The openness to the external influences—
Arab, Roman, Chinese, British, Islamic, Christian, Brahminical—that
went into the making of the Malayali (Keralite) people reflected their
trading heritage. More than two millennia ago, Keralites had trade
relations not just with other parts of India but with the Arab world, the
Phoenicians and the Roman empire, so Malayalis have had, for a long
time now, an open and welcoming attitude to the rest of humanity.
Jews fleeing Roman persecution found refuge here; there is evidence
of their settlement in Cranganore as far back as 68 CE. And 1,500
years later, the Jews settled in Kochi, where they built a magnificent
synagogue that still stands. Kerala's Christians belong to the oldest
Christian community in the world outside Palestine. And when St
Thomas, one of Jesus's twelve apostles, brought Christianity to Kerala,
it is said he was welcomed on shore by a flute-playing Jewish girl.

St Thomas made converts among the high-born elite, the Namboodiri Brahmins, which meant there were Indians whose families had practised Christianity for far longer than the ancestors of any Briton could lay claim to.

Islam came to Kerala not by the sword, as it did in northern India, but through traders, travellers and missionaries, who brought its message of equality and brotherhood to the coastal people. The new faith was peacefully embraced and encouraged, rather than rejected: indeed, as I have mentioned earlier, the Zamorin of Calicut was so impressed by the seafaring skills of this community that he issued a decree in the sixteenth century obliging each fisherman's family in his kingdom to bring up one son as a Muslim to man his all-Muslim navy, commanded by sailors of Arab descent, the Kunjali Maraicars. The first recorded instance in Kerala of violence involving the Muslim community, religiously defined as opposed to the clashing armies of contending warriors or kings, was in British India, when the 'Moplah Rebellion' occurred in 1920.

Looking at peninsular south India at the time of the Muslim invasions (from the fourteenth to the seventeenth centuries), Cynthia Talbot observed that since a majority of medieval South India's population continued to be non-Muslim, even within the regions where Muslims were politically dominant, the two societies always overlapped. A certain degree of cooperation and collaboration was inevitable in these circumstances. The Muslim polities of the peninsula were dependent on Hindu officials and warriors for tax collection and maintenance of order in the countryside. As to the rhetorical portrayal of each other, 'both denigrating and tolerant representations of the Other coexisted at any given phase', but they tended to highlight foreignness rather than religion. And foreignness, of course, was an attribute that tended to fade, if not entirely disappear, with time.

The political consequences of this British denial of the precolonial past and the deliberate imperial construction of a 'Hindu–Muslim divide' after 1857 became vividly apparent in the late nineteenth century. When Allan Octavian Hume founded the Indian National Congress he actively welcomed Indians of all faiths to the organization; its first few presidents included Hindus, Christians, Parsis and Muslims. The British did not approve of Hume's liberal attitude. (Had they been sincere about empowering a cooperative class of English-educated Indians, they could easily have done so, co-opting these liberal lawyers, as they mostly were, into the British governance of India.) Instead, the British watched the rise to prominence of Congress, a secular body transcending religion, with growing disapproval, and pronounced it a Hindu-dominated organization. They instigated a Muslim nobleman, Nawab Khwaja Salimullah of Dacca, to start a rival organization in 1906 for his co-religionists alone, the Muslim League.

Meanwhile Lord Curzon's decision in 1905 to partition Bengal, ostensibly for administrative reasons but in reality to create a Muslim-majority province in the east, aroused fierce opposition from all segments of Bengali society and from Indian nationalists everywhere, who saw it as a transparent attempt to divide the country. The British deliberately 'sold' the partition of Bengal to the Muslims as promoting their interests, so that the Nawab of Dacca, who had initially condemned the division of his province as 'beastly', was persuaded to change his mind under the influence of Lord Curzon's visit to him. This followed speeches in which the Viceroy promised that the partition 'would invest the Mohammedans of Eastern Bengal with a unity which they had not enjoyed since the days of the old Mussulman viceroys and kings'. To sweeten the pill further the British government advanced the nawab a private loan of £100,000 at a concessional rate of interest, and soon the nawab and his followers did a U-turn to become staunch supporters of the Partition of Bengal.

The British made no effort to hide their partiality. Herbert Risley, the architect of the scheme, admitted frankly that 'one of our main objects is to split up and thereby weaken a solid body of opponents to our rule.' The Lieutenant Governor of Bengal, Sir Bampfylde Fuller, said publicly—he later claimed that he had done so in jest—'that of his two wives (meaning the Muslim and Hindu sections of his province) the Mohammedan was the favourite'. His 'jest' was taken rather too seriously by some Muslim elements, who concluded that by these words the British authorities were ready to grant them impunity for anti-Hindu violence, which then proceeded to spread in East Bengal. Assaults, rape and abductions against the Hindu minority followed: 'thus', reported Henry Nevinson, 'a new religious feud was established in Eastern Bengal'. Administrative division, as the protestors saw clearly, served as an assault upon the social unity of Bengali communities.

Nevinson goes on:

I have almost invariably found English officers and officials on the side of the Mohammedans where there is any rivalry of race or religion at all. And in Eastern Bengal this national inclination is now encouraged by the Government's open resolve to retain the Mohammedan support of the Partition by any means in its power. It was against the Hindus only that all the petty persecution of officialdom was directed. It was they who were excluded from Government posts; it was Hindu schools from which Government patronage was withdrawn. When Mohammedans rioted, the punitive police ransacked Hindu houses, and companies of little Gurkhas were quartered on Hindu populations. It was the Hindus who in one place were forbidden to sit on the riverbank. Of course, the plea was that only the Hindus were opposed to the Government's policy of dividing them from the rest of their race, so that they alone needed suppression.

Yet the Congress initially chose to take this development in its stride: seeing the League as representing merely the landed aristocracy and upper-class merchants and landlords among the Muslim population, it deemed it not to be a threat. Indeed, the election of the moderate Aga Khan as its first president seemed to confirm this judgement. The Congress declared membership of the League not to be incompatible with membership of the Congress, continued to invite League members to Congress meetings, and on three remarkable occasions, elected Muslim League members to preside over the Congress. (Hakim Ajmal Khan, Maulana Mohammed Ali and Dr M. A. Ansari enjoy the remarkable distinction of having been presidents of both the Congress and the League without having to give up either.)

In 1916, Motilal Nehru was chosen by the Congress to draft, together with a brilliant young Muslim lawyer called Muhammad Ali Jinnah, the principles that would govern cooperation with the Muslim League. Their work, recognizing the principle that decisions would not be taken affecting the interests and beliefs of a minority community without the agreement of a majority of that community's representatives, formed the foundation of what was widely hailed as the Lucknow Pact. The Congress's leading literary light, the poetess Sarojini Naidu, hailed Jinnah as the 'ambassador of Hindu–Muslim unity' and set about editing a compilation of his speeches and writings.

Indeed, for all the British encouragement, the Muslims of India as a whole did not think of their futures as anything but entwined with their Hindu compatriots. It is striking that, as late as 1918, in his most substantial book on 'the Indian question', the Aga Khan articulated a vision of India as a confluence of four civilizations—'Western', 'Far Eastern', 'Brahmanical' and 'Mohamedan'—and expressed an 'Indian patriotism' that assumed close understanding between Hindus and Muslims (including a common desire for India, rather than Britain, to colonize East Africa!). Similarly, he is dismissive of 'political Pan-Islamism', speaking of Islam as a social, cultural and spiritual force that unites believers morally around the world, but stressing that 'religion has more and more become a spiritual force in the modern world, and less and less a temporal one. In this [era] national and material interests have predominated over religious ties'. These were views widely held by other educated Indian Muslims, and had been expressed in almost identical terms by Justice Syed Mahmud four decades previously.

Mahatma Gandhi, upon assuming the leadership of the Congress, also sought to make common cause with Muslim opinion by spearheading a Khilafat agitation in support of Indian Muslim demands to restore the Caliphate in Turkey after the collapse during World War I of the Ottoman Empire. That movement fizzled out when it was overtaken by domestic developments (including some assaults by Caliphate enthusiasts on Hindus deemed insufficiently supportive of the cause) and was, in any case, made irrelevant by events in Turkey, but it was an earnest display of the Congress's determined effort to represent all Indians, irrespective of faith, and not to surrender to the British project of religious division.

The British-conducted censuses had overt political significance, since the census numbers were crucial to the political debates at the beginning of the twentieth century. They were ignored in constituting the British Indian Army, in which Muslims accounted for 50 per cent of the Indians serving in uniform despite being only 20 per cent of the population. (The Dalit leader Dr B. R. Ambedkar suggested this disproportionate representation in the army was deliberately designed 'to counteract the forces of Hindu agitation' against the British Raj.) But when it came to politics, the census figures proved most useful to the British in heightening a sense among some Muslims of being an endangered minority. Communal identity and representation became major issues, by design, when separate electorates were being defined based on religious identity for the first time by the Minto–Morley Reforms. Similarly, as we have seen, census numbers engendered a huge upheaval in colonial governance when the British sought to partition the province of Bengal.

In exactly the same way, when a limited franchise was finally extended to ordinary Indians by the Montagu–Chelmsford Reforms to vote for positions of limited authority in British-approved bodies, imperial officials provided political franchise to several of the communal identities the British government had created within Indian society, each one competing against the other to gain favour with the colonialists. Thus there were seats reserved for Hindus, Muslims, Sikhs and so on. This resulted in the aggravation of communal identities, since what little politics was permitted could quickly devolve into a communal competition for limited resources. Public sentiments could be aroused to exaggerate differences amongst Indians, which redounded to the benefit of the British, who, of course, were above it all. So Englishmen who would have shuddered at the idea of allowing the Jews of Golders Green to vote separately in London elections enthusiastically arranged separate electorates for the Muslims of India, where Muslim voters could only vote for Muslim candidates, Sikhs for Sikhs and Christians for Christians. The practice prompted Will Durant to observe that the British approach 'intensifies and encourages the racial and religious divisions which statesmanship would seek to heal'.

But healing was not the object of government policy, as we have seen from the outset of this chapter: a divided people were easier to subjugate. Lord Olivier, Secretary of State for India in the 1920s, openly admitted to a 'predominant bias in British officialdom in favour of the Moslem community... Largely as a make-weight against Hindu nationalism'. This was compounded by the British tendency to give the Muslims even more than they had asked for. Thus, when the Muslim League demanded one of two possible privileges in the five Muslim-majority provinces, either statutory majorities, enshrined in law, with joint electorates, or separate electorates for Muslims the British gave them statutory majorities with separate electorates in their Communal Award, letting the Muslim Leaguers have it both ways.

Ironically, had Indian politics been encouraged to develop as British politics had, along ideological lines, one could have seen the emergence of a conservative party and a socialist one, with some liberals in between; these tendencies were all present among Indian public men. This kind of conventional political contention could have kept India united, with Jinnah and Nehru becoming the Disraeli and Gladstone of their era in an emerging Indian Dominion. But colonial policies drove conservatives and socialists alike to define themselves primarily in relation to the communal question, leading ultimately to the tragic sundering of the country.

The alterations this brought about to Indian sensibilities were profound. Most scholars of Indian history blame the British for the gradual whittling away of the shared syncretic traditions described earlier. As Alex von Tunzelmann noted in her history, *Indian Summer: The Secret History of the End of an Empire*, when 'the British started to define "communities" based on religious identity and attach political representation to them, many Indians stopped accepting the diversity of their own thoughts and began to ask themselves in which of the boxes they belonged'.

Such divisions were heightened not just between religious communities, but also within them. Thus the British can be largely blamed for the creation of previously non-existent Shia-Sunni tensions within the Muslim population of Lucknow. Prior to the British annexation of Oude (Avadh), the two sects had lived in harmony under a Shia nawab, whose celebrations of the Shia festival of Muharram had included Sunnis and Hindus as well in a public affirmation of his people's fraternity. Once the British had deposed the nawab in 1856, the unifying symbol of the throne was lost, and the relationship between the ruling Shia nobility and the non-Shia subjects of the kingdom (Sunnis and Hindus) irrevocably transformed. The exaggeration by the British of communal identities now embraced sectarian differences between the two Muslim sects.

As the scholar Keith Hjortshoj recounts: 'By 1905, religious rhetoric between Shias and Sunnis had reached such heights that Sunnis in Lucknow did not join in the Marsiyah elegies during Muharram, but instead recited a praise of the first three Caliphs called the Madhe-Sahaba. Shias responded with Tabarra curses upon the Sahaba.' Shia leaders also managed to persuade the British government that Sunni practices during Muharram were largely irrelevant, so the British enacted strict laws against practices by Sunnis that could be offensive to Shias. Before long the British had decided to authorize separate Shia and Sunni processions to commemorate Muharram.

The British-sponsored Shia-Sunni divide in Lucknow is one of the clearest examples of how the British encouraged differences, and how Indians sought to create communities that the Raj would recognize and to which it would give political weight. This occurred, as it happened, at the very time when various political groups were competing for space in the expanded Indian representation announced for the viceroy's and governors' councils under the Minto-Morley Reforms. 'When the British authorities assumed responsibility for banning or approving commemorations, arbitrating disputes, and regulating procession routes,' Hjortshoj has explained, 'they transformed religious differences into public, political, and legal issues. And so they have remained.'

Far from promoting Indian political unity, British policies identified, accentuated and legitimized such divisions. One can lay not only a Hindu–Muslim divide at their door, but also credit them for giving legal definition to a new political division between the Sunni and Shia communities.

The British-promoted cleavage also divided the Muslim community. A prominent Deobandi cleric who opposed the communal polarization promoted by the British and fought against the League's Pakistan project, Maulana Husain Ahmad Madani, wrote passionately to a co-religionist as late as 1945:

Muslims have been together with the Hindus since they moved to Hindustan. And I have been with them since I was born. I was born and raised here. If two people live together in the same country, same city, they will share [a] lot of things with each other. Till the time there are Muslims in India, they will be together with the Hindus. In the bazaars, in homes, in railways, in trams, buses, lorries, in stations, colleges, post offices, jails, police stations, courts, councils, assembles, hotels, etc. You tell me where and when we don't meet them or are not together with them? You are a zamindar. Are not your tenants Hindus? You are a trader; you don't buy and sell from Hindus? You are a lawyer: don't you have Hindu clients? You are in a district or municipal board; won't you be dealing with Hindus? Who is not with the Hindus?

The creation and perpetuation of Hindu–Muslim antagonism was the most significant accomplishment of British imperial policy: the project of *divide et impera* would reach its culmination in the horrors of Partition that eventually accompanied the collapse of British authority in 1947.

A Saint Among Sinners

The great Indian opponent of the British Raj, Mahatma Gandhi, opposed colonial rule in an unusual way: not by violence but by the strength of moral force. Gandhi's life was, of course, his lesson. He was unique among the statesmen of the twentieth century in his determination not only to live his beliefs but also to reject any separation between beliefs and action. Gandhi was a philosopher who was constantly seeking to live out his own ideas, whether they applied to individual self-improvement or social change: his autobiography was typically subtitled *The Story of My Experiments with Truth*. Truth could not be obtained by 'untruthful' or unjust means, which included inflicting violence upon one's opponent. The means had to be worthy of the ends; if they were not, the ends would fail too.

To describe his method, Gandhi coined the expression *satyagraha*, literally, 'holding on to truth' or, as he variously described it, truth-force, love-force or soul-force. He disliked the English term 'passive resistance' because *satyagraha* required activism, not passivity. If you believed in Truth and cared enough to obtain it, Gandhi felt, you could not afford to be passive: you had to be prepared actively to suffer for Truth. So non-violence, like many later concepts labelled with a negation, from non-cooperation to non-alignment, meant much more than the denial of an opposite; it did not merely imply the absence of violence. Non-violence was the way to vindicate the truth not by the infliction of suffering on the opponent, but on one's self. It was essential to willingly accept punishment in order to demonstrate the strength of one's convictions.

This was the approach Gandhi brought to the movement for India's independence and it worked. Where sporadic terrorism and moderate constitutionalism had both proved ineffective, Gandhi took the issue of freedom to the masses as one of simple right and wrong and gave them a technique to which the British had no response. By going beyond the councils and the meeting rooms he seized the public imagination. By abstaining from violence the Mahatma wrested the moral advantage. By breaking the law non-violently he showed up the injustice of the law. By accepting the punishments imposed on him he confronted his captors with their own brutalization. By voluntarily imposing suffering upon himself in his hunger strikes he demonstrated the lengths to which he was prepared to go in defence of what he considered to be right. In the end he made the perpetuation of British rule an impossibility.

In this, Gandhi was embodying what the doughty nationalist Lala Lajpat Rai had propounded in 1905:

'The British are not a spiritual people,' the Lala had said. 'They are either a fighting race or a commercial nation. It would be throwing pearls before swine to appeal to them in the name of the higher morality or justice or on ethical grounds. They are a self-reliant, haughty people, who can appreciate self-respect and self-reliance even in their opponents.' (Despite this insight, Lajpat Rai was himself killed, aged sixty-three, by repeated blows to the head by the stave of a superintendent of police, James A. Scott, while leading a peaceful, non-violent protest against the British in 1928.)

As the non-violent Indian nationalist movement gained traction, public sympathy and international attention in the 1920s and 1930s, with Gandhi seizing the world's imagination through his *satyagraha*, his fasts and the Empire-defying Salt March, the British felt obliged to grant improved measures of self-governance through the Government of India Act, 1935. Even then, however, the franchise was extended to less than 10 per cent of the population and, as before, Indians voted not as citizens of a single country but as members of different religious groups, with Muslim voters choosing Muslim members from a reserved list—a further confirmation of *divide et impera*. Separate electorates were part of the British attempt to thwart Mahatma Gandhi's mass politics, which for the first time had created a common national consciousness not just among the educated elite who had formerly dominated the Congress but amongst the general public he had successfully mobilized.

The British decision to declare the community then known as 'Untouchables' (today as Dalits, or more bureaucratically as 'Scheduled Castes') to be a minority community entitled to separate representation, distinct from other Hindus, in a new category called the 'Depressed

Classes', was seen by Indian nationalists as a ploy to divide the majority community in furtherance of imperial interests. Dalits, in turn, saw the nationalist movement as dominated by the same 'upper' castes that had long discriminated against them, and Dalit leaders like Ambedkar, a brilliant constitutional scholar who had risen from hard-scrabble poverty by sheer dint of merit, embraced separate electorates as a means of asserting their right to choose their own representatives.

The Indian National Congress, led by Mahatma Gandhi, was already opposed to separate electorates for Muslims, Sikhs and Christians, since it saw the practice as designed to promote a sense that they were separate communities whose interests were somehow different from the general mass of Indians. Still, the Congress could not formally oppose separate electorates for fear of antagonizing minority groups while the British were busy stoking minority fears of Hindu domination if and whenever self-government came to India. The Congress, therefore, confined its opposition to the principle that separate electorates were wrong and unnecessary but could only be abandoned with the consent of the minorities.

However, the British attempt to separate the Depressed Classes was of a different order, since it was the first time that separate electorates were being proposed within a religious community, and the strategy of fragmenting Indian nationalism and breaking the incipient unity of the Indian masses was clearly apparent to Congress leaders. Gandhi demanded that the representatives of the Depressed Classes should be elected by the general electorate under a wide, and if possible universal, common franchise, and undertook a fast unto death in 1932 that riveted the nation and compelled the British and the Dalit leadership to give in. Under a political compromise, known as the Poona Pact, that year separate electorates for the Depressed Classes were abandoned but additional seats were reserved for them in the provincial and central legislatures—an increase from 71 to 147 in the former and to 18 per cent of the Central Legislature.

(Interestingly enough, the leader of the Dalits who clashed with Gandhi over the issue, Dr B. R. Ambedkar, went on to serve after Independence as chairman of the Drafting Committee for India's Constitution, and ensured that his country would have the world's first and farthest-reaching affirmative action programme for his community.

Though separate electorates were dropped for good, 85 seats in independent India's 543-seat lower house were reserved for Scheduled Castes and Tribes, as were a quota of places in government service and universities—guaranteeing not just opportunities but assured outcomes.)

If the Dalits did not end up with separate electorates, the Muslim League found it difficult initially to profit from them. 'The ambassador of Hindu–Muslim unity' was not an appellation destined to endure for Jinnah. Disdaining the populism and the mass appeal of Gandhi, Jinnah had retreated to his law practice in England, only to return, after a long political sulk, as the leader determined to take the Muslim League towards separatism. Jinnah began to claim that India's Muslims represented a nation unto themselves: 'We are different beings,' he declared in barefaced denial of his entire upbringing, career, social relations and personal life. 'There is nothing in life which links us together. Our names, our clothes, our foods—they are all different; our economic life, our educational idea, our treatment of women, our attitude to animals... We challenge each other at every point of the compass.' For the Savile Row-suit-wearing, sausage-eating, whisky-swilling Jinnah to go on about clothes and food was a bit rich, as was the reference to women's habits coming from the lips of a man who had been famously indulgent of his young wife's scandalously 'bold' attire.

But the political choice had been made to accentuate difference, and that is what the Muslim League leader set out to do. He sought to establish the League as the 'sole representatives' of India's Muslims, but Muslim voters, inconveniently enough, demurred, voting for Muslims of other political allegiances, including, most gallingly, for Muslim members of the Indian National Congress, as well as for the League.

The 1937 elections saw the Indian National Congress being elected to rule eight provinces; the party won an astonishing 617 of the 739 'general' seats it contested, and even 25 of the 59 seats, reserved exclusively for Muslims, that the Congress contested. Several other parties, and 385 Independents, also won seats. Trailing a distant second to the Congress was the Muslim League, which failed to win even a plurality of the seats reserved for Muslims, winning just 106 of the 1,585 seats at stake and failing to take control of any province. The domestic political contest, it seemed, had been decisively settled in favour of the inclusive, pluralist, multi-ethnic party, the Congress.

But those who saw it that way had spoken too soon. The Congress's victory was far from determinant. Though the elections involved some 15.5 million voters and marked a significant step forward in the creation of representative governance, most key powers were still retained by the Viceroy, and no elections were held to the central government, which continued to be run by him. This was deliberate: alarmed by the growing popularity of the Congress, the British counted upon what the viceroy, Lord Linlithgow, called 'the potency of provincial autonomy to destroy the effectiveness of the Congress as an all-India instrument of revolution'. The hope was to give the party's provincial leaders enough of a taste of the loaves and fishes of office to wean them away from their national leadership and give them a personal stake in collaboration with the Raj. The electoral system was also stacked in favour of rural representation in order to get more landlords elected whose interests would diverge from the socialist programmes of the Congress's national leaders.

So much of the talk of self-government was hollow, and its hollowness was confirmed when it was the Viceroy, and not the elected representatives of the Indian people, who declared war on Germany on behalf of India in 1939. This promptly precipitated the resignation of the elected Congress ministries, in protest at not being consulted on such a vital matter. The pretence of developing responsible political institutions in India was laid to rest. And soon a rough beast, in Yeats' immortal words, arose amid the Muslims of India, slouching towards a new Bethlehem to be born.

Stumbling Towards Armageddon

To the surprise of both their supporters and their critics, the Congress ministries in the nine provinces had conducted themselves as able stewards of the governmental system of the British Raj. For the most part they did little to dismantle oppressive British laws, and in some cases proved as zealous in arresting radicals as the British themselves had been.

Meanwhile, both during his party's electoral setback and then when the Congress opened the window of opportunity by resigning its ministries, Muhammad Ali Jinnah, the increasingly hard-line leader of the Muslim League, had proven to be a skilled tactician, making up for the

League's defeat in the Muslim-majority provinces of Punjab and Bengal by in effect co-opting the victorious leaders there (Sir Sikandar Hayat Khan of the Unionist Party and Fazlul Huq of the Krishak Praja Party, respectively) onto the League platform. The Congress itself was riven by infighting. Its acceptance of office had both alienated its left wing and made it vulnerable to largely specious charges of imposing 'Hindu majority rule' on the Muslim minority.

Ironically, when war came, the Viceroy would have found ready support from the Congress, whose leader, Jawaharlal Nehru, had declared that in any conflict between democracy and fascism, 'our sympathies must inevitably be on the side of democracy... I should like India to play its full part and throw all her resources into the struggle for a new order'. Nehru's abhorrence of fascism was so great that he would gladly have led a free India into war on the side of the democracies, provided that choice was made by Indians and not imposed upon them by the British. But when Germany's invasion of Poland on 1 September 1939 led Britain to declare war upon it, Indians noted the irony of the English fighting to defend the sovereignty of a weak country resisting the brute force of foreign conquest—precisely what Indian nationalists were doing against British imperialism. So Britain would fight Germany for doing to Poland what Britain had been doing to India for nearly two hundred years.

Nehru blamed British appeasement for the fall of Spain to the fascists, the betrayal of Ethiopia to the Italians, and the selling out of Czechoslovakia to the Nazis: he wanted India to have no part of the responsibility for British policy, which he saw as designed to protect the narrow class-interests of a few imperialists. Despite his stated antipathy for fascism and the Nazis, Nehru saw no reason why Indians should be expected to make sacrifices to preserve British rule over them. How could a subject India be ordered to fight for a free Poland? A free and democratic India, on the other hand, would gladly fight for freedom and democracy.

Under his direction, the Congress Working Committee adopted a resolution making this case (while rejecting former President Subhas Chandra Bose's demand that civil disobedience be launched immediately). Nehru made no secret of his own anti-Nazi views; all he wanted was some indication from the British government of respect for his position so that India and Britain could then gladly 'join in a struggle for freedom'. The Congress leaders made it clear to the viceroy that all they needed was a declaration that India would be given the chance to determine its own future after the war. The Congress position was greeted with understanding and even some approval in left-wing circles in Britain, but though he would have found allies in the anti-fascist Congress governments in the provinces and amongst Congress legislators in the Central Assembly, Lord Linlithgow did not so much as make a pretence of consulting India's elected leaders before declaring war on Germany on behalf of India. Instead, he turned to the Muslim League for support.

The Congress had, in fact, hoped for a joint approach on the war issue with the League. The Viceroy's statement in October 1939 emphatically rejecting the Congress position, however, prompted the working committee, with Nehru in the lead, to order all its provincial ministries to resign rather than continue to serve a war effort in which they had been denied an honourable role. The decision was taken on a point of principle, but politically it proved a monumental blunder. It deprived the Congress of their only leverage with the British government, cast aside the fruits of their electoral success, and presented Jinnah with a golden opportunity. He broke off talks with the Congress—declaring the day of the Congress resignations a 'day of deliverance'—and turned to the viceroy instead.

Two years in the political wilderness after the electoral setbacks of 1937 had already transformed the League. Congress rule in many provinces had unwittingly increased Muslim concern, even alarm, about the implications of democratic majoritarian rule in a country so overwhelmingly Hindu. Many Muslims began to see themselves as a political and economic minority, and the League spoke to their insecurities. Jinnah had begun to come to the conclusion that the only effective answer to the Congress's political strength would be separation—the partition of the country to create an independent state in the Muslim-majority areas of the northwest and east. This demand would be enshrined in the League's Lahore Resolution of 23 March 1940 calling for the creation of Pakistan. Nehru and his fellow Congress leaders were largely oblivious of the change of thinking amongst many League members, manifest in an increasingly populist political strategy (it was only in 1939, for instance, that Jinnah began to learn Urdu and to don the 'Muslim' *achkan* (a knee-length coat buttoned down the front) for official photographs, actions reminiscent of that old saw from the French tumult of 1848: 'I am their leader—I must follow them').

In October 1939, Jinnah persuaded Lord Linlithgow, the Viceroy, to enlist the League as an interlocutor equal to the Congress and as the sole representative of India's Muslims, a position to which its electoral results did not yet entitle it. The Viceroy, anxious to prevent Congress–League unity on the war issue, consented. The League's policy, he observed, was now the most important obstacle to any talk of Indian independence, and therefore needed to be encouraged. That November Jinnah was invited, for the first time, to broadcast a special message to Muslims on the occasion of the Id festival; an explicit recognition of the League president as the spokesman of the Muslim community. Nehru and the Congress simply saw such claims as illegitimate and premised on bigotry; however, they did not do enough to address the real crisis of confidence brewing in the Muslim community at the prospect of majority rule.

Through much of 1940 the Congress played a waiting game, hoping for British concessions. Some Congressmen were prepared to go even farther and extend direct support to the war effort if there was a national government established in India to support it. But Linlithgow was a large, slow-moving and slow-witted man: his thinking was far removed from even the most basic of Indian aspirations. (He wrote to London in April 1940: 'I am not too keen to start talking about a period after which British rule will have ceased in India. I suspect that that day is very remote and I feel the [less] we say about it in all probability the better.' Indeed that was the year in which Churchill confidently expressed the belief that the British empire would last a thousand years.[9]) When the official response of the government came in August 1940, it was a derisory offer to associate a few 'representative Indians' with the Viceroy's toothless advisory councils. Nehru rejected this utterly. Civil disobedience seemed the only answer.

[9] Brigadier Enoch Powell (the future Conservative politician) wrote as late as May 1946 that 'India would need British control of one kind or another for at least 50 years more.'

The government decided not to wait for what Nehru might do. They arrested him on 30 October 1940 and, after a trial distinguished by a magnificent statement by the accused ('it is the British empire itself that is on trial before the bar of the world'), sentenced him to four years in prison. The conditions of his detention were unusually harsh, with a number of petty indignities inflicted upon him, in particular relating to his ability to send or receive mail, which deprived him of the solace that letters had provided over the years. In December 1941, however, despite the opposition of Winston Churchill, the War Cabinet in London authorized the release of all the imprisoned Congressmen. Nehru hoped in vain for some policy declaration by the British that would enable him to commit India to the Allied cause, but the reactionary Churchill and his blinkered representatives in New Delhi went the other way, with Churchill (whose subsequent beatification as an apostle of freedom seems all the more preposterous) explicitly declaring that the principles of the Atlantic Charter would not apply to India. This was all the more inexplicable in the face of the rout of British forces in Asia: Singapore fell in February, Burma in March; the Japanese were at India's gates in the east, and Netaji Subhas Chandra Bose, who had fled British India, had fashioned an 'Indian National Army' in mid-1941 out of prisoners of war, to fight alongside the Japanese. Nehru had no desire to see one emperor's rule supplanted by another's: he started organizing the Congress to prepare for resistance to the Japanese. American sympathy was matched by that of the Labour Party in the War Cabinet. Clement Attlee persuaded his colleagues to send the socialist Sir Stafford Cripps to India in early 1942 with an offer of Dominion status after the war, with the possibility of partition.

Cripps was already a legend in British politics, a former Solicitor General who had been expelled from the Labour Party in 1939 for advocating a united front with the Conservatives (which, of course, came to pass during the war), and who combined an ascetic vegetarianism with a flamboyant ego ('there, but for the grace of God, goes God,' Churchill remarked of him). Cripps had visited India after the outbreak of war in 1939 and knew many Indian leaders; he considered Nehru a friend. Yet the Cripps Mission was welcomed by Jinnah, but foundered on the opposition of the Congress. Mahatma Gandhi objected principally because the British proposal appeared to concede the idea of

Partition; he memorably called the offer 'a post-dated cheque' (an imaginative journalist added, 'on a crashing bank') and urged its rejection. Congress President Maulana Azad insisted that the defence of India should be the responsibility of Indian representatives, not the unelected Government of India led by the British Viceroy, and it was on this issue that Nehru refused to compromise. Cripps was inclined to give in, and spoke of an Indian national government running the country's defence with the viceroy functioning as a figurehead (like the British king). But he had exceeded his instructions: Churchill ('I hate Indians. They are a beastly people with a beastly religion.'), abetted by the hidebound Viceroy, Linlithgow, and the often hapless commander-in-chief, Lord Archibald Wavell, scuttled the negotiations.

Churchill had strong views on Gandhi. Commenting on the Mahatma's meeting with the viceroy of India, 1931, he had notoriously declared: 'It is alarming and nauseating to see Mr Gandhi, a seditious Middle Temple lawyer, now posing as a fakir of a type well known in the east, striding half naked up the steps of the viceregal palace, while he is still organising and conducting a campaign of civil disobedience, to parlay on equal terms with the representative of the Emperor-King.' (Gandhi had nothing in common with fakirs, Muslim spiritual mendicants, but Churchill was rarely accurate about India.) 'Gandhi-ism and all it stands for,' declared Churchill, 'will, sooner or later, have to be grappled with and finally crushed.' In such matters Churchill was the most reactionary of Englishmen, with views so extreme they cannot be excused as being reflective of their times: in fact Churchill's statements appalled most of his contemporaries. Even the positive gloss placed on him today seems inexcusable: 'He put himself at the head of a movement of irreconcilable imperialist romantics,' wrote Boris Johnson in his recent admiring biography of Churchill. 'Die-hard defenders of the Raj and of the God-given right of every pink-jowled Englishman to sit on his veranda and...glory in the possession of India'.

Mahatma Gandhi, increasingly exasperated by the British, argued that Nehru's pro-Allied position had won India no concessions. His public message to the government was to 'leave India to God or anarchy'. Nehru, ever the Harrovian Anglophile, quoted Cromwell (in a conscious echo of the Harrovian Amery, who had used the same words just two years earlier in Parliament in calling for Neville Chamberlain's resignation as prime minister): 'You have sat too long here for any good you have been doing. Depart, I say, and let us have done with you. In the name of God, go!' On 7 August 1942 in Bombay, the All-India Congress Committee, at Gandhi's urging, adopted a resolution moved by Nehru, and seconded by Patel, calling upon Britain to—in a journalistic paraphrase that became more famous than the actual words of the resolution—'Quit India'. (Gandhi's own preferred phrase was 'Do or Die'.) Within thirty-six hours the Congress leaders were arrested.

For all of Gandhi's devotion to non-violence, his jailing, together with the rest of the Congress leadership, left the Quit India movement in the hands of the young and the hot-headed. An underground movement was born, which actively resorted to acts of sabotage. Ordinary people took improbable risks to hoist the national flag on government buildings. Young newspaper-boys added sotto voce subversion to their sales cries: '*Times of India*. Quit India! *Times of India*. Quit India!' In the weeks after the arrests, no day passed without reports of clashes between demonstrators and police. The British responded with ruthless repression, firing upon unarmed protestors, killing dozens every week, flogging offenders, and censoring (and closing down) nationalist newspapers. 'Quit India' became the drumbeat of a national awakening, but all it did was prolong the nation's continued subjugation.

Wartime hardened British attitudes to the prisoners as well. Gandhi 'should not be released on the account of a mere threat of fasting', Churchill told the Cabinet. 'We should be rid of a bad man and an enemy of the Empire if he died.' He was quite prepared to facilitate the process, suggesting that the Mahatma should be 'bound hand and foot at the gates of Delhi, and let the viceroy sit on the back of a giant elephant and trample [the Mahatma] into the dirt.'

What became Nehru's longest spell in prison, a total of 1,040 days, or over thirty-four months, from 9 August 1942 to 15 June 1945, saw the British moving to strengthen the position of Jinnah and the Muslim League, pressuring Jinnah's critics within the party to remain in the League and under his leadership. Muslim opponents of the Pakistan idea were dissuaded or sidelined. Others who could have made a difference (like Sir Sikandar Hayat Khan in Punjab and Allah Bux in Sindh) died before they were able to influence the outcome. The League formed governments (often with the votes of British members, and with Congress legislators in jail) in provinces where it had been routed in the elections, and enjoyed patronage appointments where formal office was not possible. In this effort the British were complicit: as Lord Linlithgow, Britain's viceroy during the fraught years of World War II, admitted of Jinnah, 'He represents a minority, and a minority that can only effectively hold its own with our assistance.' As the League grew with British patronage, its membership swelled from 112,000 in 1941 to over 2 million members in 1944.

The futility of the Quit India movement, which accomplished little but the Congress's own exclusion from national affairs, compounded the original blunder of the Congress in resigning its ministries. It had left the field free for the Muslim League, which emerged from the war immeasurably enhanced in power and prestige. Both the resignations of the Congress ministries in 1939 and the Quit India movement in 1942 turned out to be futile gestures of demonstrative rather than far-sighted politics. They paved the way for the triumph of the Muslim League.

On 15 June 1945, Nehru and his Congress colleagues emerged from prison, blinking in the sunlight. The war was over, and they had been freed. But they would be taking their first steps in, and towards, freedom in a world that had changed beyond recognition.

Endgame: Election, Revolt, Division

The British had not covered themselves with glory during the war. They had run a military dictatorship in a country that they had claimed to be preparing for democracy. They had presided over one of the worst famines in human history, the Bengal Famine of 1943, while diverting food (on Churchill's personal orders) from starving civilians to well-supplied Tommies. (More on this in the next chapter.) Even Lord Wavell, who had been rewarded for military failure (in both the deserts of North Africa and the jungles of Burma) by succeeding Linlithgow as viceroy, considered the British government's attitude to India 'negligent, hostile and contemptuous to a degree I had not anticipated'.

The Labour victory in the British general election of 1945 meant that the egregious Churchill was soon to be replaced as prime minister by Attlee, but this did not precipitate any change in the anti-Congressism of the British authorities in India. Wavell convened a conference in Simla from late June 1945, which the Viceroy allowed Jinnah to wreck. In this atmosphere of frustration and despair, the British called elections in India at the end of 1945, for seats in the central and provincial assemblies.

The Congress was woefully unequipped to contest them. Its blunder in surrendering the reins of power in 1939 and then losing its leadership and cadres to prison from 1942 meant that it went into the campaign tired, dispirited and ill-organized. The League, on the other hand, had flourished during the war; its political machinery was well oiled with patronage and pelf, while the Congress's was rusty from disuse. The electoral fortunes of 1937 were now significantly reversed. The Congress still carried a majority of the provinces. But except for the North-West Frontier Province, where the Congress won nineteen Muslim seats to the League's seventeen, the League swept the reserved seats for Muslims across the board, even in provinces like Bombay and Madras which had seemed immune to the communal contagion. Whatever the explanation—and Nehru could have offered a few— there was no longer any escaping the reality that Jinnah and the Muslim League could now legitimately claim a popular mandate to speak for the majority of India's Muslims.

Nehru did not believe that this meant that the partition of the country, which he thought totally impractical, was inevitable. In speeches, interviews and articles throughout late 1945 and early 1946, he expressed the belief that, free of foreign rule, the Muslims of India would relinquish any thought of secession. The Muslims of India, he wrote, 'are only technically a minority. They are vast in numbers and powerful in other ways, and it is patent that they cannot be coerced against their will... This communal question is essentially one of protection of vested interests, and religion has always been a useful stalking horse for this purpose'. He even argued that Congress should grant the right of secession just to allay any Muslim fears, not in the expectation that the Muslim League-ruled provinces would actually exercise it. But whether, as many Indian analysts have suggested, Jinnah had really meant to establish a separate state or was merely advocating Pakistan to obtain leverage over the Congress, his followers had taken him at his word. A state of their own was what they were determined to have, and by the spring of 1946 Nehru's idealism appeared naïve, even dangerously so.

Tragically, *divide et impera* had worked too well. A device to maintain the integrity of British India had made it impossible for that integrity to be maintained without the British.

* * *

Britain's time in India was almost up. Even Indian soldiers and policemen openly expressed their support for the nationalist leaders, heedless of the reaction of their British officers. Mutinies broke out in the air force and the British Indian Navy. The latter was serious, affecting seventy-eight ships and twenty shore establishments, involving 20,000 naval personnel. Violence erupted at political events. In one incident in Bombay, 233 demonstrators were killed by British soldiers putting down an anti-British riot. The demand for freedom was all but drowned out by the clamour for partition.

In a gesture so counterproductive that it could almost have been an act of expiation, the Raj clumsily gave the warring factions a last chance of unity. It decided to prosecute the defectors of Bose's Indian National Army. Bose himself had died in a fiery plane crash at war's end in Formosa (Taiwan), so the Raj sought to find scapegoats amongst his lieutenants. In a desire to appear even-handed, the British chose to place three INA soldiers on trial in Delhi's historic Red Fort: a Hindu, a Muslim and a Sikh. The result was a national outcry that spanned the communal divide. Whatever the errors and misjudgements of the INA men (and Nehru believed freedom could never have come through an alliance with foreigners, let alone foreign fascists), they had not been disloyal to their motherland. Each of the three defendants became a symbol of his community's proud commitment to independence from alien rule. Both the Congress and the League rose to the trio's defence; for the first time in their long careers, Nehru and Jinnah accepted the same brief, Nehru donning a barrister's gown after twenty-five years.

But the moment passed: the defence of three patriots was no longer enough to guarantee a common definition of patriotism. The ferment across the country made the result of the trials almost irrelevant. The trials were eventually abandoned, because by the time they had begun it was apparent that the ultimate treason to the British Raj was being contemplated in its own capital.

London, under the Labour Party, exhausted by war, was determined to rid itself of the burdens of its Indian empire. In February 1946,

Prime Minister Attlee announced the dispatch of a Cabinet Mission to India 'to discuss with leaders of Indian opinion the framing of an Indian Constitution'. The endgame had begun.

In April 1946, Nehru was elected unopposed as president of the Congress, with an interim Indian government being formed in advance of talks with the Cabinet Mission in Simla in May. The Mission, a trium- virate of Sir Stafford Cripps, Lord Pethick-Lawrence and A. V. Alexander, was besieged. The vultures, sensing that the Raj was close to its end, began gathering for the feast. The negotiations and confabulations, intrigue and manoeuvring amongst and within the various interested parties—the British, the Congress, the Muslim League, the Hindu Mahasabha, the loyalists, the communists, the civil servants—became more intense and more convoluted with each passing day. Wavell's astonishingly candid diaries reveal his distaste for, and distrust of, prac- tically every Indian politician he had to deal with, each (in his eyes) proving more dishonest than the next. Though he was, like most of the British administration, hostile to the Congress and sympathetic to the League his government had helped nurture, he was scathing in his con- tempt for the mendacity of the League's leaders, and of their 'hymn of hate against Hindus'. (No Congress leader expressed any hatred of Muslims to the viceroy.)

Even the idea of Pakistan seemed to take many forms in the minds of its own advocates, with several seeing it as a Muslim state within a united India, and others advocating assorted forms of decentralized confederation rather than outright secession. (The American journalist Phillips Talbot told me of Sir Abdullah Haroon of the League showing him, in 1940, eight separate plans for Pakistan then being debated by the League's high command.) Jinnah was steadfast in his demand for a separate state in the northwest and east of the country, but avoided giving specific answers as to how the creation of such a state could serve its declared purpose of protecting Muslims in the Hindu-majority provinces. Nehru, meanwhile, sought nothing less than an act of abdi- cation from the British: India's political arrangements should, he declared, be left to Indians to determine in their own constituent assembly, free of British mediation.

Part of the problem at the time may well have lain in a profound miscalculation on Nehru's part about the true intentions of the British.

Cut off by imprisonment from the political realities of world affairs, Nehru came to Simla believing (as he asserted to Phillips Talbot) that perfidious Albion was still trying to hold on to her prized imperial possession by encouraging division amongst the Indian parties. Talbot felt that Nehru had simply not realized that Britain was exhausted, near bankrupt, unwilling and unable to despatch the 60,000 British troops the government in London estimated would be required to reassert its control in India. London wanted to cut and run, and if the British could not leave behind a united India, they were prepared to 'cut' the country quite literally before running. Nehru, still imagining an all-powerful adversary seeking to perpetuate its hegemony, and unaware of the extent to which the League had become a popular party amongst Indian Muslims, dealt with both on erroneous premises. 'How differently would Nehru and his colleagues have negotiated,' Talbot wondered, 'had they understood Britain's weakness rather than continuing to be obsessed with its presumed strength?' The question haunts our hindsight.

When the Simla Conference began on 9 May 1946, Jinnah who was cool but civil to Nehru refused to shake hands with either of the two Muslim Congressmen, Maulana Azad or Khan Abdul Ghaffar Khan; he wished to be seen as the sole spokesman of Muslim India. Nonetheless, when the Cabinet Mission proposed a three-tier plan for India's governance, with a weak centre (limited to defence, external affairs and communications), autonomous provinces (with the right of secession after five years) and groups of provinces (at least one of which would be predominantly Muslim), the League accepted the proposal, even though it meant giving up the idea of a sovereign Pakistan.

The viceroy, without waiting for the Congress's formal acceptance of the scheme, invited fourteen Indians to serve as an interim government. While most of the leading Muslim Leaguers and Congressmen were on the list, there was a startling omission: not a single Muslim Congressman had been invited to serve. The Congress replied that it accepted the plan in principle, but could not agree to a government whose Muslim members were all from the League. Jinnah made it clear he could not accept anything else, and the resultant impasse proved intractable. The Cabinet Mission left for London with its plan endorsed but this dispute unresolved, leaving a caretaker viceroy's council in charge of the country. Ironically, its only Indian member (along with seven Englishmen) was a

Muslim civil servant, Sir Akbar Hydari, who had made clear his fundamental opposition in principle to the idea of Pakistan.

Meanwhile, the problem of the Cabinet Mission's proposed government remained to be addressed. Both Congress and the League had
accepted the plan in principle; the details were yet to be agreed upon.
Nehru, newly restored to the presidency of the Congress, chaired a
meeting of the AICC in Bombay at which he rashly interpreted
Congress's acceptance of the plan as meaning that 'we are not bound
by a single thing except that we have decided to go into the Constituent
Assembly'. The implications of his statement were still being parsed
when he repeated it at a press conference immediately afterwards,
adding that 'we are absolutely free to act'. Nehru stated specifically that
he did not think the grouping of provinces, so important to the League,
would necessarily survive a free vote. An incensed Jinnah reacted by
withdrawing the League's acceptance of the Cabinet Mission Plan.

Nehru was widely blamed for his thoughtlessness in provoking the
end of the brief hope of Congress–League cooperation in a united
Indian government, even on the League's terms. But even had Nehru
held his tongue in July 1946, it is by no means clear that a common
Congress–League understanding would have survived. Azad had been
willing to relinquish the claims of Muslim Congressmen to office in the
interests of unity, but the party as a whole was not prepared to concede
the point to Jinnah. In stating that the grouping of provinces was not
immutable, Nehru was echoing the letter of the Plan if not its spirit.
(The League could have been accused of doing the same thing when it
declared that the Plan gave it the basis to work for Pakistan). To see him
as wrecker-in-chief of the country's last chance at avoiding partition is,
therefore, to overstate the case. As his biographer M. J. Akbar put it,
'Pakistan was created by Jinnah's will and Britain's willingness'—not
by Nehru's wilfulness.

On 8 August 1946, the Congress Working Committee, bolstered by
the admission of fresh faces appointed by the new president (including
two relatively youthful women, Kamaladevi Chattopadhyay and
Rajkumari Amrit Kaur), declared that it accepted the Cabinet Mission
Plan with its own interpretations on issues of detail. But this was not
enough to bring Jinnah back into the game. Nehru met with him (at
Jinnah's home in Bombay) to seek agreement on an interim govern-

ment, but Jinnah proved obdurate: he was determined to obtain Pakistan. The Muslim League leader declared 16 August 1946 as 'Direct Action Day' to drive home this demand. Thousands of Muslim Leaguers took to the streets in an orgy of violence, looting and mayhem, and 16,000 innocents were killed in the resulting clashes, particularly in Calcutta. The police and army stood idly by: it seemed the British had decided to leave their former imperial capital to the mob. Three days of communal rioting in the city left death and destruction in their wake before the army finally stepped in. But the carnage and hatred had also ripped apart something indefinable in the national psyche. Reconciliation now seemed impossible.

Yet a week later Wavell and Nehru were discussing the composition of an interim government for India, to consist of five 'Caste Hindus', five Muslims, a Scheduled Caste member, and three minority representatives. They agreed that Jinnah could nominate his representatives but could have no say in the Congress's nominations including, in principle, of a nationalist Muslim. Though the League was still deliberating about whether to join, an interim government of India was named, and its Congress members sworn in, on 2 September 1946. Nehru, in a broadcast on 7 September, saw this as the culmination of a long struggle: 'Too long have we been passive spectators of events, the playthings of others. The initiative comes to our people now and we shall make the history of our choice.'

But the British remained supportive of the League and of its government in Bengal, which had allowed the horrors of Direct Action Day to occur. 'What is the good of our forming the Interim Government of India,' Nehru wrote indignantly to Wavell about conditions in Bengal in the wake of the Calcutta killings, 'if all that we can do is to watch helplessly and do nothing else when thousands of people are being butchered...?' But he went too far in insisting upon visiting the overwhelmingly Muslim, though Congress-ruled, North-West Frontier Province. The British connived in League-organized demonstrations against him at which stones were flung and Nehru was bruised. More importantly, the fiasco suggested that Nehru, as a Hindu, could never be acceptable to the province's Muslims as a national leader.

Meanwhile, British pressure on Congress to make more concessions to Jinnah in order to secure the League's entry into the interim government prompted Gandhi and Nehru to relinquish voluntarily their right to nominate a Muslim member. This had been a deal-breaker for Jinnah, and he now seemed ready, in discussions with Nehru, to find a compromise. But after their talks had made headway, Jinnah once again insisted that Congress recognize the League as the sole representative of Indian Muslims. Nehru refused to do this, saying it would be tantamount to a betrayal of the many nationalist Muslims in Congress, and a stain on his own as well as the country's honour. The viceroy thereupon went behind the Congress's back and negotiated directly with Jinnah, accepting his nominations of Muslims as well as of a Scheduled Caste member. On 15 October, the Muslim League formally announced that it would join the interim government.

But the League had done so only to wreck it from within. Even before its nominees were sworn in on the 26th, they had made speeches declaring their real intention to be to work for the creation of Pakistan. The League's members met by themselves separately prior to each Cabinet meeting and functioned in Cabinet as an opposition group rather than as part of a governing coalition. On every issue, from the most trivial to the most important, the League members sought to obstruct the government's functioning, opposing every Congress initiative or proposal. Meanwhile, the party continued to instigate violence across the country; as riots broke out in Bihar in early November (with Gandhi walking through the strife-torn province single-handedly restoring calm), Jinnah declared on 14 November that the killing would not stop unless Pakistan was created. The British convened talks in London in December to press the Congress to make further concessions to the League in order to persuade it to attend the Constituent Assembly. Nehru, still burned by the reaction to his Bombay press conference, was at his most conciliatory, but Jinnah saw in the British position confirmation that his party's fortunes were in the ascendant, and escalated his demands. To Nehru it seemed the British had learned nothing from the failure of the policy of appeasement in Europe in the 1930s.

The Constituent Assembly met as scheduled on 9 December, without League participation, but was careful not to take any decisions that might alienate Jinnah. Nonetheless, on 29 January 1947, the Muslim League Working Committee passed a resolution asking the British government to declare that the Cabinet Mission Plan had failed, and to dissolve the assembly. The Congress members of the interim government in turn demanded that the League members, having rejected the Plan, resign. Amid the shambles of their policy, the British government announced that they would withdraw from India, come what may, no later than June 1948, and that to execute the transfer of power, Wavell would be replaced.

Into the midst of this stalemate came His Excellency Rear Admiral the Right Honourable Lord Louis Francis Albert Victor Nicholas, Viscount Mountbatten of Burma, KCG, PC, GMSI, GMIE, GCFO, KCB, DSO, the outgoing Supreme Allied Commander in Southeast Asia. A blue-blooded patrician of royal lineage (Queen Victoria was his great-grandmother and he was therefore the reigning monarch's cousin), Mountbatten was also vain, charming, superficial and impulsive. 'I've never met anyone more in need of front-wheel brakes,' his own Chief of Staff, General Ismay, admitted.

Sadly, such brakes were what India needed, as it plunged headlong into disaster.

Two Surrenders: The British Give Up and the Congress Gives In

It was now increasingly apparent even to Nehru that Pakistan, in some form, would have to be created; the League was simply not going to work with the Congress in a united government of India. He nonetheless tried to prod leaders of the League into discussions on the new arrangements, which he still hoped would fall short of an absolute partition. By early March, as communal rioting continued across northern India, even this hope had faded. Both Sardar Vallabhbhai Patel and Nehru agreed that, despite Gandhi's refusal to contemplate such a prospect, the Congress had no alternative but to agree to partitioning Punjab and Bengal; the option of a loose Indian union including a quasi-sovereign Pakistan would neither be acceptable to the League nor result in a viable government for the rest of India. By the time Mountbatten arrived on 24 March 1947 the die had been cast. It was he, however, who rapidly ended the game altogether.

Mountbatten later claimed he governed by personality, and indeed both his positive and negative attributes would prove decisive. On the one hand he was focused, energetic, charming and free of racial bias,

unlike almost every one of his predecessors; on the other, he was astonishingly vain, alarmingly impatient, and easily swayed by personal likes
and dislikes. His vicereine, Edwina, was a vital partner, one who took
a genuine interest in Indian affairs. Theirs was a curious marriage,
marked by her frequent infidelities, which he condoned, and it has
been suggested that her affection for Nehru played a part in some of his
(and Mountbatten's) decisions relating to Indian independence. There
is no question that Nehru and Edwina indeed became close, but it does
not seem likely that this had any political impact.

Meanwhile, the breakdown of governance in India was gathering
pace. Communal violence and killings were a daily feature; so was
Jinnah's complete unwillingness to cooperate with the Congress on any
basis other than that it represented the Hindus and he the Muslims of
India. The British gave him much encouragement to pursue this position: the governor of the North-West Frontier Province, the pro-
League Sir Olaf Caroe, was unconscionably pressing the Congress
government of this Muslim-majority state to make way for the League,
since its continuation would have made Pakistan impossible.

As the impasse in the interim government continued, Mountbatten
and his advisers drew up a 'Plan Balkan' that would have transferred
power to the provinces rather than to a central government, leaving them
free to join a larger union (or not). The British kept Nehru in the dark
while Plan Balkan was reviewed (and revised) in London—all the more
ironic for an empire that liked to claim it had unified India. When he was
finally shown the text by Mountbatten at Simla on the night of 10 May,
Nehru erupted in indignation, storming into his friend Krishna Menon's
room at 2 a.m. to sputter his outrage. Had the plan been implemented,
the idea of India that Nehru had so brilliantly evoked in his writings
would have been sundered even more comprehensively than Jinnah was
proposing. Balkanization would have unleashed civil war and disorder on
an unimaginable scale, as provinces, princely states and motley political
forces contended for power upon the departure of the Raj.

A long, passionate and occasionally incoherent note of protest from
Nehru to Mountbatten killed the plan. But the only alternative was
partition. In May, Nehru saw the unrest in the country as 'volcanic': the
time had come for making hard and unpleasant choices, and he was
prepared to make them. Reluctantly, he agreed to Mountbatten's pro-

posal for a referendum in the North-West Frontier Province and in the Muslim-majority district of Sylhet, gave in on a Congress counter-proposal for a similar approach in regard to Hindu-majority districts of Sindh, and most surprisingly, agreed to Dominion status for India within the British Commonwealth, rather than the full independence the Congress had long stood for.

As long as the British gave Jinnah a veto over every proposal he found uncongenial, and as long as they were about to give up the ghost, there was little else Nehru could do but give in to Partition. Nor is there evidence in the writings and reflections of the other leading Indian nationalists of the time that any of them had any better ideas. The only exception was Mahatma Gandhi: Gandhi went to Mountbatten and suggested that India could be kept united if Jinnah were offered the leadership of the whole country. Nehru and Patel both gave that idea short shrift, and Mountbatten did not seem to take it seriously.

There is no doubt that Mountbatten seemed to proceed with unseemly haste, picking a much earlier date than planned—15 August, a date he chose on a whim because it was the date he had accepted the Japanese surrender as Supreme Allied Commander in Southeast Asia—and that in so doing he swept the Indian leaders along. Nehru was convinced that Jinnah was capable of setting the country ablaze and destroying all that the nationalist movement had worked for: a division of India was preferable to its destruction. 'It is with no joy in my heart that I commend these proposals,' Nehru told his party, 'though I have no doubt in my mind that it is the right course.' The distinction between heart and head was poignant, and telling.

On 3 June, Nehru, Jinnah, and the Sikh leader Baldev Singh broadcast news of their acceptance of partition to the country. The occasion again brought out the best in Nehru: 'We are little men serving a great cause,' he said. 'Mighty forces are at work in the world today and in India... [It is my hope] that in this way we shall reach that united India sooner than otherwise and that she will have a stronger and more secure foundation... The India of geography, of history and tradition, the India of our minds and hearts, cannot change.' But of course it could change: geography was to be hacked, history misread, tradition denied, minds and hearts torn apart.

Nehru imagined that the rioting and violence that had racked the country over the League's demand for Pakistan would die down once that demand had been granted, but he was wrong. The killing and mass displacement worsened as people sought frantically to be on the 'right' side of the lines the British were to draw across their homeland. Over a million people died in the savagery that bookended the freedom of India and Pakistan; some 17 million were displaced, and countless properties destroyed and looted. Lines meant lives. What Nehru had thought of as a temporary secession of certain parts of India hardened into the creation of two separate and hostile states that would fight four wars with each other and be embroiled in a nuclear-armed, terrorism-torn standoff decades later.

Gandhi was not the only one to be assailed by a sense of betrayal. The Congress government in the North-West Frontier Province, let down by the national party, chose to boycott the referendum there, which passed with the votes of just 50.49 per cent of the electorate (but nearly 99 per cent of those who voted). Mountbatten, who had seen himself serving for a while as a bridge between the two new Dominions by holding the governor-generalship of both, was brusquely told by Jinnah that the League leader himself would hold that office in Pakistan. The outgoing viceroy would therefore have to content himself with the titular overlordship of India alone.

Amidst the rioting and carnage that consumed large sections of northern India, Jawaharlal Nehru found the time to ensure that no pettiness marred the moment: he dropped the formal lowering of the Union Jack from the independence ceremony in order not to hurt British sensibilities. The Indian tricolour was raised just before sunset, and as it fluttered up the flagpole a late-monsoon rainbow emerged behind it, a glittering tribute from the heavens. Just before midnight, Nehru rose in the Constituent Assembly to deliver the most famous speech ever made by an Indian:

> Long years ago we made a tryst with destiny, and now the time comes when we shall redeem our pledge, not wholly or in full measure, but very substantially. At the stroke of the midnight hour, when the world sleeps, India will awake to life and freedom. A moment comes, which comes but rarely in history, when we step out from the old to the new, when an age ends, and when the soul of a nation long suppressed finds utterance.

There were no harsh words for the British, whose Raj was ending at midnight. 'This is no time...for ill-will or blaming others,' he added.

'We have to build the noble mansion of free India where all her children may dwell.'

Quitting India, Creating Pakistan

In that last mad headlong rush to freedom and partition, the British emerge with little credit. Before the war they had no intention of devolving power so rapidly, or at all. The experience of the elected governments in the last years of the Raj confirmed that the British had never been serious about their proclaimed project of promoting the responsible governance of India by Indians. When the Congress ministries quit, the British thought little of appointing unelected Muslim Leaguers in their place and in many cases assuming direct control of functions that had supposedly been devolved to Indians. The British, who had been dismayed by the League's inability to win a majority of Muslim seats anywhere, thereby undermining the strength of divide and rule, welcomed the opportunity to assume the power they had partly ceded, and to shore up the League as the principal alternative to the Indian National Congress in the process. They openly helped the Muslim League take advantage of this unexpected opportunity to exercise influence and patronage that their electoral support had not earned them, and to build up support while their principal opponents languished in jail.

This was all part of official policy: no one in any responsible position in London or New Delhi as late as 1940 had any serious intention whatsoever of relinquishing the Empire or surrendering India to a rabble of nationalists clad in homespun. But the devastation of World War II meant that only one half of the phrase could survive: bled, bombed and battered for six years, Britain could divide but it could no longer rule.

The British—terrorized by German bombing, demoralized by various defeats and large numbers of their soldiers taken prisoner, shaken by the desertion of Indian soldiers and the mutiny of Indian sailors, shivering in the record cold of the winter of 1945–46, crippled by power cuts and factory closures resulting from a post-War coal shortage—were exhausted and in no mood to focus on a distant empire when their own needs at home were so pressing. They were also more or less broke: American loans had kept the economy afloat and needed to be repaid, and even India was owed a sizable debt. Overseas commitments were no longer sustainable or particularly popular. Exit was the only viable option: the question was what they would leave behind—one India, two or several fragments?

Britain's own tactics before and during the war—compounded, as we have seen, by the Congress's folly in relinquishing all its leverage and going to jail—ensured that by the time departure came, the prospects of a united India surviving a British exit had essentially faded. *Divide et impera* had worked too well: two Indias is what it would be.

The task of dividing the two nations was assigned to Sir Cyril Radcliffe, a lawyer who had never been to India before and knew nothing of its history, society or traditions. Radcliffe drew up his maps in forty days, dividing provinces, districts, villages, homes and hearts—and promptly scuttled home to Britain, never to return to India. 'The British Empire did not decline, it simply fell', as Alex von Tunzelmann put it. The British were heedless of the lives that would be lost in their headlong rush to the exits.

So much has already been written about the tragic disruption of Partition that it seems otiose to add new words to describe what has already been so devastatingly depicted by so many. It may suffice for now to quote the British Muslim scholar Yasmin Khan, in her well-regarded history *The Great Partition: The Making of India and Pakistan*. Khan writes that Partition 'stands testament to the follies of empire, which ruptures community evolution, distorts historical trajectories and forces violent state formation from societies that would otherwise have taken different and unknowable paths'.

It is difficult, therefore, to buy the self-serving imperial argument that Britain bequeathed to India its political unity and democracy.

Yes, it allied a variety of states under a system of common law and administration, but with a number of distortions (outlined in the previous chapters) occasioned by the fitful and hypocritical nature of British conquest and rule, and by the British determination to deny Indians the opportunity to exercise genuine political authority in representative institutions.

Yes, it brought in a supposedly free press, but ensured it operated under severe constraints, and planted the seeds of representative parliamentary institutions while withholding the substance of power from Indians.

Far from introducing democracy to a country mired in despotism and tyranny, as many Britons liked to pretend, it denied political freedom to a land that had long enjoyed it even under various monarchs, thanks to a cultural tradition of debate and dissent even on vital issues of spirituality and governance.

Yes, India has emerged as a thriving pluralist democracy, though both Pakistan and Bangladesh have encountered difficulties in doing so, and Pakistan officially and undemocratically discriminates against its non-Muslim citizens even under civilian rule. But India's flourishing democracy of seven decades is no tribute to British rule. It is a bit rich, as I pointed out in Oxford, for the British to suppress, exploit, imprison, torture and maim a people for 200 years and then celebrate the fact that they are a democracy at the end of it.

Finally, the most painful question of all: what political unity can we celebrate when the horrors of Partition were the direct result of the deliberate British policy of communal division that fomented religious antagonisms to facilitate continued imperial rule? If Britain's greatest accomplishment was the creation of a single political unit called India, fulfilling the aspirations of visionary emperors from Ashoka to Akbar, then its greatest failure must be the shambles of that original Brexit— cutting and running from the land they had claimed to rule for its betterment, leaving behind a million dead, thirteen million displaced, billions of rupees of property destroyed, and the flames of communal hatred blazing hotly across the ravaged land. No greater indictment of the failures of British rule in India can be found than the tragic manner of its ending.

5

THE MYTH OF ENLIGHTENED DESPOTISM

There has been a tendency on the part of many, including several Anglophile Indians, to see British colonial rule as essentially benign, a version of the 'enlightened despotism' that characterized the Enlightenment of the eighteenth and nineteenth centuries. In this view, the British may have been imperialists who denied Indians democracy, but they ruled generously and wisely, for the greater good of their subjects. To paraphrase Emperor Joseph II of Austria, who famously said: 'Everything for the people, nothing by the people', the British, in this reading, may not have let the Indians do anything, but they did everything for them.

This view is either naïve or self-serving, it is difficult to decide which. A few examples of how the British actually ruled in India are therefore worth examining, for they give the lie to this narrative. The most obvious example relates to the famines the British caused and mismanaged; to the system of forced emigration of Indians by transportation and indentured labour; and to the brutality with which dissent was suppressed. We shall examine each of these briefly.

Feast and Famine: The British and 'Starving India'

As India became increasingly crucial to British prosperity, millions of Indians died completely unnecessary deaths in famines. As a result of

what one can only call the British Colonial Holocaust, thanks to economic policies ruthlessly enforced by Britain, between 30 and 35 million Indians needlessly died of starvation during the Raj. Millions of
tonnes of wheat were exported from India to Britain even as famine
raged. When relief camps were set up, the inhabitants were barely fed
and nearly all died.

It is striking that the last large-scale famine to take place in India was
under British rule; none has taken place since, because Indian democracy has been more responsive to the needs of drought-affected and
poverty-stricken Indians than the British rulers ever were. As the
scholar and Nobel Laureate Amartya Sen has explained, there has never
been a famine in a democracy with a free press, because public accountability ensures effective response. Sen's work, informed by compassion as well as solid quantitative research, has established the now
widely-accepted doctrine that famines are nearly always avoidable; that
they result not from lack of food but lack of access to food; that distribution is therefore the key, and that democracy is the one system of
government that enables food to be distributed widely and fairly. Lack
of democracy and public accountability, however, is what characterized
British rule in India.

A list of major famines during British rule makes for grim reading:
the Great Bengal Famine (1770), Madras (1782–83), Chalisa Famine
(1783–84) in Delhi and the adjoining areas, Doji bara Famine (1791–
92) around Hyderabad, Agra Famine (1837–38), Orissa Famine
(1866), Bihar Famine (1873–74), Southern India Famine (1876–77),
the Indian Famine (1896–1900 approx.), Bombay Famine (1905–06)
and the most notorious of the lot, the Bengal Famine (1943–44).[10] The
fatality figures are horrifying: from 1770 to 1900, 25 million Indians
are estimated to have died in famines, including 15 million in the five
famines in the second half of the nineteenth century. The famines of the
twentieth century probably took the total well over 35 million. William
Digby pointed out that in the entire 107 years from 1793 to 1900, only

---

[10] Lists vary. The *Oriental Herald* in February 1838 reported on fifteen famines
in British India in the course of seven decades: 'Famines prevailed in India,
in 1766, 1770 (when half the inhabitants perished in Bengal), 1782, 1792,
1803, 1804, 1819, 1820, 1824, 1829, 1832, 1833, 1836, 1837, and now
in 1838.'

an estimated 5 million people had died in all the wars around the world combined, whereas in just ten years 1891–1900, 19 million had died in India in famines alone. While comparisons of human deaths are always invidious, the 35 million who died of famine and epidemics during the Raj does remind one of the 25 million who died in Stalin's collectivization drive and political purges, the 45 million who died during Mao's cultural revolution, and the 55 million who died world-wide during World War II. The death toll from the colonial holocausts is right up there with some of the most harrowing examples of man's inhumanity to man in modern times.

In late colonial India, famines became an important area of political contestation. Their repeated occurrence, the failures of the British to fulfil their promises of good governance, and the resultant mass starvations, provided a strong rallying point for Indian nationalist leaders: Dadabhai Naoroji began his research into the famous 'economic drain' theory and 'un-British rule in India' after being moved by the horror of the Orissa deaths. He had hitherto been seen as an Anglophile and an admirer of British liberalism, but now he could no longer hide his disillusionment. 'Security of life and property we have better in these times, no doubt,' Naoroji wrote. 'But the destruction of a million and a half lives in one famine [the toll in Orissa in 1866] is a strange illustration of the worth of the life and property thus secured.'

The British tended to base their refusal to intervene in famines with adequate governmental measures on a combination of three sets of considerations: free trade principles (do not interfere with market forces), Malthusian doctrine (growth in population beyond the ability of the land to sustain it would inevitably lead to deaths, thereby restoring the 'correct' level of population) and financial prudence (don't spend money we haven't budgeted for). On these grounds, Britain had not intervened to save lives in Ireland, or prevent emigration to America, during the famine there. In the mid-nineteenth century, as Dinyar Patel points out, 'it was common economic wisdom that government intervention in famines was unnecessary and even harmful. The market would restore a proper balance. Any excess deaths, according to Malthusian principles, were nature's way of responding to overpopulation'.

Thus the Governor of Bengal, Sir Cecil Beadon (who on a visit to the area had declared, 'Such visitations of providence as these no government can do much either to prevent or alleviate'), when criticized for doing nothing to reduce food prices during the Orissa Famine of 1866, declared that 'If I were to attempt to do this, I should consider myself no better than a dacoit or a thief.' The governor was more concerned with fealty to the free-market principles of Adam Smith, and the damage to his political reputation, were he seen to be intervening in the 'natural laws' of economics, than the tragedy of the deaths of people in Orissa.

This did, it must be said, trouble some Englishmen of conscience: the Marquess of Salisbury, Secretary of State for India during the Orissa Famine of 1866, is said to have reproached himself daily for his failure to act for two months after he had been informed of the onset of the crisis; his inaction was blamed for one million famine-related deaths. British administrators largely acknowledged, from at least the 1860s, that the frequent famines were not the result of food shortages per se, but the inability of people to purchase food or, in a scholar's words, 'complex economic crises induced by the market impacts of drought and crop failure.' The reasons for that inability, however, went well beyond those the British liked to cite, and inculpated the colonial rulers themselves. During the very 1866 Orissa Famine that would so disturb Salisbury's sleep, while a million and a half people starved to death, the British insouciantly exported 200 million pounds of rice to Britain.

On the one hand, the persistence of famines contributed to the British narrative too, since they could be cited to make the argument that Indians needed British oversight and supervision that, indeed, the Indians would all be dying of starvation were it not for the benevolence of British rule. On the other, the British, in their official reports and reviews of famine, took care to blame everything but themselves—the burgeoning population, declining rice production, the role of climate and other uncontrollable factors, lack of transportation, even indigenous culture. All these elements were emphasized as causes that thwarted the noble attempts by good British administrators to prevent food shortages, with very little consideration given to the role that colonial policies and practices played in shaping the events that led to those shortages, destroying the purchasing power of the Indian peasantry and failing to mitigate the ravages of the climate.

This was not merely a nineteenth-century phenomenon, but characterized British colonial policy throughout. As late as 1943, the last paragraph of the official report into the Bengal Famine provides an interesting example of this:

> We have criticized the Government of Bengal for their failure to control the famine. It is the responsibility of the Government to lead the people and take effective steps to prevent avoidable catastrophe. But the public in Bengal, or at least certain sections of it, have also their share of blame. We have referred to the atmosphere of fear and greed which, in the absence of control, was one of the causes of the rapid rise in the price level. Enormous profits were made out of the calamity, and in the circumstances, profits for some meant death for others. A large part of the community lived in plenty while others starved, and there was much indifference in face of suffering. Corruption was widespread throughout the province and in many classes of society... Society, together with its organs, failed to protect its weaker members. Indeed there was a moral and social breakdown, as well as an administrative breakdown.

As against this self-exculpation—when you blame a tragedy on everybody, you blame it on nobody—there lies the uncompromising denunciation of a Will Durant: 'Behind all these as the fundamental source of the terrible famines in India, lies such merciless exploitation, such unbalanced exportation of goods, and such brutal collection of high taxes in the very midst of famine, that the starving peasants cannot pay what is asked for... American charity has often paid for the relief of famine in India while the Government was collecting taxes from the dying.' Romesh Chunder Dutt argued accurately that 'there has never been a single year when the food-supply of the country was insufficient for the people'. Durant quotes an American theologian, Dr Charles Hall, as echoing this view and adding: 'The Indian starves [so] that India's annual revenue may not be diminished by a dollar. 80 per cent of the whole population has been thrown back upon the soil because England's discriminating duties have ruined practically every branch of native manufacture. We send shiploads of grain to India, but there is plenty of grain in India. The trouble is that the people have been ground down till they are too poor to buy it.'

Before the British came, Indian rulers had supported the people in times of food scarcity by policies of tax relief, fixing grain prices and banning food exports from famine-affected regions. There was also a strong tradition of personal charity, especially during periods of scarcity. In tough times, wealthier Indians, including landowners and merchants, often took on the responsibility of helping the poor by offering them work, giving them food or even subsidizing the cost of grain by selling it below market prices. The East India Company took a dim view of this kind of Indian almsgiving, dismissing it as undiscerning charity which irresponsibly attracted the wandering poor; one writer called it 'indiscriminate indigenous almsgiving motivated by superstition and ostentation'. The British therefore declared that they would 'provide employment for the able-bodied' but not 'gratuitous relief' to the general public.

The Company's governmental successors were no better. Throughout, the imperial rulers were far less concerned about the welfare of the Indian poor than about their fear—based, at least partly, on the experience of the British poor laws, reformed in 1834, which many feared had encouraged pauperism—that institutionalized famine relief would create a culture of dependence on government support.

Many British officials also drew a distinction between the 'necessitous poor' and the 'religious mendicants' whom they considered undeserving of assistance. Indian donors drew no such lines; they had been used for millennia to sants and sadhus, monks and renunciates, going respectably from door to door and village to village, expecting to be fed by householders on the way. The British may have considered them 'mendicants', social leeches undeserving of assistance, but Indians were happy to help them. Indian ideas of charity differed greatly from prevalent British mores. Affluent Indians were meant to help the general public in ways that did not come naturally to the British in India. Indeed some Indians in the eighteenth and early nineteenth centuries were critical of the British for returning home with their vast Company fortunes without having done a thing for the people they had exploited and left without digging wells, making reservoirs, building bridges or planting trees, in the long-established Indian tradition.

In keeping with established British policy, Viceroy Lord Lytton notoriously issued orders prohibiting any reduction in the price of food during a famine. 'There is to be no interference of any kind on the part of Government with the object of reducing the price of food', he declared, instructing district officers to 'discourage relief works in every possible way... Mere distress is not a sufficient reason for opening a relief work'. The historian Professor Mike Davis notes that Lytton's pronouncements were noteworthy for combining non-intervention with a unique aversion to 'cheap sentiment' the prerogative of the unaccountable appointee to high office who is immune to public needs. (Ironically, Lord Lytton's only qualification for the job of viceroy was that, as Robert Bulwer-Lytton, he was Queen Victoria's favourite poet.)

Lytton was more outspoken than many, accusing his British critics of indulging in 'humanitarian hysterics' and inviting them to foot the bill if they wanted to save Indian lives. In keeping with his determination to encourage fiscal prudence and cut down government costs, Lytton dispatched an official named Sir Richard Temple to Madras during the famine of 1876–77 with instructions not to listen to the 'humanitarian humbugs' and to reduce the cost of relief measures. This was achieved, of course, with little regard for popular suffering; the condition of the populace was secondary to the state of the government's account books. When Temple had, in the earlier Orissa Famine of 1866, imported rice from Burma for starving Oriyas, *The Economist* bitterly attacked him for allowing Indians to think 'it is the duty of the Government to keep them alive'. The Temple of 1877 was a different man. Though the British created 'work camps' as a form of famine relief (so the starving could use their labour to earn their bread), the most significant legacy this official left behind was the 'Temple wage' which, in Mike Davis's words, 'provided less sustenance for hard labour' in British labour camps during the famine than the infamous Buchenwald concentration camp's inmates would receive eighty years later.

In other words, the British cannot be accused of 'doing nothing' during the 1876–77 famine, but rather of doing much to worsen its impact. India's grain continued to be exported to global markets, just as Stalin was to do during the 'collectivization famines' that beset Russia and Ukraine in the 1930s: in effect, as Professor Mike Davis has written, 'London was eating India's bread' while Indians were dying in a famine. To add insult to injury, the British increased taxes on the peasantry, and railed against those too hungry to be productive as 'indolent' and 'unused to work'. When some Englishmen of conscience objected and mounted relief operations of their own, the British government threatened them with imprisonment. A Mr MacMinn, who out of his own money distributed grain to the starving, was 'severely reprimanded, threatened with degradation, and ordered to close the work immediately'.

One first-hand witness, Lieutenant Colonel Ronald Osborne, has written movingly of the horror in 1877: 'Scores of corpses were tumbled into old wells, because the deaths were too numerous for the miserable relatives to perform the usual funeral rites. Mothers sold their children for a single scanty meal. Husbands flung their wives into ponds, to escape the torment of seeing them perish by the lingering agonies of hunger. Amid these scenes of death, the government of India kept its serenity and cheerfulness unimpaired. The [newspapers] were persuaded into silence. Strict orders were given to civilians under no circumstances to countenance the pretence that civilians were dying of hunger.'

In fact, in addition to keeping a tight leash on expenditure during the 1877–78 South Indian famine, the British government was also anxious not to appear to rely on charitable donations to save lives. As Georgina Brewis describes it: 'When in August 1877 the leading citizens of Madras, both Indian and European, appealed in Britain for donations to a famine relief fund, Lytton viewed this as an act of insubordination and acted swiftly to suppress the fund, sending a coded telegram to the Lieutenant-Governor of Bengal. This move provoked outcry when leaked to the Indian and British press. As the newspapers were quick to point out, Lytton's opposition to the fund placed all donors in the wrong, including the newly designated "Empress" of India and a host of former Governor-Generals who had headed the subscription lists in Britain. A leader in *The Times* expressed great regret that "the Viceroy should have interposed to repress the impulses of private charity" and denounced his policy of pursuing famine relief "solely with economy in mind". Lord Lytton was eventually forced to sanction the existence of the relief fund and to donate Rupees 10,000 (£1,000) himself, a gesture he admitted privately he made with "an ill will". The fund, which eventually totalled £820,000, was raised through millions of small contributions from individuals, schools, churches and regiments throughout the British world. However, until December 1877, Lytton continued to describe the fund as "a complete nuisance" and to issue dire warnings that all the money would be wasted by an irresponsible committee.'

After this episode the British Government of India took command of famine relief more formally, drawing up rules defining the 'legitimate' objectives of charitable relief, giving itself the power to sanction international appeals and oversee volunteers. When a fresh famine broke out in October 1896, with Lytton mercifully long gone, the government engaged itself studying the rules rather than responding to the suffering. It was only when public opinion in England could no longer be ignored that an international appeal was finally issued in January 1897, four months after the famine began and many lives had been lost.

The facts of British culpability, even at the height of the 'civilizing mission' in the late nineteenth century, are overwhelming, but some continue to gloss over it. Lawrence James writes, in blithe disregard of the evidence, that British imperial rulers of India 'were humane men and, although hampered by inadequate administrative machinery and limited resources, they made a determined effort to feed the hungry' during the famines of the 1870s and 1890s. The only proof he offers for this is that during the famine period of 1871–1901, India's population increased by 30 million. India is a big country and famine did not strike everywhere; in the regions where it did, the effect was calamitous and millions died, but elsewhere life went on, and as a result the total population of India rose. But this does not mean people did not die in the millions where famine struck. By James's logic the increase in China's population under Mao and the Soviet Union's under Stalin should equally give the lie to the gory tales of mass starvation in those countries. The rise in both deaths and malnutrition in the famine-affected years would be a better indicator, but James avoids mentioning those figures.

Human beings were not the only victims of British-induced famines; cattle died too. It is striking that the export trade in hides and skins rose from 5 million rupees in 1859 to nearly 115 million rupees in 1901, an astonishing increase especially in a culture where the death of a cow was devastating, not only for religious reasons but because cows were crucial to farming, and also served as a means of transportation and as status symbols in rural society. The deaths of quite so many cows suggest severe rural distress; farmers know few setbacks worse than the death of their cattle, which would be a major blow to their present prospects and darken their future hopes. Indeed, some officials seemed to consider the deaths of cows worse than those of people: one report on famines noted that '[i]n its influence on agriculture, [cattle mortality] is perhaps a more serious and lasting evil than the loss of population. As a rule, those who die of hunger must be old or helpless, whereas the able-bodied and useful escape. But if the cattle perish, cultivation is almost impossible.'

The loss of cattle directly impacted agricultural productivity, which would take years, if not decades, to be restored to pre-famine levels. The poorest farmers suffered most, since their existence was always on the margins of economic viability, but their loss of livestock was never compensated by official relief policies, which preferred to target 'healthy' cattle for help, usually the cattle of those who could afford to feed them better. Even when 'cattle camps' were set up during famines, the aim was to keep their expenses to a bare minimum and recover most of the expenditure from charitable contributions. Though nine camps were established in the Bombay Presidency during the famine of 1899–1900, for instance, 75 per cent of the costs to run them were recovered by the government. Fiscal prudence consistently trumped 'humanitarian humbug'. Indians proved more generous whenever they were not themselves laid low by famine, and 'native charity' was often available to rescue cattle, including often aid from the village zamindar, who felt a social obligation to provide whatever relief he could to save his people and their cows.

It is instructive, too, that one of the challenges faced in pre-British India—the lack of adequate infrastructure and transportation to get food from areas where it was plentiful to areas of scarcity, which was cited by Florence Nightingale as a major reason for famines—was irrelevant to British India after the advent of the railways. And yet the worst famines of the nineteenth century occurred after thousands of miles of railway lines had been built. There could be no more searing proof that the responsibility for famines lay with the authorities and their policies.

Even as the British Crown failed Indians, in some quarters in Britain it became fashionable to be seen as generous benefactors dropping glittering coins into the begging bowls of India. The *Daily Mail* declared in 1897 that 'it falls to us to defend our Empire from the spectral armies of hunger…our weapon is good honest British money'. In the same breath Indian charity was dismissed, as I have pointed out earlier. No matter how it was regarded by the British, the truth was that it was Indians who supported the majority of organized relief efforts during famines, where the inadequacy of the government was compounded by its official reluctance to act generously. The Indian diaspora contributed large sums to the funds raised in British colonies: Mahatma Gandhi, for instance, organized collections in South Africa for Indian famines in 1897 and 1900. Various Indian relief organizations arose to fill the breach left by the inattentive or unsupportive British government in India. Kitchens, orphanages, inexpensive grain shops for the poor, and poor-houses were constructed by Indian donors during the famines. Several non-governmental organizations, associations and sabhas, as well as reformist religious societies like the Arya Samaj, Brahmo Samaj and the Ramakrishna Mission saw relief work as a form of *seva* and worked with a will to compensate for the deficiencies of official relief efforts.

Aside from indifference to the human victims of suffering, famine relief in India brought out another negative feature of the colonial regime—its unwillingness to acknowledge its own limitations and its ability to disguise mismanagement as wise policy. The British tended to dress up their inaction and the feebleness of their relief measures by a great show of statistical precision, as if to confirm that with the numbers at their fingertips, they had matters well in hand.

One such example of what a scholar calls 'numerical rhetoric' as a tool in debates on famine could be discerned in a statement by Leopold Amery, the then secretary of state for India, to the members of the House of Commons in 1943 about the Bengal Famine, which by the time the good Lord Amery spoke had taken close to 3 million lives. Amery compared the significant rise in India's population with the general downturn in the food production rates: 'In the past 12 years the population of India had increased by about 60 millions, and it had been estimated that the annual production of rice per head in Bengal had fallen from 384 lb to 283 lb in the last 30 years'. The British were doing their best but could not stave off a Malthusian catastrophe. Amery frequently resorted to numbers at the Commons, once in December giving figures for hospital admissions and deaths, carefully adding the caveat that some deaths may not have been due to starvation. There was, all too often, an inverse correlation between the precision of the numbers provided by the government and the effectiveness of the relief measures it was supposedly undertaking.

As we have seen, by the time it ended, nearly 4 million Bengalis starved to death in the 1943 famine. Nothing can excuse the odious behaviour of Winston Churchill, who deliberately ordered the diversion of food from starving Indian civilians to well-supplied British soldiers and even to top up European stockpiles in Greece and elsewhere. 'The starvation of anyway underfed Bengalis is less serious' than that of 'sturdy Greeks', he argued. Grain for the Tommies, bread for home consumption in Britain (27 million tonnes of imported grains, a wildly excessive amount), and generous buffer stocks in Europe (for yet-to-be-liberated Greeks and Yugoslavs) were Churchill's priorities, not the life or death of his Indian subjects. When reminded of the suffering of his victims his response was typically Churchillian: The famine was their own fault, he said, for 'breeding like rabbits'. When officers of conscience pointed out in a telegram to the prime minister the scale of the tragedy caused by his decisions, Churchill's only reaction was to ask peevishly: 'why hasn't Gandhi died yet?'

As Madhusree Mukerjee's richly-documented account of the Bengal Famine demonstrates, India's own surplus foodgrains were exported to Ceylon; Australian wheat was sent sailing past Indian cities (where the bodies of those who had died of starvation littered the streets) to storage depots in the Mediterranean and the Balkans, to create stockpiles that could ease the pressure on post-War Britain, and offers of American and Canadian food aid were turned down. The colony was not permitted to spend its own sterling reserves, or indeed use its own ships, to import food. Even the laws of supply and demand couldn't help: in order to ensure supplies for its troops elsewhere, the British government paid inflated prices for grain in the Indian open market, thereby making it unaffordable for ordinary Indians.

From the behaviour of British officials and ministers during the Bengal Famine, a picture emerges that strips away the last shred of moral justification for the Empire. The way in which Britain's wartime financial arrangements and Indian supplies to the war effort laid the ground for famine; the exchanges between Secretary of State Amery and the bumptious Churchill, whose love of war trumped 'such dreary matters as colonial economics'; the amoral racism of Churchill's reprehensible aide, Paymaster-General Lord Cherwell, who denied India famine relief and recommended most of the logistical decisions that were to cost so many lives—all these are the culmination of two centuries of colonial cruelty. The only difference is that the evidence for British callousness and racism in 1943 is far better documented than for the dozen grotesque famines that preceded it.

I have dwelt at length on famines because they offer such an outstanding example of British colonial malfeasance. One could have cited epidemic disease as well, which constantly laid Indians low under British rule while the authorities stood helplessly by. To take just the first four years of the twentieth century, as Durant did: 272,000 died of plague in 1901, 500,000 in 1902, 800,000 in 1903, and 1 million in 1904 the death toll rising every year. During the Spanish Influenza epidemic of 1918, 125 million cases of 'flu were recorded (more than a third of the population), and India's fatality rate was higher than any Western country's: 12.5 million people died. As the American statesman (and three-time Democratic presidential candidate) William Jennings Bryan pointed out, many Britons were referring to the deaths caused by plague as 'a providential remedy for overpopulation'. It was ironic, said Bryan, that British rule was sought to be justified on the grounds that 'it keeps the people from killing each other, and the plague praised because it removes those whom the Government has saved from slaughter!'.

Arguably, epidemics existed before colonialism as well, and cannot be said to have been caused or worsened by colonial policy; so they are not comparable, for the purposes of my argument, with famines. But their persistence, and the tragically high human toll they exacted, remain a severe indictment of the indifference to Indian suffering of those who ran the British Raj. This is all the more true because 'marked improvements in public health' are often cited by defenders of British rule in India. There is not a great deal of evidence for this claim, which rests largely on the introduction of quinine as an anti-malarial drug (though its principal use was in the tonics with which the British in jungle outposts drowned and justified their gin), public programmes of vaccination against smallpox (so inadequate that it was only well after Independence that a free India eradicated this scourge from the country) and improvements in water supplies (done so ineffectually, in fact, that cholera and other waterborne diseases persisted throughout the Raj). It is also telling that there were no great hospitals established by the Raj anywhere in the country: strikingly, every one of the major modern medical establishments of British India was established by the generosity of Indian benefactors, even if, for understandable reasons, these Indian donors often named their hospitals after British colonial grandees.

Forced Migration: Transportation and Indentured Labour

In the British empire, transportation to penal colonies became a preferred method of dealing with overcrowded prisons in England as well as ensuring the supply of manpower to the underpopulated colonies. The flow of convict labour, run by the government, was soon integrated with the privately-controlled trade in indentured labourers to the Caribbean and the American colonies. This policy was also applied to India.

From 1787, Indian convicts were transported, initially to the penal colonies in Southeast Asia, particularly Bencoolen in Sumatra (1787–1825, when the British and the Dutch swapped Bencoolen for Malacca to consolidate their holds on Malaysia and Indonesia respectively), Penang, otherwise known as Prince of Wales Island (1790–1860), Mauritius (1815–53), Malacca and Singapore (1825–60), and the Burmese provinces of Arakan and Tenasserim (1828–62). Since they were largely put to work in infrastructure-building projects, Indian convicts were in great demand, especially in Singapore, the fastest growing of the Straits Settlements. In the East India Company's heyday they were called the 'Botany Bays of India'. Indian convict labour, put to work as low-cost workers in all public projects, was vital to Penang's successful colonization. Between 1852 and 1854, when labour costs in the region rose by an estimated 30 per cent, the Company's government in the Straits Settlements relied almost entirely on Indian convict labour for the construction of public works. Between 1825 to 1872, Indian convicts made up the bulk of the labour force for all public works projects in Singapore.

Indian convicts—and the term embraces many charged with petty crimes, from theft to indebtedness—were also transported to Mauritius once the British had taken the island from the French in the Napoleonic Wars, though their initial introduction in 1829 was not a success. The plantation economy of Mauritius largely ran on slavery, but the labour crisis that followed the abolition of slavery led to a demand for workers from India, and the British started shipping them anew in 1834. By 1838, 25,000 Indians had arrived; a brief ban, brought about by the anti-slavery campaigners, stopped Indian emigration from 1839–42, but this was overturned, and in 1843 officials reported that 30,218 male and 4,307 female indentured immigrants entered Mauritius. The females were considered essential to encourage labourers to remain after the period of their indentured servitude. By 1868, regulations had increased the share of female migrants to a minimum of forty women for every hundred men.

Some 500,000 labourers from India were transferred to Mauritius under the contract system for indentured labour; many were convicts, but others came voluntarily, though their willingness was sometimes obtained by coercion. In the words of one scholar, 'Whether labour were predominantly enslaved, apprenticed or indentured, incarceration was part of a broader process through which the regulation of [the] colonial workforce was taken from the private to the public sphere.'

An attempt was also made to start a penal colony closer to the Indian mainland in the Andaman Islands, but the first attempt was not successful and 700 convicts were transferred in 1796 from the penal settlement of the Andamans to Penang. Once the Straits Settlements were separated from British India in the 1860s, however, the British had no choice, if they wished to continue to transport Indian offenders, but to redevelop the penal settlement, which they did after 1858; the Andamans soon became the preferred destination for Indians the British deemed to be political troublemakers.

Besides the Straits Settlements and Mauritius, destitute Indians were also shipped as indentured labour to other British colonies around the world, from Guyana and the Caribbean Islands to South Africa and Fiji in the Pacific. Some 1.9 to 3.5 million Indians (the numbers vary in different sources, depending on who is counted) moved halfway across the globe, most involuntarily, under the colonial project. They played their roles as cogs in the wheels of the imperial machinery, toiling on sugar plantations, building roads and buildings, clearing jungle. Many suffered horribly on harrowing journeys and some perished en route; others endured terrible privations. Recent work by Professor Clare Anderson has established the extent of the horrors: in just one year,

1856–57, and on one route, Kolkata to Trinidad, the percentage of deaths of indentured labour on the transportee ships reached appalling levels: 12.3 per cent of all males, 18.5 per cent of the females, 28 per cent of the boys and 36 per cent of the girls perished, as did a tragic 55 per cent of all infants. To make an admittedly invidious comparison, the deaths of slaves on the notorious 'Middle Passage' was estimated at around 12.5 per cent. To be an indentured Indian labourer transported to the Caribbean on British ships was to enter a life-and-death lottery in which your chances of survival were significantly worse than those of a shackled African slave.

The cultural result of this tragic experience, though, was the creation of a common sorrow-filled bond between slavery-induced and indentured labour. The 'Brotherhood of the Boat' became the subject of poetry, shared folklore and, above all, music that persists to this day.

All those thus transported were cut off from any hope of return to India, or contact with the families they had left behind at home. Though many of the indentured labourers had the right to demand passage home after five years' bonded labour, this was largely theoretical and few, if any, were allowed to exercise such a right. (Clever tweaks in the regulations, such as the right being forfeit if not claimed within six months after the expiry of the original contract, or a stiff and unaffordable fare being charged for the journey, discouraged many as well.) Some—a tiny minority of Indian transportees—are said to have successfully returned, but the only case I am aware of is a handful of survivors who returned to India from a shipload of unfortunates transported to the Caribbean island of St. Croix in 1868, a majority of whom perished on board.

In the period 1519–1939, an estimated 5,300,000 people, whom scholars delicately dub 'unfree migrants', were carried on British ships, of whom approximately 58 per cent were slaves, mainly from Africa, 36 per cent were indentured labour, mainly from India, and 6 per cent were transported convicts, both from India and other colonies. If nothing else, this British endeavour, motivated as always by the simple exigencies of the colonial project, transformed the demography of dozens of countries, with consequences that can still be seen today.

Many of the volunteers, as opposed to convicts and others transported, signed up for indentured servitude as a result of their immiseration under Company rule; thousands of Indian farmers were driven off their land and forced into migration by the taking over of their fertile lands for opium cultivation. Some were former sepoys and recruits on the run from the ruthless British reprisals that followed the 'mutiny' of 1857. (It made little difference to the British, for whom mutineers, 'criminals' and those seeking to escape poverty were all the same.) Niall Ferguson dismisses this immensely painful and disruptive displacement as 'this mobilisation of cheap and probably underemployed Asian labour to grow rubber and dig gold'. Perhaps a more humane view comes from the Indian novelist Amitav Ghosh, who has written that the migration of peasants from the Gangetic plains 'was as if fate had thrust its fist through the living flesh of the land in order to tear away a piece of its stricken heart'. The wrenching of people from their homes amid scenes of desolation and despair was a crime that would haunt the history of British rule in India for generations to come.

The Brutish Raj

British imperialism had long justified itself with the pretence that it was enlightened despotism, conducted for the benefit of the governed. Churchill's inhumane conduct in the summer and autumn of 1943 gave the lie to this myth. But it had been battered for two centuries already: British imperialism had triumphed not just by conquest and deception on a grand scale but, as I have mentioned, by ruthlessly suppressing dissent, executing rebels and deserters and chopping off the thumbs of skilled weavers so they could not produce the fine cloth that made Britain's manufactures look tawdry. The suppression of the 1857 'mutiny' was conducted with extreme brutality, with hundreds of rebels being blown to bits from the mouths of cannons or hanged from public gibbets, women and children massacred (in retaliation, it must be admitted, for the killing of British women and children) and over 100,000 lives lost.

'British brutality' seems to many a contradiction in terms: the British are, after all, a byword for gentility, understatement, irony. They triumph through brilliance, not the blunderbuss. Surely they could not have behaved in India like the murderous Belgians in the Congo?

They did. Not all the time, and not with the sustained and inhuman brutality consistently deployed by King Leopold's amoral killers, but they were no exception to the basic rule that imperialism extends itself through brute force. 'Most of the time,' says the historian Jon Wilson, 'the actions of British imperial administrators were driven by irrational passions rather than calculated plans. Force was rarely efficient. The assertion of violent power usually exceeded the demands of any particular commercial or political interest.'

Brutality was an early feature of the military campaigns of the East India Company. Historians attribute the early viciousness of the British to 'their sense of vulnerability and inability to get their way, in the absence of strong relationships with local society, by asserting power through petty acts of humiliation'. (Such misbehaviour led to the Anjengo massacre of 1721, when several British soldiers and Company men were slaughtered by Nair warriors seething after repeated assaults on their honour.) The perpetrators were punished and the British doubled down on their superior power of violence. Constant paranoia fuelled a preference for force over negotiation, which the British always sought to justify by the circumstances. One of the English officers reported to the Company's council during the campaign against the Raja of Tanjore in the 1790s: 'I can only [subdue resistance] by reprisals, which will oblige me to plunder and burn the villages, kill every man in them, and take prisoners the women and children. These are actions which the nature of this war will require.'

When the Vellore mutiny occurred in 1806, sparked by changes in the uniforms of the Company's Indian sepoys that were found offensive by both Hindus and Muslims, the British put it down with ruthless ferocity. Three hundred (some versions say 350) of the mutineers were tied together, lined up against the wall of a fives court and shot at a range of thirty yards; this happened without even a summary trial or an opportunity to explain themselves. After a more formal court-martial process of the rest, six mutineers were blown away from the mouths of cannons, five were shot by firing squad, eight were hanged and five transported to a penal colony.

During the Revolt of 1857, thousands of mutineers were killed by similar means, as were large numbers of civilians of both sexes. General James George Smith Neill, in Allahabad and Kanpur, was particularly bloodthirsty, as was Sir Hugh Rose in Jhansi, where some 5,000 civilians were massacred, with no 'maudlin clemency' shown to the inhabitants of the rebel city of the redoubtable Rani Lakshmibai. When Delhi was retaken, the savagery was pitiless: in one neighbourhood alone, Kucha Chelan, some 1,400 unarmed citizens were massacred. 'The orders went out to shoot every soul,' recorded one young officer. 'It was literally murder.' So many civilians were killed that an eyewitness reported 'dead bodies in every street, rotting in the burning sun'. Refugees sheltering in mosques were plucked out and executed. Mass hangings were the norm. Delhi, the Mughal capital, a rich and bustling city of half a million inhabitants, was left a desolate ruin.

Casual murder was hardly unknown as the British killed Indians with impunity. Denis Judd recounts an incident in which a British soldier overheard two Indians sitting on a cart discussing Kanpur, site of one of the more brutal battles of the 1857 revolt. In the soldier's own words: 'I knowed what that meant. So I fetched Tom Walker, and he heard 'em say, "Cawnpore", and he knowed what that meant. So we polished 'em both off.'

Some of these killings might be sought to be explained, if not excused, by the heat of battle, particularly in putting down a rebellion. But some reprisals were in cold blood. Though the family of Mughal Emperor Bahadur Shah Zafar surrendered peacefully to the British forces that captured Delhi, they were treated abominably. Most of his sixteen sons were tried and hanged, while several were shot in cold blood, after first being stripped of their arms and, of course, their jewels. Atrocities also took place under civilian rule, on official orders and against civilian victims. In 1872, in Malerkotla, Punjab, some 65 Namdhari Sikhs were blown to bits from the mouths of cannons; in Peshawar's Qissa Khwani Bazaar in 1930, 400 Indians were butchered; and innumerable smaller incidents of beatings, floggings, racial abuse and assaults, shootings, hangings and transportation of Indians for a varied list of offences speckle the bloody history of British colonialism.

Such examples of brutality from the days of the East India Company or the early days of Crown rule tend to lay themselves open to the defence that those were other times, when other mores applied. But they continued even in the twentieth century. The brutal force used to repress the Quit India movement in 1942 involved tactics that, in the words of a British governor, if 'dragged out in the cold light of [day], nobody could defend'. Gang rape by the police was not uncommon:

73 women were violated by police in a bid to terrorize the satyagrahis, prisoners were forced to lie naked on blocks of ice till they lost consciousness, and thousands were beaten in jail. Even strafing of civilian protestors from the air was authorized. At the beginning of the century, Ruskin declared that 'every mutiny, every danger, every terror, and every crime, occurring under, or paralyzing, our Indian legislation, arises directly out of our national desire to live on the loot of India'. Reprisals against Indians challenging continued British exploitation, he pointed out, had no moral basis. Still, they continued to be exacted.

One instance of British colonial conduct from the twentieth century deserves detailed description to illustrate the larger point I am making. The incident took place just after the end of World War I (the war to 'make the world safe for democracy', in that ringing phrase of Woodrow Wilson's). I refer, of course, to Jallianwala Bagh.

It was 1919. The Ottoman and Austro-Hungarian empires had collapsed; new nations were springing up from their ruins; talk of self-determination was in the air. India had just emerged from World War I having made enormous sacrifices, and a huge contribution in men and materiel, blood and treasure, to the British war effort, in the expectation that it would be rewarded with some measure of self-government. Those hopes were belied, as explained in Chapter 2; the dishonest Montagu–Chelmsford 'reforms' and the punitive Rowlatt Acts were India's only reward.

This is what happened next.

In March and April 1919, Indians rallied across the Punjab to protest the Rowlatt Acts; they shut down normal commerce in many cities, including Amritsar, through hartals on 30 March and 6 April that demonstrated, through empty streets and shuttered shops, the dissatisfaction of the people at the British betrayal. This was a form of Gandhian non-violent non-cooperation; no violence or disorder was reported during the hartals (strikes). But on 9 April, with no provocation, the British government in the Punjab arrested two nationalist leaders, Dr Saifuddin Kitchlew and Dr Satyapal, who had addressed the protest meetings. As news of the arrests spread, the people of Amritsar came out onto the streets and sought to push their way to police headquarters to protest the arrests. The police barred their way, some stones were thrown by agitated civilians, and the police retaliated by opening fire, killing ten demonstrators. This inflamed the crowd, which reacted to the police killing by venting their fury on any visible symbol of the British empire. In the riot that ensued, five Englishmen were killed and a woman missionary assaulted (however, she was rescued, and carried to safety, by Indians).

The British promptly sent troops to Amritsar to restore order; by 11 April, 600 soldiers arrived, followed the next day by their commander, Brigadier General Reginald Dyer. By then the city was calm and whatever demonstrations and protest meetings were occurring were entirely peaceable. Nonetheless, Dyer made several arrests to assert his authority, and on the 13th he issued a proclamation that forbade people to leave the city without a pass, to organize demonstrations or processions, or even to gather in groups of more than three. The city was seething under these restrictions, but there were no protests. Meanwhile, unaware of the proclamation, some 10–15,000 people from outlying districts gathered in the city the same day to celebrate the major religious spring festival of Baisakhi. They had assembled in an enclosed walled garden, Jallianwala Bagh, a popular spot for public events in Amritsar but accessible only through five narrow passageways.

When Dyer learned of this meeting he did not seek to find out what it was about, whether the attendees were there in open defiance or merely in ignorance of his orders. He promptly took a detachment of soldiers in armoured cars and equipped with machine guns, and parked his vehicles in front of the gate to the Bagh. Without ordering the crowd to disperse or issuing so much as a warning—and though it was apparent it was a peaceful assembly of unarmed civilians—Dyer ordered his troops, standing behind the brick walls surrounding the Bagh, to open fire from some 150 yards away. The crowd, of thousands of unarmed and non-violent men, women and children gathered peacefully in a confined space, started screaming and pressing in panic against the closed gate, but Dyer ordered his men to keep firing till all their ammunition was exhausted. When the troops had finished firing, they had used 1,650 rounds, killed at least 379 people (the number the British were prepared to admit to) and wounded 1,137.[11] Barely a bullet was wasted, Dyer noted with satisfaction.

[11] The unofficial Indian numbers are higher: most converge at a figure of 1,499 killed. However, the figures of 1,650 rounds used, and 1,137 injured, are

There was no warning, no announcement that the gathering was illegal and had to disperse, no instruction to leave peacefully: nothing. Dyer did not order his men to fire in the air, or at the feet of their targets. They fired, at his orders, into the chests, the faces, and the wombs of the unarmed and defenceless crowd.

History knows the event as the Jallianwala Bagh massacre. The label connotes the heat and fire of slaughter, the butchery by bloodthirsty fighters of an outgunned opposition. But there was nothing of this at Jallianwala Bagh. Dyer's soldiers were lined up calmly, almost routinely; they were neither threatened nor attacked by the crowd; it was just another day's work, but one unlike any other. They loaded and fired their rifles coldly, clinically, without haste or passion or sweat or anger, emptying their magazines into the shrieking, wailing, then stampeding crowd with trained precision. As people sought to flee the horror towards the single exit, they were trapped in a murderous fusillade. Sixteen hundred and fifty bullets were fired that day into the unarmed throng, and when the job was finished, just ten minutes later, hundreds of people lay dead and several thousand more lay injured, many grotesquely maimed for life.

The Jallianwala Bagh massacre was no act of insane frenzy but a conscious, deliberate imposition of colonial will. Dyer was an efficient killer rather than a crazed maniac; his was merely the evil of the unimaginative, the brutality of the military bureaucrat. But his action that Baisakhi day came to symbolize the evil of the system on whose behalf, and in whose defence, he was acting. In the horrified realization of this truth by Indians of all walks of life lay the true importance of the Jallianwala Bagh massacre. It represented the worst that colonialism could become, and by letting it occur, the British crossed that point of no return that exists only in the minds of men—that point which, in any unequal relationship, both master and subject must instinctively respect if their relationship is to survive.

---

not disputed. The truth of the deaths may lie somewhere in between; 379, the official figure, is the minimum. Even if the official figures are accurate, though, that makes for 1,516 casualties from 1,650 bullets, a measure of how simple, and how brutal, Dyer's task was.

The massacre made Indians out of millions of people who had not thought consciously of their political identity before that grim Sunday. It turned loyalists into nationalists and constitutionalists into agitators, led the Nobel Prize-winning poet Rabindranath Tagore to return his knighthood to the king and a host of Indian appointees to British offices to turn in their commissions. And above all it entrenched in Mahatma Gandhi a firm and unshakable faith in the moral righteousness of the cause of Indian independence. He now saw freedom as indivisible from Truth, and he never wavered in his commitment to ridding India of an empire he saw as irremediably evil, even satanic. The historian A. J. P. Taylor calls the massacre 'the decisive moment when Indians were alienated from British rule'. No other 'punishment' in the name of law and order had similar casualties: 'The Peterloo Massacre had claimed about eleven lives. Across the Atlantic, British soldiers provoked into firing on Boston Commons had killed five men and were accused of deliberate massacre. In response to the self-proclaimed Easter Rebellion of 1916 in Dublin, the British had executed sixteen Irishmen.' Jallianwala confirmed how little the British valued Indian lives.

In describing his own actions to the official Hunter Commission enquiry, Dyer never showed the slightest remorse or self-doubt. This was a 'rebel meeting', he claimed, an act of defiance of his authority that had to be punished. 'It was no longer a question of merely dispersing the crowd' but one of producing a 'moral effect' that would ensure the Indians' submission. Merely shooting in the air to disperse the crowd would not have been enough, because the people 'would all come back and laugh at me'. He noted that he had personally directed the firing towards the exits (the main gate and the five narrow passageways) because that was where the crowd was most dense: 'the targets,' he declared, 'were good'. The massacre lasted for ten minutes, and the toll amounted to an extraordinary kill-rate, akin to a turkey-shoot. When it was over and the dead and wounded lay in pools of blood, moaning on the ground, Dyer forbade his soldiers to give any aid to the injured. He ordered all Indians to stay off the streets of Amritsar for twenty-four hours, preventing relatives or friends from bringing even a cup of water to the wounded, who were writhing in agony on the ground calling for help.

A reign of colonial terror followed. Salman Rushdie has suggested that, after the assault on the lady missionary, 'the calumny...that frail

English roses were in constant sexual danger from lust-crazed wogs' may also have played a part in General Dyer's mind. Be that as it may, and since it is impossible for an Indian to write objectively about the massacre and its aftermath, let me turn to the American Will Durant to provide the gruesome details:

> General Dyer issued an order that Hindus using the street in which the woman missionary had been beaten should crawl on their bellies; if they tried to rise to all fours, they were struck by the butts of soldiers' guns. He arrested 500 professors and students and compelled all students to present themselves daily for roll-calls, though this required that many of them should walk sixteen miles a day. He had hundreds of citizens, and some schoolboys, quite innocent of any crime, flogged in the public square. He built an open cage, unprotected from the sun, for the confinement of arrested persons; other prisoners he bound together with ropes, and kept in open trucks for fifteen hours. He had lime poured upon the naked bodies of *sadhus* (saints), and then exposed them to the sun's rays that the lime might harden and crack their skin. He cut off the electric and water supplies from Indian houses and ordered all electric fans possessed by [Indians] to be surrendered, and given *gratis* to the British. Finally he sent airplanes to drop bombs upon men and women working in the fields.

While the official commission of enquiry largely whitewashed Dyer's conduct, Motilal Nehru was appointed by the Congress to head a public enquiry into the atrocity, and he sent his son Jawaharlal to Amritsar to look into the facts. Jawaharlal Nehru's diary meticulously records his findings; at one point he counted sixty-seven bullet marks on one part of a wall. He visited the lane where Indians had been ordered by the British to crawl on their bellies and pointed out in the press that the crawling had not even been on hands and knees but fully on the ground, in 'the manner of snakes and worms'. On his return journey to Delhi by train he found himself sharing a compartment with Dyer and a group of British military officers. Dyer boasted, in Nehru's own account, that 'he had [had] the whole town at his mercy and he had felt like reducing the rebellious city to a heap of ashes, but he took pity on it and refrained... I was greatly shocked to hear his conversation and to observe his callous manner'.

No doubt some good Englishmen will say that Brigadier General Reginald Dyer was an aberration, one of those military sadists that every army throws up from time to time, and not typical of the enlightened men in uniform who normally served the Raj. The excuse will not wash. Not only was Dyer given a free hand to do as he pleased, but news of his barbarism was suppressed by the British for six months, and when outrage at reports of his excesses mounted, an attempt was made to whitewash his sins by the official commission of enquiry, Hunter Commission, which only found him guilty of 'grave error'. It was only when a thoroughly documented report was prepared by the investigative team of the Indian National Congress that the British admitted what had happened. Dyer was relieved of his command and censured by the House of Commons, but promptly exonerated by the House of Lords and allowed to retire on a handsome pension. Rudyard Kipling, winner of the Nobel Prize for Literature and the poetic voice of British imperialism, hailed him as 'The Man Who Saved India'.

Even this did not strike his fellow Britons in India as adequate recompense for his glorious act of mass murder. They ran a public campaign for funds to honour his cruelty and collected the quite stupendous sum of £26,317 1s 10d, an astonishing sum for those days and worth over a quarter of a million pounds today. It was presented to him together with a jewelled sword of honour. In contrast, after many months of fighting for justice, the families of the victims of the Jallianwala Bagh massacre were given 500 rupees each in compensation by the government—at the prevailing exchange rate, approximately £37 (or in today's money £1450) for each human life.

For Jawaharlal Nehru, the English reaction to the massacre—and Dyer being publicly feted—was almost as bad as the massacre itself. 'This cold-blooded approval of that deed shocked me greatly,' he later wrote. 'It seemed absolutely immoral, indecent; to use public school language, it was the height of bad form. I realized then, more vividly than I had ever done before, how brutal and immoral imperialism was and how it had eaten into the souls of the British upper classes.'

It was no longer possible to claim that Dyer did not represent the British in India: they had claimed him as one of their own—their saviour.

* * *

Famine, forced migration and brutality: three examples of why British rule over India was despotic and anything but enlightened. But why should one be surprised? Sir William Hicks, home minister in the Conservative government of Prime Minister Stanley Baldwin, had stated the matter bluntly in 1928: 'I know it is said in missionary meetings that we conquered India to raise the level of the Indians. That is cant. We conquered India as an outlet for the goods of Britain. We conquered India by the sword, and by the sword we shall hold it. I am not such a hypocrite as to say we hold India for the Indians. We went with a yardstick in one hand and a sword in the other, and with the latter we continue to hold them helpless while we force the former down their throats.'

In Dyer's case, the sword was a bejewelled one; the yardstick measured the account books in the British treasury. One should never reproach a government for the candour of its high representatives.

6

THE REMAINING CASE FOR EMPIRE

What, then, remains of the case for the British empire in India?

Alex von Tunzelmann's clever start to her book *Indian Summer* made my point most tellingly:

> In the beginning, there were two nations. One was a vast, mighty and magnificent empire, brilliantly organized and culturally unified, which dominated a massive swath of the earth. The other was an undeveloped, semi-feudal realm, riven by religious factionalism and barely able to feed its illiterate, diseased and stinking masses. The first nation was India. The second was England.

The historian Andrew Roberts rather breathtakingly claimed, given this background, that British rule 'led to the modernisation, development, protection, agrarian advance, linguistic unification and ultimately the democratisation of the sub-continent.' We have dealt with the suggestion that it is to Britain that India owes its political unity and democracy; we have shown the severe limitations in the British application of rule of law in the country; we have laid bare the economic exploitation of India and the despoliation of its lands which give the lie to Roberts's claims of 'modernisation, development [and] agrarian advance'; and we have dispensed with the notion that there was something benign and enlightened about British despotism in India.

But the idea that such modernization could not have taken place without British imperial rule is particularly galling. Why would India, which throughout its history had created some of the greatest (and most modern for their time) civilizations the world has ever known, not have acquired all the trappings of developed or advanced nations today, had it been left to itself to do so? As I have pointed out earlier in the book, the story of India, at different phases of its several-thousand-year-old civilizational history, is replete with great educational institutions, magnificent cities ahead of any conurbations of their time anywhere in the world, pioneering inventions, world-class manufacturing and industry, a high overall standard of living, economic policies that imparted prosperity, and abundant prosperity—in short, all the markers of successful 'modernity' today—and there is no earthly reason why this could not again have been the case, if it had had the resources to do so which were instead drained away by the British. An Englishman writing for European social democratic readers in 1907 put it clearly: 'Wherever they are allowed a free outlet they [the Indians] display the highest faculties; and it is absurd to contend that great States which managed their own business capably for thousands of years, which outlived and recovered from invasions and disasters that might have crushed less vigorous countries, would be unable to control their own affairs successfully if a handful of unsympathetic foreigners were withdrawn, or driven out, from their midst.'

The clinching proof of this argument, after all, lies in the fact that despite having had to climb out of the deep socio-economic trough that colonialism had plunged the country into, and despite having made its own mistakes in the years after Independence, India has become the world's third-largest economy in less than seven decades since the British left, and is currently its fastest-growing one; it has also piled up an impressive list of 'modern' distinctions including that of being the first country in the world to have successfully sent a spacecraft into Mars orbit at the first attempt (a feat even the US could not accomplish and one which China and Japan have failed trying to do). How much better would India have done if it hadn't had the succubus that was the British empire fastened to it for twenty decades?

Apologists for Empire point to a number of other benefits they say the British left India with: the railways, above all; the English language; the education system and even organized sport, especially cricket, the one sport at which, in recent years, Indians have twice been world champions. Let us examine these in turn.

THE REMAINING CASE FOR EMPIRE

The Great Indian Railway Bizarre

The construction of the Indian railways is often pointed to by apologists for Empire as one of the ways in which British colonialism benefited the subcontinent, ignoring the obvious fact that many countries also built railways without having to go to the trouble and expense of being colonized to do so. But the facts are even more damning.

The railways were first conceived of by the East India Company, like everything else in that firm's calculations, for its own benefit. Governor-General Lord Hardinge argued in 1843 that the railways would be beneficial 'to the commerce, government and military control of the country'. Ten years later, his successor Lord Dalhousie underscored 'the important role that India could play as a market for British manufacturers and as a supplier of agricultural raw materials'. Indeed, the vast interior of India could be opened up as a market only by the railways, labourers could be transported to and from where they were needed by the new enterprises, and its fields and mines could be tapped to send material to feed the 'satanic mills' of England.

In its very conception and construction, the Indian railway system was a big colonial scam. British shareholders made absurd amounts of money by investing in the railways, where the government guaranteed returns on capital of 5 per cent net per year, unavailable in any other safe investment. That was an extravagantly high rate of return those days, possible only because the government made up the shortfall from its revenues, payments that of course came from Indian, and not British, taxes. These excessive guarantees removed any incentive for the private companies constructing the railways to economize—the higher their capital expenditure, the higher would be their guaranteed return at a high and secure rate of interest. As a result each mile of Indian railway construction in the 1850s and 1860s cost an average of £18,000, as against the dollar equivalent of £2,000 at the same time in the United States. In the event, it was twenty years or more before the first lines earned more than 5 per cent of their capital outlay, but even after the government had taken over railway construction in the 1880s, thanks to the rapacity of private British firms contracted for the task, a mile of Indian railway cost more than double the same distance in the equally difficult and less populated terrain of Canada and Australia.

It was a splendid racket for everyone, apart from the Indian tax-payer. In terms of a secure return, Indian railway shares offered twice as much as the British government's own stock. Guaranteed Indian railway shares absorbed up to a fifth of British portfolio investment in the twenty years to 1870—the first line opened in 1853—but only 1 per cent of it originated in India. Britons made the money, controlled the technology and supplied all the equipment, which meant once again that the profits were repatriated. It was a scheme described at the time as 'private enterprise at public risk'. All the losses were borne by the Indian people, all the gains pocketed by the British trader—even as he penetrated by rail deep into the Indian economy. The steel industry in England found a much-needed outlet for its overpriced products in India, since almost everything required by the railways came from England: steel rails, engines, rail wagons, machinery and plants. Far from supporting the proposition that the British did good to India, the railways are actually evidence for the idea that Britain took much more out of its most magnificent colony than it put in.

Nor was there any significant residual benefit to the Indians. The railways were intended principally to transport extracted resources, coal, iron ore, cotton and so on, to ports for the British to ship home to use in their factories. The movement of people was incidental, except when it served colonial interests; and the third-class compart-ments, with their wooden benches and total absence of amenities, into which Indians were herded, attracted horrified comment even at the time. (And also questions in the toothless legislatures: there were four-teen questions on this issue in the legislative assembly every year between 1921 and 1941, and eighteen more annually in the Council of State. The concern kept mounting as conditions worsened: the yearly averages for 1937–1941 were sixteen and twenty-five respectively. Mahatma Gandhi's first crusade on his return to India was on behalf of the third-class traveller.) Yet the third-class passengers became a source of profit for the railways, since British merchants in India ensured that freight tariffs were kept low (the lowest in the world, in fact) while third-class passengers' fares were made the railway companies' princi-pal source of profit. No effort was made, in building the railway lines, to ensure that supply matched the demand for popular transport.

And, of course, racism reigned; though whites-only compartments were soon done away with on grounds of economic viability, Indians found the available affordable space grossly inadequate for their numbers. (A marvellous post-Independence cartoon captured the situation perfectly: it showed an overcrowded train, with people hanging off it, clinging to the windows, squatting perilously on the roof, and spilling out of their third-class compartments, while two Britons in sola topis sit in an empty first-class compartment saying to each other, 'My dear chap, there's *nobody* on this train!')

As Durant pointed out, the railways were built, after all, for 'the purposes of the British army and British trade...Their greatest revenue comes, not, as in America, from the transport of goods (for the British trader controls the rates), but from third-class passengers—the Hindus; but these passengers are herded into almost barren coaches like animals bound for the slaughter, twenty or more to one compartment...'

Nor were Indians employed in the railways. The discriminatory hiring practices of the Indian Railways meant that key industrial skills were not effectively transferred to Indian personnel, which might have proved a benefit. The prevailing view was that the railways would have to be staffed almost exclusively by Europeans to 'protect investments'. This was especially true of signalmen, and those who operated and repaired the steam trains, but the policy was extended to the absurd level that even in the early twentieth century all the key employees, from directors of the Railway Board to ticket-collectors, were white men—whose salaries and benefits were also paid at European, not Indian, levels and largely repatriated back to England. Moreover, when the policy was relaxed and expensive European labour reduced, there was a continuing search for the most 'British-like' workers. Thus came the long-lasting identification of the Anglo-Indian community with railway employment, since at first it was these Eurasians from military orphanages, the product of liaisons between British 'other ranks' and local Indian women, who were trained to do the jobs that only Europeans had been assumed to be capable of doing previously. (In keeping with British notions of eugenics, and since the Anglo-Indians were not a very large community, 'martial' Sikhs and pale-skinned Parsis were then employed as well, although they were only put in charge of driving engines within station yards and employed in stations with infrequent traffic.)

British racial theories were in full flow on railway matters: it was believed that Indians did not have the 'judgement and presence of mind' to deal with emergencies and that they 'seldom have character enough to enforce strict obedience' to railway rules. When Indianization was attempted for economic reasons in the 1870s, railway officials argued that it would take three Indians to do the job of a single European. So great was the racist resistance to Indian employees that the project of training drivers was discontinued after a three-year trial, and the drivers who had been trained were once again restricted to yard work.

Here, too, the double standards of British colonial justice described previously were much in evidence, as with the 1861 collision of a mail train and a goods train between Connagar and Bally in Bengal. The European driver and guard of the goods train were both drunk and went to sleep, leaving the fireman in charge of the train while they slept. The poor man kept doing his job—stoking coal—and his train duly crashed into a mail train. When the accident was investigated, blame was placed on the absence of the Bengali stationmaster, rather than the behaviour of the comatose Europeans.

Double standards prevailed in other ways: whereas in Britain it was common practice to ensure the merit-based promotion of firemen to drivers, or of station-masters of small rural stations to large stations, this did not happen in India because these junior positions were occupied by Indians, whose promotion would be to posts otherwise occupied by Europeans. By 1900, in the regulations for pay, promotion, and suitability for jobs, or what we would today describe as the human resource management rules, employees were subdivided into 'European, Eurasian, West Indian of Negro descent pure or mixed, Non-Indian Asiatic, or Indian'. On employment the local medical officer would certify the race and caste identity of a candidate and write it on his history sheet—thus determining his future pay, leave, allowances, and possible promotions as well as place in the railway hierarchy for the rest of his career.

The Royal Indian Engineering College at Cooper's Hill near London, established in 1872 to produce engineers for India, allowed as candidates only those capable of passing examinations in mathematics, sciences, Latin, Greek, German, English literature and history—stipulations designed to exclude the majority of Indian candidates. These rules had the desired effect: In 1886, out of 1,015 engineers in the Public Works Department (PWD), only 86 were Indians.

Racism combined with British economic interests to undermine efficiency. The railway workshops in Jamalpur in Bengal and Ajmer in Rajputana were established in 1862 to maintain the trains, but their Indian mechanics became so adept that in 1878 they started designing and building their own locomotives. Their success increasingly alarmed the British, since the Indian locomotives were just as good, and a great deal cheaper, than the British-made ones. In 1912, therefore, the British passed an Act of Parliament, explicitly making it impossible for Indian workshops to design and manufacture locomotives. The Act prohibited Indian factories from doing the work they had successfully done for three decades; instead, they were only allowed to maintain locomotives imported from Britain and the industrialized world. Between 1854 and 1947, India imported around 14,400 locomotives from England (some 10 per cent of all British locomotive production), and another 3,000 from Canada, the US and Germany, but made none in India after 1912. After Independence, thirty-five years later, the old technical knowledge was so completely lost to India that the Indian Railways had to go cap-in-hand to the British to guide them on setting up a locomotive factory in India again.

There was, however, a fitting postscript to this saga. The principal technology consultants for British Railways, the London-based Rendel Palmer & Tritton, today rely almost entirely on Indian technical expertise, provided to them by RITES, a subsidiary of the Indian Railways.

This is far from being a retrospective critique from the comfortable perspective of a twenty-first-century commentator. On the contrary, nineteenth-century Indians were quite conscious at the time of the abominable role of the railways in the crass exploitation of their country. The Bengali newspaper *Samachar* wrote on 30 April 1884 that 'iron roads mean iron chains' for India—foreign goods could flow more easily, it argued, killing native Indian industry and increasing Indian poverty. Nationalist voices like those of G. V. Joshi, G. S. Iyer, Gopal Krishna Gokhale and Dadabhai Naoroji were raised publicly in the 1890s, pointing out how limited were the benefits of the railways to India, how the profits all went to foreigners abroad, and how great was the burden on the Indian exchequer. The money that was being sent to England every year as interest, they pointed out unfailingly, could have been used for productive investments in Indian industry, in infrastructure work like irrigation (especially irrigation, which would help the Indian farmer, and which received only one-ninth of the government funding the railways did), or simply just spent in India to stimulate the local economy. Gokhale declared that 'the Indian people feel that [railway] construction is undertaken principally in the interests of the English commercial and moneyed classes, and that it assists in the further exploitation of our resources'. Indians also pointed out at the time that the argument that the railways would be an instrument against famine, and improve the general economic condition of the people, was fraudulent: in fact, famines persisted despite the railways, which only facilitated the export of grain and other agricultural products, effectively removing the very food surpluses that might have served as a buffer against famine.

There were other critiques. Gandhi argued in *Swaraj* that the railways spread bubonic plague. The ecological impact of railway construction aroused concern even at the time. In building the Sara-Sirajganj line in the Bengal delta, massive earthworks were put in place to block waterways, in order to reduce the outlay on bridges and the effect of damp. In doing so, very large arable areas to the northwest were waterlogged, ruining their agricultural potential. During the 1918 floods, railway embankments blocked natural water channels resulting in catastrophic flooding.

Market distortions also occurred with railway development. The railways were responsible, for instance, for sharply raising the price of rice. Before the railways came, slow water-based transport spread surpluses around the districts, keeping prices in any given areas low. But railways allowed surpluses to be cleanly extracted, essentially making peasants in the rice growing areas (and participating in an informal economy) compete directly with urban Indians and exporters for rice. The same was true of the fish markets.

And there are other examples to show how the interests of Indians were never a factor in railway operations: during World War I, several Indian rail lines were dismantled and shipped out of the country to aid the Allied war effort in Mesopotamia!

On the whole, therefore, the verdict of the eminent historian Bipan Chandra stands. British motives in building railways in India, he wrote, were 'sordid and selfish…the promotion of the interests of

British merchants, manufacturers and investors...at the risk and expense of Indian revenues'; their 'essential purpose' being to 'assist British enterprise in the exploitation of the natural resources of India.' *Quod erat demonstrandum.*

Education and the English Language

'Britain provided India with the necessary tools for independence,' wrote a British blogger on an Indian youth website in response to my Oxford speech. 'The idea of a modern democracy, of a self-governed country with a constitution and the guarantee of civil rights, was brought to India by Indians educated abroad, with the most famous example being barrister Mohandas Karamchand Gandhi, whose contribution to independence is, well, not insignificant. Not to forget the English language, without which pan-Indian protest and, later, communication and culture, is simply unimaginable.'

This case is often made by well-meaning individuals, and perhaps it should not be necessary to point out that Mahatma Gandhi's ideas of democracy and civil rights were developed in resistance to British rule, not in support of it. Still, the gift of the English language cannot be denied—I am, after all, using it as I write—and nor can the education system, of which again I am a beneficiary. So let us look at both closely.

The British left India with a literacy rate of 16 per cent, and a female literacy rate of 8 per cent—only one of every twelve Indian women could read and write in 1947. This is not exactly a stellar record, but educating the masses was not a British priority. As Will Durant points out, 'When the British came, there was, throughout India, a system of communal schools, managed by the village communities. The agents of the East India Company destroyed these village communities, and took no steps to replace the schools; even today [1930]... they stand at only 66 per cent of their number a hundred years ago. There are now in India 730,000 villages, and only 162,015 primary schools. Only 7 per cent of the boys and 1 per cent of the girls receive schooling, i.e. 4 per cent of the whole. Such schools as the Government has established are not free, but exact a tuition fee which...looms large to a family always hovering on the edge of starvation.'

Britain's education policy, in other words, had very little to commend itself. It supplanted and undermined an extensive Indian tradition: traditional methods of *guru-shishya parampara* (in which students lived with their teachers and imbibed an entire way of thinking) had thrived in India, as did the many monasteries which went on to become important centres of education, receiving students from distant lands, notably as far from our shores as China and Turkey. The Pala period [between the eighth and the twelfth century CE], in particular, saw several monasteries emerge in what is now modern Bengal and Bihar, five of which—Vikramashila, Nalanda, Somapura Mahavihara, Odantapuri, and Jaggadala—were premier educational institutions which created a coordinated network amongst themselves under Indian rulers.

Nalanda University, which enjoyed international renown when Oxford and Cambridge were not even gleams in their founders' eyes, employed 2,000 teachers and housed 10,000 students in a remarkable campus that featured a library nine storeys tall. It is said that monks would hand-copy documents and books which would then become part of private collections of individual scholars. The university opened its doors to students from countries ranging from Korea, Japan, China, Tibet, and Indonesia in the east to Persia and Turkey in the west, studying subjects which included the fine arts, medicine, mathematics, astronomy, politics and the art of war. Amongst them were several famous Chinese scholars who studied and taught at Nalanda University in the seventh century. Hsuan Tsang (Xuanzang from the Tang dynasty) studied in the university and then taught there for five years, while leaving detailed accounts of his time in Nalanda.

In the period of Muslim rule, in addition to madrasas, schools of religious instruction essentially open to Muslims, there were also *maktabs* (schools), which imparted Persian-Islamic education to Indian students, usually in Urdu (though Arabic and/or Persian were also taught). Before the British took over, the court language of the Mughals was Persian and the Muslim section of the population used Urdu—a mixture of Persian, Arabic and Hindi. Many Hindus in northern India also studied in Urdu or Persian. (In the south, various regional languages prevailed.) A *maktab* was an elementary (and secondary for some) educational institution before the 1850s that was used for secular education: the subjects taught included public administration, trade and intellectual and cultural pursuits, such as poetry. *Maktab*s were open to members of the elite class and included both Hindus and Muslims (in some places, many more of the former than the latter). Many *maktab*s closed in the mid-nineteenth century as their elite students gravitated to colonial schools in the hope of greater opportunities for advancement after their schooling.

As late as the late eighteenth/early nineteenth century, Raja Rammohan Roy, who would be hailed by the British as a progressive and modern-minded reformer, started his formal education in a village school or *pathshala*, where he learned Bengali, some Sanskrit and Persian; later, at age nine, he studied Persian and Arabic in a madrasa in Patna, and two years later went to Benares (Kashi) to learn Sanskrit and Hindu especially the scriptures, *Vedas* and *Upanishads*. Only then did he learn English and adapt to the British system of education in India, at which he excelled. But this kind of extensive grounding in traditional Indian learning, followed by English education, was already becoming quite rare.

In addition to monasteries and formal establishments of learning, informal institutions and methods of education also flourished in India. Oral education has always enjoyed an honoured place in Indian culture. Gandhi memorably advocated oral education in place of the prevailing emphasis on textbooks: 'Of textbooks...' he said, 'I never felt the want. The true textbook for the pupil is his teacher.' And so, in the little ashram that he created in South Africa, named Tolstoy Farm, he adopted oral forms of communicating his ideas, disregarding the need for formal written work. Gandhi found inspiration in the ways that knowledge of the *Vedas* and other foundational Hindu texts like the *Ramayana* and *Mahabharata* were passed orally from one generation to another. The oral tradition, sustained through the generations, had allowed this ancient knowledge to live.

But while such traditions give Indian education its moorings in our culture, there is no escaping the stark fact that modern India lost much of it under British rule, achieved independence with only 16 per cent literacy, and is still struggling to educate the broad mass of its population to seize the opportunities afforded by the globalized world of the twenty-first century. At least some of the blame for this surely lies in the system of education implemented by the British. The eminent

Major General Sir Thomas Munro, hero of the Mysore and Maratha wars, no less, pointed out that 'in pursuing a system, the tendency of which is to lower the character of the whole people, we profess to be extremely anxious to improve that character by education'. The use of the word 'profess' pointed to the eminent soldier's own doubts about the sincerity of the Company's intentions.

Of course the British did give India the English language, the benefits of which persist to this day. Or did they? The English language was not a deliberate gift to India, but again an instrument of colonialism, imparted to Indians only to facilitate the tasks of the English. In his notorious 1835 *Minute on Education*, Lord Macaulay articulated the classic reason for teaching English, but only to a small minority of Indians: 'We must do our best to form a class who may be interpreters between us and the millions whom we govern; a class of persons, Indians in blood and colour, but English in taste, in opinions, in morals and in intellect.' The language was taught to a few to serve as intermediaries between the rulers and the ruled. That Indians seized the English language and turned it into an instrument for our own liberation—using it to express nationalist sentiments against the British, as R. C. Dutt, Dinshaw Wacha and Dadabhai Naoroji did in the late nineteenth century and Jawaharlal Nehru in the twentieth—was to their credit, not by British design.

The East India Company's interest in Indian education began after the publication of a report by the company evangelist, Charles Grant, in 1792, which 'believed that the introduction of Western education and Christianity would transform a morally decadent society'. After the setting up of missionary schools was legitimized in the revised Charter Act of 1813, the Company's Court of Directors, in a dispatch to the Bengal government offering guidance on the implementation of the act, also noted that English would 'improve the communication between Europeans and natives' and 'produce those reciprocal feelings of regard and respect which are essential to the permanent interests of the British empire in India'. In other words, this was not only about Christian missionary zeal; it was also to be seen from the point of view of the Company's interests. The preferences of the natives were to be taken into account only 'whenever it can be done with safety to our dominions'.

While the evangelicals saw English education as a means of supplanting the pernicious influences of both 'Hindoo and Mohemedan learning', the philosopher James Mill and his followers urged the promotion of Western science and learning in India from a utilitarian point of view. However, Mill was not of the opinion that English was the language to do it in; rather, he preferred that texts be translated to the vernacular. In this he could also find support in the Charter of 1813, which also provided for the 'revival and improvement of literature, and the encouragement of the learned natives of India'.

These seemingly contradictory objectives could not be reconciled, however, and it was rapidly apparent to those entrusted with Indian affairs that it had to be one or the other. A debate ensued between the two schools of thought, but there seemed to be little doubt where the Company's bias lay. Teaching Sanskrit or Arabic to Indians was not going to be of much practical use to the business of the Company, but Indians who could read and write English, however badly they spoke it, could indeed be of value to the British.

In this debate between 'Orientalists' and 'Anglicists', the Anglicists prevailed—thanks, it is commonly believed, to the championing of their cause by Lord Macaulay, who had been appointed chair of the Committee on Public Instruction. Some argue that Macaulay's contribution to the system of education in India is overstated, and that the forces he represented would probably have been successful anyway. Governor-General William Bentinck was an open supporter of the Anglicist cause and had begun to implement a policy of English education through Company-ruled India, and Macaulay's task, they suggest, was merely to justify the prevalent policy rather than concoct a new one. But there is no doubt that his articulation of the Anglicist cause remains the clearest and most far-reaching statement of colonial purpose in the field of education, the most notorious in India for its flagrantly contemptuous dismissal of Oriental learning, and the most liable to quotation and misquotation by critics of the entire enterprise. (To this day English-speaking Indians are denounced as 'Macaulay-putras', or 'sons of Macaulay', by their non-Anglophile critics—usually, of course, in English.)

In his *Minute on Education*[12] Macaulay took an uncompromisingly, and many would say arrogantly, ethnocentric stand on the issue. His view,

---

[12] Dubbed by an Indian wag, with a penchant for alliteration, as 'Macaulay's Moronic Minute'.

which prevailed with the reformist governor-general, was that 'the intellectual improvement of those classes of the people who have the means of pursuing higher studies can at present be affected only by means of some language not vernacular amongst them'. He did not allow his ignorance of the East to undermine his self-confidence. 'A single shelf of a good European library was worth the whole native literature of India and Arabia', he notoriously declared, while admitting he had not read a single work from the literatures he was dismissing. 'We have to educate a people who cannot at present be educated by means of their mother-tongue. We must teach them some foreign language. The claims of our own language it is hardly necessary to recapitulate. It stands pre-eminent even among the languages of the West. In India, English is the language spoken by the ruling class. It is spoken by the higher class of natives at the seats of Government...of all foreign tongues, the English tongue is that which would be the most useful to our native subjects... What the Greek and Latin were to the contemporaries of More and Ascham, our tongue is to the people of India... The languages of western Europe civilised Russia. I cannot doubt that they will do for the Hindoo what they have done for the Tartar...'

What about the practical legal aspects of governing a foreign population, many following their own customs and laws?

'The fact that the Hindoo law is to be learned chiefly from Sanscrit books, and the Mahometan law from Arabic books, has been much insisted on, but seems not to bear at all on the question. We are commanded by Parliament to ascertain and digest the laws of India. The assistance of a Law Commission has been given to us for that purpose. As soon as the [new, British-drafted legal] Code is promulgated, the Shasters and the Hedaya will be useless to a moonsiff or a Sudder Ameen. I hope and trust that, before the boys who are now entering at the Mudrassa and the Sanscrit College have completed their studies, this great work will be finished. It would be manifestly absurd to educate the rising generation with a view to a state of things which we mean to alter before they reach manhood.'

(There is irony in this justification of the dismantling of traditional education: the penal code Macaulay drafted in the 1830s would only be enacted by the British a generation later, in 1861.)

To their credit, the Anglicists did not altogether dismiss the vernacular languages. They sought that European scientific and literary knowledge should percolate down to the masses through an intermediary élite class of English-speaking Indians. Macaulay had pointed out that 'it is impossible for us, with our limited means, to attempt to educate the body of the people'. To this élite, interpretative class, therefore, 'we may leave it to refine the vernacular dialects of the country, to enrich those dialects with terms of science borrowed from the Western nomenclature, and to render them by degrees fit vehicles for conveying knowledge to the great mass of the population.' Another Anglicist 'most fully admitted that the great body of the people must be enlightened through the medium of their own languages, and that to enrich and improve these, so as to render them the efficient depositories of all thoughts and knowledge, is an object of the first importance'. Mass English education was never British policy, therefore, nor was it necessary to dispense 'European' scientific knowledge to Indians; the educated Indians would do so in their own languages.

This did happen, to some extent. The Delhi College was founded in 1825 partly with such an object in view: a Vernacular Translation Society was formed there in the 1840s, which attempted to translate English textbooks on history, law, science and medicine into Urdu, with the help of Western-educated Indians and other college officials. These were some of the earliest textbooks on 'modern' subjects that were written to propagate an updated Western curriculum, and served as vernacular education textbooks in the northwestern provinces and Punjab in the 1840s and 1850s. It is difficult to argue, however, that such education acquired as much reach or influence as English education in India, which to this day is considered the passport to success and influence in Indian society. Most Indians educated in English used that language for their own career self-advancement, not to serve as academic translators or instructors for the masses; and vernacular teaching remained an orphaned profession, reserved for those unfortunates whose own English was not good enough for professions that required the language of the colonials. The Anglicists' purpose was not served, but one wonders whether, in these circumstances, it ever could have been.

Under the British, the universities remained largely examination-conducting bodies, while actual higher education was carried out in affiliated colleges, which offered a two-year BA course (following a year of intermediate studies after high school). The colleges, like the

British schools in India, heavily emphasized rote learning, the regurgitation of which was what the examinations tested. Failing the exams was so common that many Indians proudly sported 'BA (F)' after the names as a credential, to indicate that they had got that far (the 'F' stood for 'failed'). Dropout rates were always very high, and successfully completing a bachelor's degree was widely hailed as a rare and considerable achievement.

Still, the British higher education system did little to promote analytic capacity or creative thinking and certainly no independence of mind. It produced a group of graduates with a better-than-basic knowledge of English, inadequate in ninety per cent of the cases to hold one's own with an Englishman, but adequate to get a clerical position in the lower rungs of government service or a teaching position in a government school. (The other ten per cent shone despite the limitations of the system and either excelled in various private capacities or went abroad to England for higher education.) Worse, though, it left the individual graduate—every one of them—Westernized enough to be alienated from his own Indian cultural roots. Indians educated under this system, observed a senior civil servant in 1913, 'become a sort of hybrid. This is due to their English masters, who are obsessed with the idea that the only way to "educate" anyone is to turn him into a plaster Englishman.'

The problem persisted throughout British rule. An Indian nationalist group declared, in a book published in London in 1915:

All Indian aspirations and development of strong character have been suppressed. The Indian mind has been made barren of any originality, and deliberately kept in ignorance... The people are kept under an illusion in order to make them more amenable to British control. The people's character is deliberately debased, their mind is denationalized and perpetually kept in ignorance and fed with stories of England's greatness and 'mission' in the world...

As Pankaj Mishra has observed:

European subordination of Asia was not merely economic and political and military. It was also intellectual and moral and spiritual: a completely different kind of conquest than had been witnessed before, which left its victims resentful but also envious of their conquerors and, ultimately, eager to be initiated into the mysteries of their seemingly near-magical power.

An intriguing example of the successful colonization of the Indian mind is that of the notorious Anglophile Nirad C. Chaudhuri, the Bengali intellectual and author of the bestselling *Autobiography of an Unknown Indian* (1951), with its cringe-worthy dedication to the British Empire in India:

> To the memory of the British Empire in India,
> Which conferred subjecthood on us,
> but withheld citizenship.

> To which yet every one of us threw out the challenge:

> 'Civis Britannicus sum'

> Because all that was good and living within us
> was made, shaped and quickened
> by the same British rule.

This unedifying spectacle of a brown man with his nose up the colonial fundament made Chaudhuri a poster child for scholarly studies of how Empire creates 'native informants', alienated from and even abhorring their own cultures and societies. Chaudhuri's admiration for the British empire extended to his appreciation of it for restraining Indians from defecating in public—an activity which assuredly the British did not, in fact, succeed in controlling, let alone stopping, except in the public areas of major towns. This suggests a curious correlation between dislike for one's own body and a yearning for foreign rule: 'these two processes of self-othering', the scholar Ian Almond observes, 'work in tandem to replicate a crucial distance between colonized and colonizer, Babu and native, mind and body'. One of the consequences of a colonial education was Chaudhuri's xenolatry, rooted in the conviction that he was 'a displaced European/Aryan suffering the present-day and (millennia-old) consequences of an ancestor's unwise decision to wander in the wrong direction and settle in an unsuitable climate'. Chaudhuri, at the age of seventy-three, upped sticks and moved to Oxford, there to live out his centenarian life. In his mind, of course, he had always lived there.

Chaudhuri wore his erudition anything but lightly, quoting Greek and Latin and dropping classical allusions in a style that went out with the sola topi. (No doubt woggishness loses something in translation.) It was typical that his take-no-prisoners assault on all the citadels of

Indian culture and civilization was titled *The Continent of Circe*: he had to turn to Western mythology even for his principal metaphor. Though Chaudhuri dismissed most British histories of India as little more than 'imperialistic bragging', he remained seduced by the Raj, seeing even in Clive's rapacity and theft the 'counterbalancing grandeur' of the grand imperialist project. The scholar David Lelyveld wrote in an indulgent review that 'Nirad Chaudhuri is a fiction created by the Indian writer of the same name—a bizarre, outrageous and magical transformation of that stock character of imperialist literature, the Bengali babu'. But while the British in India laughed at the typical babu for his half-successful attempts to emulate his colonial masters, Nirad babu sought to demonstrate to post-imperial Britain that he was impossible to laugh at. That there might be something faintly comical about the sight of this wizened figure, in his immaculate Bengali dhoti, strutting about Oxford lamenting the decline of British civilization, does not appear to have occurred to him.

But there was still one fatal fly in the Anglophile's ointment. Even Nirad Chaudhuri had to admit that British racism, snobbery and exclusiveness ('all the squalid history of Indo-British personal relations') had a great deal to do with the downfall of the Empire. He wrote bitterly of 'intolerable humiliation' and 'national and personal degradation' from British behaviour towards Indians. In repeated personal instances of racism, Ian Almond points out, 'the comprador intellectual discovers the precise limits of his contract'—the supposed benevolence of the Empire which he celebrates in his writings encountering the more prosaic reality of the British baton and the white man's sneer.

Textual Harassment

In 1859–60, education in Bengal received 1,032,021 rupees from the British government, which was about the same amount spent on rebuilding army barracks that year. The funding of education continued to be a low priority for the British throughout their rule. Durant noted in 1930 that the British government in India preferred to devote the limited resources it allocated to education to 'universities where the language used was English, the history, literature, customs and morals taught were English, and young [Indians]… found that they had merely let themselves in for a ruthless process that aimed to de-nationalize and de-Indianize them, and turn them into imitative Englishmen'. This was done with minimal resources: Durant observed that the total expenditure for education in India (in 1930) was less than half that in New York state alone. Between 1882 and 1897, a fifteen-year period marked by a significant expansion of public education worldwide, the appropriation for the army in India increased by twenty-one-and-a-half times the increase for education. 'The responsibility of the British for India's illiteracy,' Durant concluded, 'seems to be beyond question.'

Still, there was one unintended benefit of the British approach to Indian education. Since educating Indians was not a major British priority, it did not attract eminent Britons, and from early in the twentieth century, academia became the one available avenue for Indian advancement. With very few exceptions, the vice-chancellors of the main public universities after the 1890s were Indians, though inevitably most were staunch defenders of British imperial rule.

While English instruction acquired a position of dominance in British India, albeit for a small if well-placed elite, a British perspective also infused the study of other subjects taught to Indians through English—notably history. The British saw precolonial Mughal history as consisting of a linear narration of events devoid of context or analysis; as for pre-Mughal texts, John Stuart Mill dismissed them as 'mythological histories...where fable stands in the face of facts'. To replace these versions, the British reconstructed 'factual' accounts of Indian historiography, adding more contextual analysis in a structured 'European' style—but with the teleological purpose of serving to legitimize British rule in India. As we have seen, English histories and theoretical constructs of India not only promoted *divide et impera* by inventing the religious 'periodization' of the Indian past, but portrayed a nation waiting for the civilizing advent of British rule. By arguing that history texts should 'rely upon facts and serve a secular curriculum', they also moved away from the teaching of religious and mythological texts, including India's timeless epics, the *Mahabharata* and *Ramayana*, which at the very least could have occupied the place in Indian schoolrooms that the *Iliad* and *Odyssey* did in British ones. Independent India carried on this tradition of secular neglect of the classics, for which it is now reproached by a new, Hindu-chauvinist government that accuses the

British and their Indian Macaulayputras of promoting the intellectual and cultural deracination of Indian children.

If the teaching of history served an evident purpose, literature served the same ends in a more tangential way. Professor Gauri Vishwanathan has done pioneering work on the role of the study of English literature in colonial India as a means of socializing and co-opting Indian elites during the early nineteenth century. Indeed, she argues that the very idea of English literature as a subject of study was first devised by the British in India to advance their colonial interests. It was not only that the English felt their literature would be a way of striking awe and respect for British civilization into the minds and hearts of the colonized Indians; it was also that the British colonists considered many of the great works of Indian literature to be 'marked with the greatest immorality and impurity'—and that included Kalidas's *Shakuntala*, described by Horace Wilson, the major nine-teenth-century Sanskrit scholar, as the jewel of Indian literature, but disapproved of as a suitable text for study in Indian schools and colleges in British India.

In this, the British educationists were only echoing the biases of Macaulay and his ilk, who made no bones about their convictions regarding the superiority of English literature. Macaulay had, after all, argued in his *Minute* that 'the literature now extant in [English] is of greater value than all the literature which three hundred years ago was extant in all the languages of the world together... The literature of England is now more valuable than that of classical antiquity.' Charles Trevelyan in his 1838 book *On the Education of the People of India* admitted that the arguments made for propagating English literature through the English language were not based on any scientific notion but on the simple Macaulayan prejudice that European knowledge was axiomatically 'superior' to oriental knowledge. Nonetheless, it worked, since Indians socialized through the study of English literature were bound to be more admiringly Anglophone and therefore more willing to be complicit in British dominance.

The study of history was not only Anglo-centric, it was deliberately designed to impress upon the student the superiority of all things British, and the privilege of being the subject of a vast Empire, whose red stain spread across a map of the world on which the sun never set.

(The sun never set on the British empire, an Indian nationalist later sardonically commented, because even God couldn't trust the Englishman in the dark.)

The study of English literature served a similar purpose. Amongst the required texts was Arthur Stanley's collection of English patriotic poetry, with an introduction by the Lord Bishop of Calcutta extolling the virtue of verse ('for an Empire lives not by bread alone', he intones sagely), and commencing with Tennyson's famous lines 'The song that nerves a nation's heart / Is itself a deed.' The poems are all, of course, intended to exalt the greater glory of the British empire. The poet G. Flavell Hayward wrote in praise of 'Glory or death, for true hearts and brave / Honour in life, or rest in a grave.' The spirit of English 'fair play' was instilled in Newbolt's 'Play up! Play up! And play the game' and Kipling's odes to the White Man's Burden no doubt made the heathen feel suitably grateful for the stamp of the colonial jackboot. ('East is East and West is West / And never the twain shall meet/', I wrote bitterly after discovering the poem in college, 'Except of course when you lie crushed / Under the Briton's feet!')

In those pre-televisual days, popular fiction, too, helped the anxious English-educated reader imbibe the virtues of colonialism. Those redoubtable bestsellers by G. A. Henty, H. Rider Haggard, and Kipling himself told tales of imperial derring-do in which the intrepid Englishman always triumphed over the dark, untrustworthy savages. Kipling's notorious verse told the English (and the Americans who were conquering the Philippines) to 'Take up the White Man's Burden, Send forth the best ye breed / Go bind your sons to exile, to serve your captives' need', despite the ingratitude of the heathens they were ruling; the White Man had to bear his Burden despite 'his old reward: / the blame of those ye better, / The hate of those ye guard'. And he was to do this, in lines reeking of hypocritical paternalism, for the needs of resentful 'sullen peoples, Half-devil [*sic*] and half-child'. (A brilliant contemporary riposte, in verse, 'The Brown Man's Burden', came from the Liberal MP and theatre impresario Henry Labouchère, which deserves to be better known. I have therefore reproduced it *in extenso* later in this chapter.)

The inclusion of an Indian character in the hugely popular children's stories featuring Billy Bunter, a staple of boys' pulp-magazine fiction in the first quarter of the twentieth century, creatively sought to inveigle the colonials into a narrative of complicity. The boy was, of course, an aristocrat, improbably named Hurree Jamset Ram Singh, his royal provenance compounded (like his illustrious compatriot Ranji) by his talent at cricket. Still, his English classmates knew him as 'Inky', and the illustrations always showed him several shades darker than them; and he was usually relegated to the margins of the Bunter stories, whose real heroes remained the English boys.

Salman Rushdie has written of the creation of a 'false Orient of cruel-lipped princes and dusky slim-hipped maidens, of ungodliness, fire and the sword', endorsing Edward Said's conclusion in his path-breaking *Orientalism*, 'that the purpose of such false portraits was to provide moral, cultural and artistic justification for imperialism and for its underpinning ideology, that of the racial superiority of the Caucasian over the Asiatic'. To Rushdie, such portrayals did not belong only to the imperial past; 'the rise of Raj revisionism, exemplified by the huge success of these fictions, is the artistic counterpart to the rise of conservative ideologies in modern Britain'.

Despite the efforts of the Orientalists and their glamorous exoticizing of British imperialism, however, there was one problem: once an Indian was taught to read, study and understand, it was impossible to restrict where his mind might take him. William Howitt presciently observed in 1839 that 'it is impossible to make the English language the vernacular tongue, without at the same time producing the most astonishing moral revolution which ever yet was witnessed on the earth. English ideas, English tastes, English literature and religion, must follow as a matter of course…' And, of course, though he did not mention it, English political ideas too. By 1908, the notorious Empire apologist J. D. Rees was complaining that 'in our schools pupils imbibe sedition with their daily lessons: they are fed with Rousseau, Macaulay, and the works of philosophers, which even in Oxford tend to pervert the minds of students to socialistic and impractical dreams, and in India work with far greater force upon the naturally metaphysical minds of youths, generally quick to learn by rote, for the most part penniless, and thus rendered incapable of earning their living, except by taking service of a clerical character under rulers, whom they denounce as oppressors unless they receive a salary at their hands. The malcontents created by this system have neither respect for, nor fear of, the Indian Government. Nor is this surprising, for the literature upon which they are brought up in our schools is fulfilled with destructive criticism of any system of Government founded upon authority...' Rees urged the British government in India to 'follow Lord Curzon's courageous lead in refusing to subsidise the manufacture of half-baked Bachelors of Arts and full-fledged agitators. It is too late, I suppose, to go back upon the decision in favour of the Anglicists, but is there any particular reason why Herbert Spencer, for instance, should be given in the Indian system so prominent a place? Is there any need to fill Indian students with philosophy, the study of which, even in Oxford, induces a regrettable tendency towards vain speculative dreams and socialistic sophistries?'

By the late nineteenth century, English education had indeed created a class of Anglophone Indians well-versed in the literature, philosophy and political ideas of the British; but, as we have seen, when they began to clamour for rights, and access to positions that they believed their education had qualified them for, they met with stubborn resistance.

There were always, of course, those who argued that the real obstacle was Indian attitudes, especially those relating to caste, since the prospect of students from various castes mingling in classrooms filled Indian traditionalists with horror. On this argument—that castes would not mingle in schools—Durant points out that they already did mingle indiscriminately 'in railway coaches, tramcars and factories' and that 'the best way to conquer caste would have been through schools'. But the British chose to shelter behind imagined objections from the traditionalists, because it suited them not to have to spend more on education.

Still, there were memorable exceptions. The pioneering Dalit reformer Jyotiba Phule, born in a 'lower' caste of gardeners and florists, became an inspiring example of how a student could study in an English school with Brahmin and other high-caste friends, energize and invigorate his intellect with literature from around the world, and build on that to transform his society. Mahatma Phule, as many called him, not only became a pioneer of Dalit empowerment and women's education but also a voice for global movements and ideas of equality. He dedicated his book *Gulamgiri* ('Slavery', 1873) to the 'good people of the United States' for having abolished slavery. A few decades later, Dr B. R. Ambedkar followed in his footsteps, though after an Indian schooling he did all his higher education abroad, in both Britain and America.

It has been argued that the British were not selective, and at least theoretically favoured the education of all castes and not just the upper castes, whereas India's own leaders were divided on whether modern education should be extended to all. A bill for universal compulsory primary education was indeed tabled by the 'moderate' Congress leader Gopal Krishna Gokhale in the legislative council of the governor-general in 1911 and another by Vithalbhai Patel in the same body in 1916, but both were defeated by the votes of the British and government-appointed members. What is less known, however, is that the bills were also opposed by the likes of Mahatma Gandhi and Surendra Nath Banerjea, staunch nationalists both. Gandhiji wrote in *Hind Swaraj*: 'The ordinary meaning of education is knowledge of letters. To teach boys reading, writing and arithmetic is called primary education. A peasant earns his bread honestly. He has ordinary knowledge of the world. But he cannot write his own name. What do you propose to do by giving him a knowledge of letters? Will you add an inch to his happiness? It is not necessary to make this education compulsory. Our ancient school system is enough. We consider your modern school to be useless'.

Fortunately, on this issue, Gandhiji's somewhat eccentric views did not prevail. But perhaps his real objection was not to literacy and education as such, but to British education in particular. In 1937, when Congress ministries were elected in eight provinces and for the first time enjoyed control over education, Gandhi put forward a plan called the Wardha Scheme for Education, which envisaged seven years of basic education for rural children, including vocational training in village handicrafts. It was never fully implemented, but it would certainly have imparted the basics, including literacy in the mother tongue, mathematics, science, history, and physical culture and hygiene, in addition to crafts. It is difficult to argue against the proposition that the Wardha scheme would have been a vast improvement on what little colonial education was available in rural India.

One of the consequences of a colonial education was, as we have seen with Nirad Chaudhuri, the colonization of the minds of Indians by the languages, models and intellectual systems brought into our lives by the West. In many ways Indians judged their societies according to Western intellectual or aesthetic standards (Ashis Nandy has written pointedly of how Third Worlders construct a 'non-West which is itself a construction of the West'). Colonialism misappropriated and reshaped the ways in which a subject people saw its history and even its cultural self-definition. Nationalists sought, in reaction, to contribute towards, and to help articulate and give expression to, the cultural identity of their society, but they did so coloured, inevitably, by the influence of their own colonial education. It was only after India had emerged into Independence, awaking from the incubus of colonialism, that Indians realized how much imperial rule had also, in many ways, fractured and distorted their cultural self-perceptions. This is changing gradually over the decades, as Indians understand that development will not occur without a reassertion of identity: that this is who they are, this is what they are proud of, this is what they want to be. The task of the Indian nationalist is to find new ways (and revive old ones) of expressing his culture, just as his society strives, with the end of colonialism, to find new ways of being and becoming.

By virtue not so much of British colonization, as of American twentieth-century dominance, English has become the language of globalization, the benefits of which are also accruing to India. But though the worldwide adoption of English has 'certainly facilitated more global exchanges and business transactions among English speakers everywhere', including India, as Adrian Lester observes, 'it [has] only served to heighten the exclusion of most non-English speaking subjects and women from access to the credit and political capital that flowed through Anglophone global networks'.

I am not suggesting that India's traditional forms of education, in Indian languages, could have met the challenge of making India literate and competitive with the rest of the world. It could, of course, have given India a basic competence and self-confidence that cultures like Japan which educate themselves in their national languages have, and the foundation to set up great schools and colleges in the Nalanda mode; and an India that had grown and flourished without the ordeal of colonialism, could always have imported the best educationists, technological systems and English teachers from wherever they were, to create our own links with the globalized world. At least, without the

British having expropriated our national wealth for two centuries, we would have had the resources to do so.

One of the regrettable consequences of British rule was how colonialism suffocated any prospect of a revival of India's traditional spirit of scientific enquiry, whether by neglect or design. The destruction of the textile and steel industries has already been discussed, but it is striking that a civilization that had invented the zero, that spawned Aryabhata (who anticipated Galileo, Copernicus and Kepler by several centuries, and with greater precision) and Susruta (the father of modern surgery) had so little to show by way of Indian scientific or technological innovation even under the supposedly benign and stable conditions of Pax Britannica. The mathematical genius Ramanujan had to travel to Cambridge to have his genius recognized, and though C. V. Raman won a Nobel Prize in Physics in 1930 and S. N. Bose should have (instead, the discovery of the particle named for him, the boson, won two others the 2013 Prize), and Bose's namesake and mentor, Jagadish Chandra Bose, blazed an astonishing path as physicist, biologist, biophysicist, botanist and archaeologist (as well as an early writer of science fiction), there was little else to celebrate by way of scientific accomplishment in the two centuries of British colonial rule. Strikingly, the British themselves flourished in these fields in the nineteenth and early twentieth centuries, while funding no great institutions in India, and neglecting the enormous potential of Indian minds to excel in science and technology. It would take a while for India to make any headway in science and technology given the ground the country had to make up in these areas. The lack of facilities at home led to an exodus of sorts; several Indians went on to excel in foreign institutions, three winning science Nobels under foreign flags, while the stunted or fledgling research institutions in India were still seeking to establish themselves as worthy homes for brilliant Indian minds. (There are signs, though, that scientific studies are improving, as the remarkable innovations in space and missile technology have shown; this owes nothing to the colonial period but is a product of independent India's own efforts.)

Still, I am conscious that there is something ironic about English-speaking Indians like myself attacking the British in English for having imparted their English education to Indians. Ironic, yes, but only up to a point. I had my English schooling in India, and I learned it without the shadow of the Englishman judging my prose. I delighted in the language on its own terms, as a pan-Indian language today, and not as a symbol of colonial oppression. In any case, most English-educated Indians, including myself, will not repudiate Shakespeare and P. G. Wodehouse: we must concede we couldn't have enjoyed their masterworks without the English language.

I am told by a British-Indian friend that in a passionate public debate in London in 2015 on the merits or otherwise of my Oxford views, more than one speaker sought to discredit me in my absence (I was in India) on the grounds that I was a known aficionado of Wodehouse and the English language, who had even revived St Stephen's College's Wodehouse Society, the first of its kind in the world, and still served as patron of the London-headquartered (global) Wodehouse Society. The implication was that one cannot denounce British colonialism and celebrate the doyen of English humorists at the same time.

My critics could not have been more wrong. Yes, some have seen in Wodehouse's popularity a lingering nostalgia for the Raj. Writing in 1988, the journalist Richard West thought India's Wodehouse devotees were those who hankered after the England of fifty years before (i.e. the 1930s): 'That was the age when the English loved and treasured their own language, when schoolchildren learned Shakespeare, Wordsworth and even Rudyard Kipling... It was Malcolm Muggeridge who remarked that the Indians are now the last Englishmen. That may be why they love such a quintessentially English writer.'

Those lines are, of course, somewhat more fatuous than anything Wodehouse himself could ever write. Wodehouse is loved by Indians who loathe Kipling and detest the Raj and all its works. Indeed, despite a brief stint in a Hong Kong bank, Wodehouse had no colonial connection himself, and the Raj is largely absent from his books. (There is only one notable exception I can recall, in a 1935 short story, 'The Juice of an Orange': 'Why is there unrest in India? Because its inhabitants eat only an occasional handful of rice. The day when Mahatma Gandhi sits down to a good juicy steak and follows it up with roly-poly pudding and a spot of Stilton, you will see the end of all this nonsense of Civil Disobedience.') But Indians saw that the comment was meant to elicit laughter, not agreement.

(Mahatma Gandhi himself was up to some humorous mischief when, in 1947, far from sitting down to steak, he dined with the king's cousin and the last viceroy, Lord Mountbatten, and offered him a bowl of home-made goat's curd—perhaps from the same goat he took to England when he went to see the king in a loincloth! I reinvented the moment in my satirical *The Great Indian Novel*, only substituting a mango for the curd.)

If anything, Wodehouse was one British writer whom Indian nationalists could admire without fear of political incorrectness. Saroj Mukherji, née Katju, the daughter of a prominent Indian nationalist politician, remembers introducing Lord Mountbatten to the works of Wodehouse in 1948; it was typical that the symbol of the British empire had not read the 'quintessentially English' Wodehouse but that the Indian freedom fighter had.

Indeed, it is precisely the lack of politics in Wodehouse's writing, or indeed of any other social or philosophic content, that made what Waugh called his 'idyllic world' so free of the trappings of Englishness, quintessential or otherwise. Whereas other English novelists burdened their readers with the specificities of their characters' lives and circumstances, Wodehouse's existed in a never-never land that was almost as unreal to his English readers as to his Indian ones. Indian readers were able to enjoy Wodehouse free of the anxiety of allegiance; for all its droll particularities, the world he created, from London's Drones Club to the village of Matcham Scratchings, was a world of the imagination, to which Indians required no visa.

But they did need a passport, and that was the English language. English was undoubtedly Britain's most valuable and abiding legacy to India, and educated Indians, a famously polyglot people, rapidly learned and delighted in it—both for itself, and as a means to various ends. These ends were both political (for Indians turned the language of the imperialists into the language of nationalism) and pleasurable (for the language granted access to a wider world of ideas and entertainments). It was only natural that Indians would enjoy a writer who used language as Wodehouse did—playing with its rich storehouse of classical precedents, mockingly subverting the very canons colonialism had taught Indians they were supposed to venerate (in a country ruled for the better part of two centuries by the dispensable siblings of the

British nobility, one could savour lines like these: 'Unlike the male codfish which, suddenly finding itself the parent of three million five hundred thousand little codfish, cheerfully resolves to love them all, the British aristocracy is apt to look with a somewhat jaundiced eye on its younger sons.')

I am grateful, in other words, for the joys the English language has imparted to me, but not for the exploitation, distortion and deracination that accompanied its acquisition by my countrymen.

Tea Without Sympathy

Something similar can probably be said about those two great British colonial legacies (now that we have discredited democracy, the 'rule of law' and the railways as credible British claims): tea and cricket. Both, I freely confess, are addictions of mine, a personal tribute to the legacy of colonialism.

In an address to a joint session of the US Congress in 1985, the late Indian Prime Minister Rajiv Gandhi recalled, with a twinkle in his eye, the great affinities between the American Revolution and the Indian colonial experience. Cornwallis, after surrendering at Yorktown, triumphed in Bengal. And then, Gandhi added mischievously, 'Indian tea stimulated your revolutionary zeal'.

He got a good laugh for the allusion to the Boston Tea Party. But he was wrong. In 1773, there was no Indian tea, at least none that was properly cultivated and traded. Tea was a Chinese monopoly, and the taxed tea the colonists tossed into Boston Bay came from Amoy, not Assam. Perhaps if it had been Indian tea, the American revolutionaries might have thought of a less wasteful method of protest.

It was the British who established Indian tea as a cultivated commodity. The story is interesting, and once again commercial motives came into play. The British ruled India but not China: rather than spending good money on the Chinese, they reasoned, why not grow tea in India? Their desire to end their dependence on Chinese tea led the British to invent agricultural espionage, as a secret agent, improbably enough named Robert Fortune, slipped into China in the early 1840s, during the chaos and confusion of the Opium War years, to procure tea plants for transplantation in the Indian Himalayas. But most of the thousands of specimens he sent to British India died, and the East India Company directors were left scratching their collective heads. The solution came by accident—when a wandering Briton discovered an Indian strain of tea growing wild in Assam, tested it in boiling water, tasted the results and realized he had struck gold: he had made tea.

That gave the British their own tea industry in India. Assam tea proved superior to the Chinese imports and more palatable to the British housewife. In the 1830s, the East India Company traded about 31.5 million lbs. (14 million kilos) of Chinese tea a year; today India alone produces nearly 300 million kilos. But even tea was not exempt from colonial exploitation: the workers laboured in appalling conditions for a pittance, while all the profits, of course, went to British firms. Early in the twentieth century, the remarkable anti-imperialist Sir Walter Strickland wrote bitterly in the preface to his now-out-of-print volume *The Black Spot in the East*: 'Let the English who read this at home reflect that, when they sip their deleterious decoctions of tannin...they too are, in their degree, devourers of human flesh and blood. It is not the tea alone, but the impoverished blood of the slaves, devoid of its red seeds of life and vigour, that they are drinking.'

The British grew tea in India for themselves, not for the locals: the light, fragrant Darjeeling, the robust Assam, the heady Nilgiris tea, all reflected the soil, climate and geography of the respective parts of India for which they were named, but they were grown by Scottish planters (and picked by woefully underpaid Indian labourers) to be shipped to the mother country, where demand was strong. A modest quantity was retained for sale to the British in India; Indians themselves did not drink the tea they produced. It was only during the Great Depression of the 1930s—when demand in Britain dropped and British traders had to unload their stocks—that they thought of selling their produce to the Indians they'd ignored for a century. The Indian masses turned to tea with delight, and the taste for it spread throughout the Depression and the War years. Today, tea can be found in the remotest Indian village, and Indians drink more black tea than the rest of the world combined.

Full credit, then, to the British. And this time it is difficult to argue that one could have had extensive tea cultivation and a vast market for the product without colonization: certainly Indians hadn't ever done it before the British. Even the name is a colonial legacy. The word 'tea', common to most European languages, is from the dialect of Amoy, from where much of Britain's tea was shipped; but those who got their tea from Canton, like the Portuguese, and overland, like the Indians and the Arabs, call it by the Cantonese word 'cha'. Almost every Indian language uses a variant of 'cha', including 'chai' and 'chaya'; it is only the Anglophone Indians who speak of 'tea'.

But before I end this section on tea, a small digression. Even as they gave us tea, the British were destroying something else. The British ruthlessly exploited the land for profit, while ruining it and decimating the wildlife it sheltered. The destruction of Indian forests and wildlife occurred at a galloping pace under colonialism. The forests were destroyed for three main reasons: to convert the land into commercial plantations, especially to grow tea; to make railway sleepers; and to export timber to England for the construction of English houses and furniture.

The British cut down the forests of the Nilgiris and Assam to grow tea, and ravaged the forests of Coorg to grow coffee. Tea was not the only villain in the ecological devastation of the Nilgiris; the British also brought in several exotic species like eucalyptus, pine and wattle to produce viscose, which was sent to the UK to be made into fabric. Unfortunately, plants like eucalyptus thirstily drink up the ground water; thanks to their plantations, the British converted the once lush tropical rainforests of the Nilgiris into a water-shortage area.

The same phenomenon occurred when the British forced Indian farmers to grow poppy in order to extract opium, which involved cutting down vast areas of forests in some parts of north India. In Assam, for instance, by the mid-nineteenth century, large numbers of trees were chopped down since the opium poppy could not ripen and flower in their shade. This practice of slashing trees to protect the poppy indirectly almost wiped out some of India's most magnificent predators. The British wanted more land to be used for commercial crops, which would bring them revenue, so they put a bounty on the head of each predator, successfully erasing tigers, cheetahs, leopards and lions from vast parts of India. The tiger and leopard survived, albeit in reduced numbers, because they hid in the jungle. But the lion needed vast open spaces and could not survive—except in the one corner of the country, in Gujarat, where an Indian prince, the Nawab of Junagadh, maintained a private lion sanctuary where hunting was permitted for his invitees only. This saved the Asiatic Lion to some extent—but this majestic animal, of whom several thousand flourished before the British came to India, was down to fewer than a hundred when the Empire ended.

By destroying the forests, the British also broke the spirit of the aboriginal people or 'tribals' who lived in and utilized the natural resources of the forests. Unfortunately, their ownership of forest lands was traditional rather than documented; since they could not claim ownership in a form the British recognized, they were dispossessed and displaced, and attempts to maintain their hunter-gatherer lifestyle resulted in them being treated as poachers and therefore criminals.

Meanwhile, the British elevated the killing of wild animals into a high-status sport, one for the whites and the privileged Indian elite, and an activity whose glamour was enhanced by the access it provided the latter into British ruling circles (rather like polo might do today). Hunting in the British period became a monster sport; countless numbers of animals were killed, irretrievably transforming the ecology of many areas. For example, Madras was once called Puliyur, which means the town of tigers and leopards (the Tamil word 'puli' is used for both tiger and leopard). The British killed every tiger and leopard in this area, so that not even one was left in Madras or any of the plains of Tamil Nadu. The term Puliyur has lost its meaning, and is now largely forgotten.

Puliyur may no longer have tigers, which are hanging on precariously elsewhere in the subcontinent, but the British still drink Indian tea. In more ways than one: Tata, the Indian business conglomerate, now owns Tetley, the venerable British tea firm. So perhaps, in the ubiquitous references to 'chai' everywhere in the country, and in the milky, sweetened cups of tea that Indians thrust on every visitor, it is we who have appropriated this colonial legacy and made it our own.

The story gets a little more complicated. Tea, like other commodities, has been suffering a decline in prices, and exports are dwindling; many tea plantations, faced with rising wages and collapsing profits, are threatening to close down. The most expensive Indian tea, Castleton, was sold for over 6,000 rupees a kilo in 1991 ($231 at the then-prevailing exchange rate); the buyers were Japanese. The new record was set in 2012, when the price hit 7,200 rupees a kilo (but that meant it was down to $120 as the rupee had weakened) Castleton is the champagne of teas: other Indian teas do not fare a fraction as well. Internationally, Indian tea is competing for export markets with inferior teas from such unlikely sources as Argentina, Kenya and Malawi. But then again—if Argentina could grow tea without the British having colonized them first, couldn't India have done so as well?

So when the first Indian prime minister who had served as a *chaiwallah* (helping his father sell tea at a railway station platform), Narendra Modi, addressed the US Congress in 2016, he sprinkled his speech with humour, but unlike his predecessor thirty-one years earlier, did not breathe a word about tea. At a time when the world commodity markets are down and Indian tea producers are clamouring for relief, the Indian prime minister must have realized that tea is no longer a joking matter.

The Indian Game of Cricket

Cricket is, of course, the only sport in the world that breaks for tea (and for many amateurs, tea is the highlight of the experience). I have often thought that cricket is really, in the sociologist Ashis Nandy's phrase, an Indian game accidentally discovered by the British. Everything about the sport seems suited to the Indian national character: its rich complexity, the infinite possibilities and variations possible with each delivery, the dozen different ways of getting out, are all rather like Indian classical music, in which the basic laws are laid down but the performer then improvises gloriously, unshackled by anything so mundane as a written score. The glorious uncertainties of the game echo ancient Indian thought: Indian fatalists instinctively understand that it is precisely when you are seeing the ball well and timing your fours off the sweet of the bat that the unplayable shooter can come along and bowl you. It is almost, as has also been observed, a pastime in which the *Bhagavad Gita* is performed in the guise of a Victorian English morality play.

A country where a majority of the population still consults astrologers and believes in the capricious influence of the planets can well appreciate a sport in which an ill-timed cloudburst, a badly-prepared pitch, a lost toss of a coin or the sun in the eyes of a fielder can transform the outcome of a game. Even the possibility that five tense, exciting, hotly-contested and occasionally meandering days of cricket can still end in a draw seems derived from Indian philosophy, which accepts profoundly that in life the journey is as important as the destination.

Cricket first came to India with decorous English gentlemen idly pursuing their leisure; it took nearly a century for the 'natives' to learn the sport, and then they played it in most un-English ways. I remember being taken by my father to my first ever Test match, in Bombay in late 1963, when a weak English side was touring. I shall never forget the exhilaration of watching India's opening batsman and wicketkeeper, Budhi Kunderan, smite a huge six over midwicket, follow it soon after with another blow that just failed to carry across the rope, and then sky a big shot in a gigantic loop over mid-on. As it spiralled upwards Kunderan began running; when the ball was caught by an English fielder, he hurled his bat in the air, continued running, caught it as it came down, and ran into the pavilion. I was hooked for life.

India has always had its Kunderans, but it has also had its meticulous grafters, its plodders, its anarchists and its stoics: a society which recognizes that all sorts of people have their place recognizes the value of variety in its cricket team as well. Cricket reflects and transcends India's diversity: the Indian team has been led by captains from each of its major faiths, Hindus, Muslims, Parsis, Christians and a colourful Sikh. A land divided by caste, creed, colour, culture, cuisine, custom and costume is united by a great conviction: cricket.

Yes, the British brought it to us. But they did not do so in the expectation that we would defeat them one day at their own game, or that our film-makers would win an Oscar nomination for an improbable tale about a motley bunch of illiterate villagers besting their colonial overlords at a fictional nineteenth-century match (*Lagaan*, 2003). Sport played an important role in British imperialism, since it combined Victorian ideas of muscular Christianity, a cult of youthful vigour and derring-do in far-off lands, and the implicit mission of bringing order and civilization to the unruly East through the imposition of rules learned on the playing fields of Eton. If Empire was a field of play, then to the colonized learning the rules and trying to defeat the masters at their own game became an inevitable expression of national feeling. Scholars have demonstrated that one of the reasons why cricket acquired such a hold in Bengal society between 1880 and 1947 was as a way to discharge the allegation of effeminacy against the Bengali male by beating the English at their own game. The educated middle class of Bengal, the *bhadralok*, joined the maharajas of Natore, Cooch Behar, Mymensingh and other native states to make cricket a part of Bengali social life as a means of attaining recognition from their colonial masters. At the same time, the British, who saw cricket as a useful tool of the Raj's civilizing mission, promoted the sport in educational institutions of the province. In a somewhat different way, Parsi cricketers in Bombay undertook the sport for the purpose of social mobility within the colonial framework. The maharajas, the affluent classes and Anglicized Indians, Ashis Nandy points out, 'saw cricket as an identifier of social status and as a means of access to the power elite of the Raj. Even the fact that cricket was an expensive game by Indian standards strengthened these connections'.

Curiously, this pattern was replicated across the country, not just in the British presidencies but also in the princely states, many of which produced not inconsiderable teams, well financed by the native rulers. Some of these gentlemen played the sport themselves at a significant level of accomplishment; one, K. S. Ranjitsinhji (universally known as 'Ranji', and enviously as 'Run-get-sin-ji'), was selected to play for England against Australia in 1895, and scored a century on debut, which made him the hero of the Indian public. It is fascinating how Ranji, like Oscar Wilde and Benjamin Disraeli, became an English hero without being quite English enough himself. ('He never played a Christian stroke in his life,' as one English admirer disbelievingly put it.) Ranji described himself as 'an English cricketer and an Indian prince,' but as Buruma observes: 'As an English cricketer he behaved like an Indian prince, and as an Indian prince like an English cricketer.'

Ranji—cricketing genius, reckless spendthrift, shameless Anglophile—was an extraordinary amalgam of the virtues and defects of both gentleman and prince. His nephew, K. S. Duleepsinhji, and another prince, the Nawab of Pataudi, both emulated Ranji in 1930 and 1933 respectively, though by then Indians were beginning to ask why they had taken their talents to the other side instead of playing for the fledgling Indian Test team. (Pataudi did, in 1946, but by then he was past his prime.)

When Indians became good enough at cricket to win the occasional game, the British took care to divide them, organizing a 'Quadrangular

Tournament' that pitted teams of Hindus, Muslims, Parsis and 'the Rest' against each other, so that even on the field of play, Indians would be reminded of the differences among them so assiduously promoted by colonial rule.

The sociologist Richard Cashman notes that Indian nationalism was less radical, in a cultural sense, than Irish nationalism. In Ireland, the nationalists and Home Rule agitators attacked cricket and other English sports as objectionable elements of colonial culture, and patronized 'Gaelic sports' instead. Indian nationalist leaders, on the other hand, 'attacked the political and economic aspects of British imperialism but retained an affection for some aspects of English culture'. While traditional Indian sports like kabaddi languished in the colonial era, and polo was revived as a sport mainly for the British and a very narrow segment of the Indian aristocracy, cricket was seen as a sport where Indians could hold their own against the English. (This may explain why Ireland still has a very modest cricket team that is yet to earn 'Test' status, whereas India in the twenty-first century is one of the giants of the world game.)

That cricket was connected with the nationalist movement in Bengal of the 1910s is evident from the sporting history of Presidency College, the principal English-language institution of higher learning for Indians in Calcutta, where sports such as gymnastics and cricket were made compulsory to develop (as we have noted a little earlier) Bengali boys physically in reaction to British colonial stereotypes of 'manly' Britons and effeminate Bengalis. When the nationalist resistance in Bengal was gathering momentum, Presidency College lost a cricket match in 1914 to an all-European team of La Martinière College, an unabashedly colonial institution whose students were divided into 'Houses' named for the likes of Charnock and Macaulay. This caused much breast-beating and self-flagellation. The players of the team were publicly criticized: 'the big defeat of the college team by La Martinière College cannot be forgiven', declared the Presidency College magazine.[13]

---

[13] Of course, my football-crazy son Kanishk assures me that the single greatest moment of Indian sporting triumph against the British in the colonial period is to be found in football, not cricket: the Mohun Bagan team that defeated the East Yorkshire Regiment to win the IFA shield in 1911, barefoot!

'The contention that emulation of the colonizers is the key to explaining the origins of Indian cricket,' writes a scholar, 'fails to successfully account for the flowering of the game in Bengal.' So cricket too had nationalist overtones, and while one must concede that the British imparted it to us, today we can more than hold our own with them, and anyone else playing that sport.

7

THE (IM) BALANCE SHEET

A CODA

As I prepare to wind up my arguments, I'd like to touch on aspects of them, in brief, in this chapter. Before I do so I'd like to make it clear that it is not my intention to discredit every single thing the British did in India. As with all human enterprises, colonialism too brought positives as well as negatives. Not every British official in India was as rapacious as Clive, as ignorantly contemptuous as Macaulay, as arrogantly divisive as Curzon, as cruel as Dyer, or as racist as Churchill. There were good men who rose above the prejudices of their age to treat Indians with compassion, curiosity and respect; humane judges, conscientious officials, visionary viceroys and governors, Britons who genuinely befriended Indians across the colour barrier; and throughout the Raj there were men who devoted their lives to serve in India—to serve their country and its colonial institutions, it must be said, but also to help ordinary people lead better lives in the process. Their good works are still remembered by the Indians whose lives they changed. Sir Arthur Cotton, for instance, built a dam across the Godavari that irrigated over 1.5 million acres of previously arid land in south India, and is celebrated to this day with some three thousand statues installed by grateful farming communities in those two Andhra Pradesh districts, with even chief ministers participating in his birthday memorials. All these figures did exist; but they alleviated, rather than justified, the monstrous crime that allowed them to exist, the crime of subjugating a people under the oppressive heel of the 'stout British boot'.

Few still claim, as Lord Curzon did, that 'the British empire is under Providence the greatest instrument for good that the world has seen'; having written (or so he declared, without the slightest suggestion of irony) 'the most unselfish page in history... We found strife and we have created order.' He added that Britain had ruled India 'for the lasting benefit of millions of the human race'.

Few claim, I said, but some do. There are still Empire apologists like Ferguson and the lesser-known but surprisingly successful Lawrence James, who portrays the imperial undertaking as (to quote his literary agency) 'an exercise in benign autocracy and an experiment in altruism'. It seems preposterous that anyone today could possibly believe the twaddle that by spreading the benign blessings of free trade like so much confetti, introducing Western notions of governance by gunboat and sowing altruistic seeds of technological progress, the British empire genuinely ruled the benighted heathen in his own interest, but there are still nostalgics willing to make such an argument to the gullible, and they must be refuted, as I have tried to do throughout the book.

Imperial Pretensions, Colonial Consquences

Recent years have seen the rise of what the scholar Paul Gilroy called 'postcolonial melancholia', the yearning for the glories of Empire, reflected in such delights as a burger called the Old Colonial, a London bar named The Plantation, and an Oxford cocktail (issued during the debate on reparations in which I spoke) named Colonial Comeback. A 2014 YouGov poll revealed that 59 per cent of respondents thought the British empire was 'something to be proud of', and only 19 per cent were 'ashamed' of its misdeeds; almost half the respondents also felt that the countries 'were better off' for having been colonized. An astonishing 34 per cent opined that 'they would like it if Britain still had an empire'.

Niall Ferguson, for instance, argues that Britain's empire promoted 'the optimal allocation of labour, capital and goods in the world...no organisation in history has done more to promote the free movement of goods, capital and labour than the British empire in the nineteenth and early twentieth centuries. And no organization has done more to impose Western norms of law, order and governance around the world. For much (though certainly not all) of its history, the British Empire acted as an agency for relatively incorrupt government. Prima facie, there therefore seems a plausible case that Empire enhanced global welfare—in other words, [that it] was a Good Thing.'

This 'Good Thing' was so proclaimed at the height of globalization at the dawn of the twenty-first century, when it suited Ferguson to portray the British empire as the pioneer of this much-vaunted global economic phenomenon, its conquests dressed up as overseas investment and its rapacity as free trade—the very elements that contemporary globalizers were claiming would raise everyone's levels of prosperity. Such an argument is, of course, highly contestable, since the 'optimal allocation' of resources that Ferguson celebrates meant, to its colonial victims, landlessness, unemployment, illiteracy, poverty, disease, transportation and servitude. The British proclaimed the virtues of free trade while destroying the free trade Indians had carried on for centuries, if not millennia, by both land and sea. Free trade, of course, suited the British as a slogan, since they were the best equipped to profit from it in the nineteenth century, and their guns and laws could always stifle what little competition the indigenes could attempt to mount. A globalization of equals could well have been worth celebrating, but the globalization of Empire was conducted by and above all for the colonizers, and not in the interests of the colonized.

Ferguson also suggests that, in the long run, the victims of British imperialism will prove to have been its beneficiaries, since the Empire laid the foundations for their eventual success in tomorrow's globalized world. But human beings do not live in the long run; they live, and suffer, in the here and now, and the process of colonial rule in India meant economic exploitation and ruin to millions, the destruction of thriving industries, the systematic denial of opportunities to compete, the elimination of indigenous institutions of governance, the transformation of lifestyles and patterns of living that had flourished since time immemorial, and the obliteration of the most precious possessions of the colonized, their identities and their self-respect.

In this the likes of Ferguson are, ironically, following no less a predecessor than Karl Marx:

Indian society has no history at all, at least no known history. What we call its history is but the history of the successive intruders who founded their empires on the passive basis of that unresisting and unchanging society. The question, therefore, is not whether the English had a right to conquer India, but whether we are to prefer India conquered by the backward Turk, by the backward Persian, by the Russian, to India conquered by the Briton... England has to fulfil a double mission in India: one destructive, the other one regenerating the annihilation of old Asiatic society, and the laying of the foundations of Western society in Asia.

A more balanced account of imperial rule, broadly sympathetic to the British Raj but without glossing over its exploitative nature—while concluding that 'whether all this has been for better or worse, is almost impossible to say'—may be found in Denis Judd's short *The Lion and the Tiger*. Jon Wilson, in his recent *India Conquered*, is dismissive of most pretensions to grand imperial purpose, one way or the other. 'Its operation was driven instead by narrow interests and visceral passions,' he argues, 'most importantly the desire to maintain British sovereign institutions in India for its own sake.' In other words, Empire had no larger purpose than its own perpetuation. No wonder, then, that it did India little good.

Indians can never afford to forget the condition in which we found our country after two centuries of colonialism. We have seen how what had once been one of the richest and most industrialized economies of the world, which together with China accounted for almost 75 per cent of world industrial output in 1750, was transformed by the process of imperial rule into one of the poorest, most backward, illiterate and diseased societies on earth by the time of our independence in 1947. In 1600, when the East India Company was established, Britain was producing just 1.8 per cent of the world's GDP, while India was generating some 23 per cent. By 1940, after nearly two centuries of the Raj, Britain accounted for nearly 10 per cent of world GDP, while India had been reduced to a poor 'third-world' country, destitute and starving, a global poster child of poverty and famine. Ferguson admits that 'between 1757 and 1900 British per capita gross domestic product increased in real terms by 347 per cent, Indian by a mere 14 per cent'. Even that figure masks a steadily worsening performance by the Raj: from 1900 to 1947 the rate of growth of the Indian economy was below 1 per cent, while population grew steadily at well over 3.5 per cent, leavened only by high levels of infant and child mortality that shrank the net rate of population growth to the equivalent of economic growth, leaving a net growth rate near zero.

Freedom from Britain turned these numbers around for India. Net per capita income growth between 1900 and 1950 was nil (economic growth of 0.8 per cent minus net population growth at the same level,) but it rose to 1.3 per cent from 1950 to 1980 (growth rate of 3.5 per cent minus population growth of 2.2 per cent), to 3.5 per cent from 1981–90 and 4.4 per cent from 1991–2000, before attaining even higher levels in the following decade, twice crossing 9 per cent and averaging 7.8 per cent from 2001–10. Besides these, other key indices were also extraordinarily good after just under seven (at the time of writing) decades of independence, compared to the twenty decades of British rule that had gone before.

The British left a society with 16 per cent literacy, a life expectancy of 27, practically no domestic industry and over 90 per cent living below what today we would call the poverty line. Today, the literacy rate is up at 72 per cent, average life expectancy is nearing the Biblical three score and ten, and 280 million people have been pulled out of poverty in the twenty-first century.

To take the simple example of electricity, one of the supposed blessings of imperial rule in India: Britain governed India for five decades after the arrival of the first electricity supplies in the 1890s. In those fifty years to independence in 1947, while all of Britain, along with the rest of Europe and America, was electrified, the Raj connected merely 1,500 of India's 640,000 villages to the electrical grid. After Independence, however, from 1947 to 1991, the Indian government brought electricity to roughly 320 times as many villages as British colonialism managed in a similar time span.

The reasons were obvious: the British colonial rulers had no interest in the well-being of the Indian people. India was what the scholars Acemoglu and Robinson call, in their path-breaking *Why Nations Fail*, an 'extractive colony'. Thanks to British imperialism, the organic development of the Indian state and its scientific, technological, industrial and civic institutions could not take place, as it did between the sixteenth and eighteenth centuries in Europe. Colonial exploitation happened instead.

217

The world was aware of this disgraceful imperial record for decades before the British ended their rule after an ignominious half-century in which India's per capita income showed no growth at all. The US statesman William Jennings Bryan quotes the editor of a Calcutta magazine, *Indian World*, as writing in 1906: 'When the English came to India, this country was the leader of Asiatic civilization and the undisputed centre of light in the Asiatic world. Japan was nowhere. Now, in fifty years, Japan has revolutionized her history with the aid of modern arts of progress, and India, with 150 years of English rule, is still condemned to tutelage.' Japan had achieved 90 per cent literacy in forty years after the Meiji Restoration, whereas India languished at 10 per cent after 150 years of British rule. Every other significant socio-economic indicator worked to India's detriment.

Instead of enriching the world, Jon Wilson argues, the British empire impoverished it. 'The empire was run on the cheap. Instead of investing in the development of the countries they ruled, the British survived by doing deals with indigenous elites to sustain their rule at knockdown prices… The feudal lords now massacring villagers in the Indian state of Bihar were created by British land policy.'

It is hard not to bristle at Lawrence James's celebration of this abject performance by the British Raj: 'In return for its moment of greatness on the world stage, the Raj had offered India regeneration on British terms. It had been the most perfect expression of what Britain took to be its duty to humanity as a whole. Its guiding ideals had sprung from the late-18th and early-19th-century Evangelical Enlightenment, which had dreamed of a world transformed for the better by Christianity and reason. The former made little headway in India, but the latter, in the form of Western education and the application of science, did.'

Did India, the land of the Vedas and the Upanishads, the country of the learned theological debates at Akbar's court, the home of the 'argumentative Indian', really need British colonialism in order to be 'regenerated' by 'reason'? The claim is breathtaking in its presumption. Taken together with Ferguson's argument that economic benefits flowed from imperial rule, these Raj apologists are guilty of what might be described as an intellectual Indian rope-trick: they have climbed up their own premises. As Professor Richard Porter asks: 'Why, for example, should one assume that eighteenth-century India could not have evolved its own economic path, with distributions of capital, labour and goods "optimal" in the eyes of its own elites, however different from the criteria of liberal western political economists?' Porter, citing the detailed work of historians and scholars, questions the perceptions of Indian 'backwardness' advanced by those who see modernity as a gift of the West.

It must not be forgotten, after all, that the India the British entered was a wealthy, thriving and commercializing society: that was why the East India Company was interested in it in the first place. The Portuguese explorer Vasco da Gama, who found his way around the Cape of Good Hope to Calicut (Kozhikode), rather breathlessly spoke to King Manuel I of Portugal of large cities, large buildings and rivers, and great and prosperous populations. He talked admiringly of spices and jewels, precious stones and 'mines of gold'. The trinkets he offered were deemed unworthy gifts for the Indian monarch he offered them to, the Zamorin of Calicut; da Gama's goods were openly mocked and scorned by merchants and courtiers accustomed to far higher quality items.

Far from being backward or underdeveloped, as we have seen, pre-colonial India exported high quality manufactured goods much sought after by Britain's fashionable society. The British élite wore Indian linen and silks, decorated their homes with Indian chintz and decorative textiles, and craved Indian spices and seasonings. (Indeed, there are tales of British manufacturers in the seventeenth century trying to pass off their wares as 'Indian' to entice customers into buying their poorer quality British-made imitations.) The annual revenues of the Mughal Emperor Aurangzeb (1618–1707) were vast. Indeed, tax revenues aside, which I have mentioned earlier in the book, his total income at the time is said to have amounted to $450,000,000, more than ten times that of (his contemporary) Louis XIV.

India's highly developed banking system and vigorous merchant capital, with its well-established network of agents, brokers and middlemen and a talent for financing exports and commercial credit, featured such sophisticated financial networks as that of the Jagat Seths, the Chettiars in the south and the Gujarati Banias in the west. This banking system was as large and extensive and dealt with as much money as the Bank of England.

This was the country impoverished by British conquest. The India that succumbed to British rule enjoyed an enormous financial surplus, deployed a skilled artisan class, exported high-quality goods in great global demand, disposed of plenty of arable land, had a thriving agricultural base, and supported some 100 to 150 million without either poverty or landlessness. All of this was destroyed by British rule. As Wilson points out: 'In 1750, Indians had a similar standard of living to people in Britain. Now, average Indian incomes are barely a tenth of the British level in terms of real purchasing power. It is no coincidence that 200 years of British rule occurred in the intervening time.'

As I have said more than once in the course of the book, there is no reason to believe that, left to itself, India could not have evolved into a more prosperous, united and modernizing power in the nineteenth and twentieth centuries. Many economists blame technological backwardness rather than British malice for India's economic failure under the Raj. But even if lack of technology was the Indian economy's single biggest failing, an independent India could always have imported the technology it needed, as Japan, for instance, was to do. This the British refused to allow Indians to do till well into the twentieth century. A country that was quite willing, over the centuries, to import artists and historians from Persia, sculptors and architects from Central Asia and soldiers from East Africa, would have seen no reason not to import the trappings of modernity from Europe, from railways to industrial technology (just as China is doing today).

India's civilizational impulse throughout history was towards greatness, punctuated undoubtedly by setbacks and conflicts, but which country has been exempt from those? Trade, not conquest, could also have changed India. Something like the Meiji Restoration could have easily taken place in India without the incubus of British rule. It is at least as plausible to argue that India would have modernized, using best practices borrowed (and paid for) from everywhere and adapted to its needs, as to claim that it needed the subjection and humiliation of Empire to reach where it has now begun to.

Joseph Conrad, no radical himself, described colonialism as 'a flabby, pretending, weak-eyed devil of a rapacious and pitiless folly'. As he wrote in 1902, 'The conquest of the earth, which mostly means the taking it away from those who have a different complexion or slightly flatter noses than ourselves, is not a pretty thing when you look into it too much.' Rabindranath Tagore put it gently to a Western audience in

THE (IM) BALANCE SHEET: A CODA

New York in 1930: 'A great portion of the world suffers from your civilisation.' Mahatma Gandhi was blunter: asked what he thought of Western civilization, he replied, 'It would be a good idea'.

'The question,' Niall Ferguson writes in his defence of Empire, 'is not whether British imperialism was without blemish. It was not. The question is whether there could have been a less bloody path to modernity'. As we have seen from the sanguinary record of massacres and brutality by the Raj laid out in the previous chapters, the answer to his question could only be yes. Gurcharan Das, who is inclined to give the British the benefit of the doubt, also does not see deliberate malice in their policy, but his review of the reasons for the industrial failure of British India amount in fact to a devastating summary of what British colonial rule had done to the economy:

> The industrial revolution did not occur because [first], Indian agriculture remained stagnant, and you cannot have an industrial revolution without an agricultural surplus or the means to feed a rapidly growing urban population; second, the international trading environment turned hostile with protectionism after World War I, followed by the Depression; third, the colonial government did not educate the masses, unlike the Japanese state; finally, a colonial mindset pervaded the Indian middle class—even the hardiest potential entrepreneur lacks confidence when he is politically enslaved.

In other words, British colonial agrarian policy, its education policy in India and its racist subjugation of Indians contribute three of Das's four major reasons for India's backwardness in the period in question; and the fourth, the Great War and its consequences, only affected India as much it did because India was a British possession.

It could be argued that the great crime of the British can be understood in a more neutral way. Critics, this argument runs, muddle the idea of the West in the colonial period, because we conflate two very separate strands that are constitutive of this idea: the first consists of modern state machinery (armies, censuses, bureaucracies, railroads, hospitals, telegraph lines, educational and scientific institutions and so on) and the second is of liberal norms (individual rights; freedom of thought, speech, artistic and political expression; equality under the law; and political democracy). One does not axiomatically go with the other. (Look, after all, at China today, where the former flourishes without the latter.) What separates the British from precolonial Indian rulers, then, is not that they were more rapacious or more amoral, but simply that they were more efficient in making a state, while remaining indifferent, or insincere, about imparting their liberal values. But Britain was also the embodiment of the Enlightenment tradition of liberalism, and we judge the 'state' they created harshly on this basis. Is this a valid argument, then, since it obviously cannot be applied on its own terms to the Marathas, the Indian principalities or even the collapsing late Mughal state the British encountered? Who was holding the Maratha Peshwas to the standards of Mill and Pitt?

This is an interesting argument, but not, ultimately, a persuasive one. For the British state in India was indeed, as I have demonstrated, a totally amoral, rapacious imperialist machine bent on the subjugation of Indians for the purpose of profit, not merely a neutrally efficient system indifferent to human rights. And its subjugation resulted in the expropriation of Indian wealth to Britain, draining the society of the resources that would normally have propelled its natural growth and economic development. Yes, there may have been famines and epidemics in precolonial India, but Indians were acquiring the means to cope with them better, which they were unable to do under British rule, because the British had reduced them to poverty and destroyed their sources of sustenance other than living unsustainably on the land—in addition to which Victorian Britain's ideological opposition to 'indiscriminate' charity denied many millions of Indians the relief that would have saved their lives.

It may seem frivolous to confine my appreciation of British rule to cricket, tea and the English language. I do not mean to discount other accomplishments. In outlining the exploitation and looting of India by British commercial interests, for example, I should acknowledge that in the process the British gave India the joint stock company, long experience of commercial processes and international trade, and Asia's oldest stock exchange, established in Bombay in 1875. Indians' familiarity with international commerce and the stock market has proved a distinct advantage in the globalized world; India's entrepreneurial capital and management skills are well able to control and manage assets in the sophisticated financial markets of the developed West today, as Tatas have demonstrated in Britain by making Jaguar profitable for the first time in years, and India's businessmen and managers are familiar with the systems needed to operate a twenty-first-century economy in an open and globalizing world.

And yet one must qualify this rosy notion—that it is thanks to British colonization that India is busy overrunning the planet with skilled, experienced and English-speaking businessmen straining at the leash to take over the world economy. The fact is that the initial Indian reaction to colonial commercial exploitation was, understandably, the opposite—not imitation but rejection. The fight for freedom from colonial rule involved the overthrow of both foreign rulers and foreign capitalists (though few nationalists could tell the difference). Thanks to colonialism, the great leaders of Indian nationalism associated capitalism with slavery: the fact that the East India Company had come to trade and stayed on to rule made our nationalist leaders suspicious of every foreigner with a briefcase, seeing him as the thin end of a neo-imperial wedge.

So instead of integrating India into the global capitalist system, as a few postcolonial countries like Singapore so effectively were to do, India's leaders were convinced that the political independence they had fought for could only be guaranteed through economic independence. That is why self-reliance became the default slogan, the protectionist barriers went up, and India spent forty-five years with bureaucrats rather than businessmen on the 'commanding heights' of the economy, spending a good part of the first four and a half decades after Independence in subsidizing unproductivity, regulating stagnation and trying to distribute poverty. One cannot blame the British for the choices Indians themselves made in reaction to British rule, but it only goes to prove that one of the lessons you learn from history is that history sometimes teaches the wrong lessons. Our current economic growth and global visibility is a result of new choices made after the initial visceral rejection of British colonialism and its methods.

If there were positive by-products for Indians from the institutions the British established and ran in India in their own interests, I am happy to acknowledge them, but only as by-products, and not because they were intended to benefit Indians. The railways were set up entirely for British gain, from construction to execution, but today Indians cannot live without them; the Indian authorities have reversed British policies and the railways are used principally to transport people, with freight bearing ever higher charges in order to subsidize the passengers (exactly the opposite of British practice). Similarly the irrigation works conducted by the British were criticized for their inadequacy by Indian nationalists—since expenditure on them was barely one-ninth that on the railways—and William Jennings Bryan, the American statesman, pointed out that, 'Ten per cent of the army expenditure applied to irrigation would complete the system within five years, but instead of military expenses being reduced, the army appropriation was increased.' However, irrigation still added some twenty million acres, an area the size of France, to the country's cultivable land (almost all of it, alas, in Pakistan today). It would be idle to pretend that no good came of any of this. But when the balance sheet is drawn up, at the end, the balance weighs heavily against the colonialists.

The Indian Army is sometimes cited as a valuable British legacy, a professional fighting force held together by strong traditions of camaraderie and courage, which has remained a meritocracy and stayed out of politics. How much of the credit for this last accomplishment should go to the British is debatable: after all, the Pakistan Army is as much an inheritor of the same colonial legacy, but it has conducted three coups, as well holding the reins firmly even when elected governments are in the saddle. The essential point is, of course, that the Indian Army was not created in India's interests, but in those of Britain, both here and abroad. The Indian soldier was merely an obedient instrument: the Indian sepoy was described by a contemporary as 'temperate, respectful, patient, subordinate, and faithful'. This quiescence ended with the 1857 revolt, but the British managed to restore discipline and the British Indian Army rebuilt itself on notions of fidelity and honour for the next ninety years.

Then the British tore it apart through Partition. The poignant tale is told of Hindu and Muslim officers singing 'Auld Lang Syne' together at the army mess in Delhi at a farewell dinner for those who were leaving for the new country of Pakistan. For many of those officers, years of comradeship were irretrievably lost in the name of a faith they had been born into and a political cause they had not chosen.

A largely uncritical, indeed romanticized, account of the British Indian Army, and how a few thousand British troops held down a subcontinent of 200 million people, comes from Philip Mason, who quotes a Victorian administrator: 'Our force does not operate so much by its actual strength as by the impression which it produces'.

That today's Indian Army, a million strong, has held on to the best of British military traditions while eschewing the temptations to which its Pakistani and Bangladeshi counterparts have fallen prey, is surely more to the credit of its own officers and men, as well as of the inclusive and pluralist nature of Indian democracy.

Some point to physical evidence of the British presence—buildings, ports, trains and institutions—as evidence of a lasting contribution. The fact is the British put in the minimum amount of investment to optimize their exploitation of Indian wealth, while keeping the indigenous population from rebelling. Some of these things were basic to any society; most were created to benefit the British, whether in India or in the UK. Niall Ferguson argues that the British built 'useful' things—opulent palaces for themselves and ships to transport indentured labour, no doubt, are good examples of these—while Indians wasted their resources on 'conspicuous consumption'. Making exportable muslin? Setting global metallurgical standards with its wootz steel? Building magnificent cities and temples? Or perhaps Ferguson thinks the Taj Mahal was a colossal and conspicuous waste?

The story is told—I cannot pinpoint the source—that when the Prince of Wales, the future Edward VIII, visited India in 1921, he pointed to a few magnificent buildings, cars and electrical installations and remarked to an Indian accompanying him, 'We have given you everything here in India! What is it you don't have?' And the lowly Indian replied, gently: 'Self-respect, sir.'

That too was snatched away by colonialism: the self-respect that comes from the knowledge that you are the master of your own fate, that your problems are your own fault and that their resolution depends principally on you and not some distant person living in a faraway land. The biggest difference that freedom has made lies in this, in the establishment of democratic rights and a shared idea of empowered citizenship, in which every citizen or sub-national group can promote their own rights and ensure their voices are heard. This was always withheld from Indians by the colonial subjecthood that was all the British were willing to confer upon them.

The Moral Barrier

Jawaharlal Nehru once described British India as being like an enormous country house in which the English were the gentry living in the best parts, with the Indians in the servants' hall: 'As in every proper country house there was a fixed hierarchy in the lower regions—butler, house-keeper, cook, valet, maid, footman, etc.—and strict precedence was observed among them. But between the upper and lower regions of the house there was, socially and politically, an impassable barrier.'

The barrier was not merely social or racial: it was also a moral barrier, one of motive and interest. One claim that cannot be credibly made is that the British authorities ever, in any instance, put the interests of the Indian public above their own, or placed the needs of single suffering Indian woman above the commercial profit-seeking that had engendered her pain. There are simply no examples of this, while myriad instances tell of the opposite. Take, for example, the British policy on the cultivation and sale of opium. In China, the British desire to reduce its people to a drugged stupor in the pursuit of profit even led to a pair of Opium Wars; in India it merely became one more form of exploitation of the masses.

The East India Company ensured that both growing opium and selling it were to be British government monopolies. The facts were laid out in an 1838 account:

> Throughout all the territories within the Company's jurisdiction, the cultivation of the poppy, the preparation of the drug, and the traffic in it, [...] are under a strict monopoly...the growing of opium is compulsory on the part of the ryot. Advances are made by Government through its native servants, and if a ryot refuses the advance, 'the simple plan of throwing the rupees into his house is adopted; should he attempt to abscond, the peons seize him, tie the advance up in his clothes, and push him into his house. The business being now settled, and there being no remedy, he applies himself, as he may, to the fulfilment of his contract...'[14] The evils which the cultivation of opium entails upon our fellow-subjects in India, arise partly from the ryots in the opium districts of Patna and Benares being

---

[14] The quotes within the quotation are, says the 1838 author, William Howitt, taken from an article on the 'Cultivation of the Poppy,' in the Chinese Repository of February 1837.

compelled to give up fixed portions of their lands for the production of the poppy.

This went on well after the Chinese had thrown off the opium yoke. An 1895 Royal Commission set up in response to public outrage glossed over the horrors of opium and claimed the public's fears and concerns were exaggerated. (Sir Richard Temple of famine fame, now retired, defended the opium policy before the Commission.) In 1930, Durant found 7,000 opium shops in India, every single one of them British-government owned, and conducting their business over the protests of every Indian nationalist organization and social service group. Some 400,000 acres of fertile land were given over to opium cultivation; these could have produced food for malnourished Indians. When the elected Indian members of the impotent Central Legislature got their colleagues to pass a bill in 1921 prohibiting the growth or sale of opium in India, the government vetoed it by the simple expedient of refusing to act upon it, mindful, no doubt, of the fact that one-ninth of the government's annual revenues came from drugs. When Mahatma Gandhi, no less, mounted a campaign against opium in Assam and succeeded in halving its consumption, the British responded by jailing him and forty-four of his satyagrahis.

Various World Opium Conferences were held to demand the abolition of this pernicious drug, but Britain refused to accede to their exhortations; in order to appease global outrage, it agreed to reduce its export of opium by 10 per cent a year, but not to restrict or dilute its production and sale in India. (Indeed, a Government Retrenchment Commission, examining economy measures, underscored 'the importance of safe-guarding opium sales as an important source of revenue', and recommended 'no further reduction'.) The result was that opium became the drug of choice of the masses, used recklessly by those who knew no better; mothers gave opium to their children to keep them quiet when they trudged off to construction sites to labour for their daily pittance.

Should the British policy on opium be excused as reflecting the attitudes of their times? Is it wrong to condemn it from the vantage point of today? No: the British were roundly condemned during their execution of their opium policy by every contemporary Indian nationalist grouping, by dozens of foreign delegates at international conferences, and by thoughtful foreign observers and reporters like the indignant Will Durant. Ironically, the most effective broadside against opium came from none other than Lord Macaulay himself, in an 1833 speech to the House of Commons:

> [It was] the practice of the miserable tyrants whom we found in India, [...] when they dreaded the capacity and the spirit of some distinguished subject...to administer to him daily [a] dose of...a preparation of opium, the effect of which was in a few months to destroy all the bodily and the mental powers of the wretch who was drugged with it, and turn him into a helpless idiot. That detestable artifice, more horrible than assassination itself, was worthy of those who employed it... It is no model for the English nation. We shall never consent to administer [opium] to a whole community, to stupefy and paralyze a great people.

Little did he realize that, for more than a century after he spoke, his own British government would give the lie to his words, for what he inveighed against is exactly what it did.

The British government's refusal to halt the sale of opium was of a piece, of course, with its official disinclination to take any steps to reform Indian society, even while its policies transformed and distorted it beyond measure. It justified this as being out of respect for native customs and traditions, but its main consideration was, of course, that reform would cost money and stir up trouble, which in turn would require the expenditure of money and time to redress. As a result British rule witnessed the entrenching of the caste system, the domination of the Muslim community by preachers and conservative religious figures, the persistence of child marriage and untouchability, and a host of other social evils within India which the British preferred to keep at arm's length rather than risk disturbing. The British interfered with social customs only when it suited them. The gap between liberal principles of universalism and the actual colonial practice of justice and governance was vast.

Such reform as did occur was strongly impelled by Indian social reformers whom the British acceded to, rather than initiated by the British themselves (with the exception of the suppression of Thuggee, which the British undertook to solve a law-and-order problem rather than a religious one). The call for the abolition of sati (widow immolation) was initiated by Raja Rammohan Roy and enacted by Bentinck, knowing he had the support of right-thinking Indians, rather than being the product of the British conscience imposing its will on the barbarous native. The modest increase in the age of marriage (to fourteen for women and eighteen for men) that took place under the British Raj was voted by the Indians in the legislature against the opposition, but later acquiescence, of the British authorities. And the persecution of widows, the worst practices of untouchability, and social evils like ritual sacrifice, were first raised and campaigned against by Indian reformists like Ishwar Chandra Vidyasagar, the Brahmo Samaj and the Arya Samaj; these evils were all continuing unhampered under the indifferent gaze of the British. Three impressive women presided over the Indian National Congress during an era in which not a single governor, secretary or other British high official was female and the very notion of a female authority figure, let alone a female viceroy, would have been a fantasy. The British, as the government of the day, had the right to permit changes to be enacted and implemented, but very rarely did they initiate them themselves.

Lawrence James brags, 'Unlike Stalin's Russia, the British empire was always an open society.' The comparator is amusing for a stalwart defender of the Raj, but we shall let that pass. For whom was the British empire an open society? Not for non-whites, as we have seen; not for women of any race; not, indeed, for Indians.

For, as I have pointed out repeatedly, behind everything lay one inescapable fact: unlike every previous conqueror of India (not counting transient raiders like Mahmud of Ghazni, Timur and Nadir Shah), unlike every other foreign overlord who stayed on to rule, the British had no intention of becoming one with the land. The French ruled foreign territories and made them French, assimilating them in a narrative of Frenchness; the Portuguese settled in their colonies and intermarried with the locals; but the British always stayed apart and aloof, a foreign presence, with foreign interests and foreign loyalties.

The Delhi Sultans and the Mughals may have arrived from abroad, and their progenitors might initially have harked back to distant cities in the Ferghana Valley as their idea of 'home', but they settled in India and retained no extraterritorial allegiance. They married women from India and diluted their foreign blood to the point that in a few generations no trace remained of their foreign ethnicity. Akbar's son Jehangir was half-Rajput; Jehangir's son Shah Jehan also came from an Indian bride; Aurangzeb was only one-eighth non-Indian. Of course, the Mughal emperors were all deeply aware of their connections to Ferghana; they would ask emissaries from there about the conditions of their ancestors' Chingisid tombs and donate money for their upkeep. The past was part of the Mughal identity, but their conceptions of themselves in the present and for the future became more rooted and embedded in India. The British, in contrast, maintained racial exclusivity, practised discrimination against Indians and sneered at miscegenation.

Yes, the Mughal emperors taxed the citizens of India, they claimed tributes from subordinate princes, they plundered the treasuries of those they defeated in battle—all like the British—but they spent or saved what they had earned in India, instead of 'repatriating' it to Samarkand or Bukhara as the British did by sending their Indian revenues to London. They ploughed the resources of India into the development of India, establishing and patronizing its industries and handicrafts; they brought painters, sculptors and architects from foreign lands, but they absorbed them at their courts and encouraged them to adorn the artistic and cultural heritage of their new land.

The British did little, very little, of such things. They basked in the Indian sun and yearned for their cold and fog-ridden homeland; they sent the money they had taken off the perspiring brow of the Indian worker to England; and whatever little they did for India, they ensured India paid for it in excess. And at the end of it all, they went home to enjoy their retirements in damp little cottages with Indian names, their alien rest cushioned by generous pensions provided by Indian taxpayers.

The question never honestly confronted by the apologists of Empire is the classic 'cui bono'—who benefited from British imperial rule? The answer is evidently Britain itself.[15] Let's look at the numbers one last time, widening the lens a little. A fascinating comparative chart of countries' share of global GDP throughout history is instructive. In 1 CE, as Christianity lay literally in swaddling clothes, India accounted for 33 per cent of global GDP, while the UK, France and Germany

---

[15] Just as this book was going to press, a new work has emerged that makes much the same case: Jon Wilson, *India Conquered: Britain's Raj and the Chaos of Empire*, London: Simon & Schuster, 2016.

combined scored barely 3 per cent. By 1700, the equivalent figures were 25 per cent and 11 per cent; by 1870, at Empire's peak, 12.5 per cent for India and 22 per cent for the three European countries; in 1913, with India's further impoverishment, 9 per cent versus 22.5 per cent. In 1950, just after the British left, India stood at 4 per cent; in 2008, this figure was above 7 per cent and climbing. The UK, France and Germany, having dropped to 16 per cent in 1950, are hovering at 9 per cent today. As of 2014 Britain accounted for 2.4 per cent of global GDP, down from 6 per cent twenty-five years ago. History administers its own correctives.

This is the reality that Raj apologists seek to put lipstick on. As one reviewer of Ferguson's pro-imperialist screed put it: 'Ferguson's "history" is a fairy tale for our times which puts the white man and his burden back at the centre of heroic action. Colonialism—a tale of slavery, plunder, war, corruption, land-grabbing, famines, exploitation, indentured labour, impoverishment, massacres, genocide and forced resettlement—is rewritten into a benign developmental mission marred by a few unfortunate accidents and excesses.'

When Kipling wrote his racist poem, *The White Man's Burden*, as I have noted, a contemporary, Henry Labouchère, published an immediate rejoinder, *The Brown Man's Burden*, that encapsulated much of what was wrong with imperialism—British, or anybody else's (the Americans were just launching into their conquest of the Philippines). It is worth reproducing extensively, though not quite in full:

> *Pile on the brown man's burden*
> *To gratify your greed;*
> *Go, clear away the 'niggers'*
> *Who progress would impede;*
> *Be very stern, for truly*
>
> *'Tis useless to be mild*
> *With new-caught, sullen peoples,*
> *Half devil and half child.*
>
> *Pile on the brown man's burden;*
> *And, if ye rouse his hate,*
> *Meet his old-fashioned reasons*
> *With Maxims up to date.*
> *With shells and dumdum bullets*

A hundred times made plain
The brown man's loss must ever
Imply the white man's gain.

Pile on the brown man's burden,
compel him to be free;
Let all your manifestoes
Reek with philanthropy.
And if with heathen folly
He dares your will dispute,
Then, in the name of freedom,
Don't hesitate to shoot.
Pile on the brown man's burden,
Nor do not deem it hard
If you should earn the rancour
Of those ye yearn to guard.
The screaming of your
Eagle Will drown the victim's sob—
Go on through fire and slaughter.
There's dollars in the job.

Pile on the brown man's burden,
And through the world proclaim
That ye are Freedom's agent—
There's no more paying game!
And, should your own past history
Straight in your teeth be thrown,
Retort that independence
Is good for whites alone.

Pile on the brown man's burden,
With equity have done;
Weak, antiquated scruples
Their squeamish course have run,
And, though 'tis freedom's banner
You're waving in the van,
Reserve for home consumption
The sacred 'rights of man'!

And if by chance ye falter,
Or lag along the course,
If, as the blood flows freely,
Ye feel some slight remorse,
Hie ye to Rudyard Kipling,

THE (IM) BALANCE SHEET: A CODA

Imperialism's prop,
And bid him, for your comfort,
Turn on his jingo stop.

The fact that, despite all these wrongs and injustices, Indians readily forgave the British when they left, retaining with them a 'special connection' that often manifests itself in warmth and affection, says more about India than it does about any supposed benefits of the British Raj.

There is a story—perhaps apocryphal—of Jawaharlal Nehru, who had cumulatively spent 3,262 days (nearly ten years of his life) in eight terms of imprisonment between 1922 and 1945 in British jails, being asked by the arch-imperialist Winston Churchill how it was that he felt so little rancour for his jailers and tormentors. 'I was taught by a great man,' Nehru was said to have replied, in a reference to the recently assassinated Mahatma Gandhi, 'never to hate—and never to fear.'

8

THE MESSY AFTERLIFE OF COLONIALISM

I shall say one last time that, in laying out this case against British colonialism in India, I do not seek to blame the British for everything that is wrong in my country today, nor to justify some of the failures and deficiencies that undoubtedly still assail India. There is a statute of limitations on colonial wrongdoings, but none on human memory, especially living memory, for as I have pointed out there are still millions of Indians alive today who remember the iniquities of the British empire in India. History belongs in the past; but understanding it is the duty of the present.

Imperial Amnesia

It is, thankfully, no longer fashionable in most of the developing world to decry the evils of colonialism in assigning blame for every national misfortune. Internationally, the subject of colonialism is even more passé, since the need for decolonization is no longer much debated, and colonialism itself no longer generates much conflict. (There are, after all, no empires left whose maintenance or withdrawal might trigger extensive warfare.) Still, it is striking how quickly amnesia has set in among citizens of the great imperial power itself. A 1997 Gallup Poll in Britain revealed the following: 65 per cent did not know which country Robert Clive or James Wolfe was associated with, 77 per cent did not know who Cecil Rhodes was, 79 per cent could not identify a famous poem Rudyard Kipling had written, and 47 per cent thought Australia was still a colony. Over 50 per cent did not know that the United States of America had once been part of the British empire.

Yet those who follow world affairs would not be entirely wise to consign colonialism to the proverbial dustbin of history. Curiously enough, it remains a relevant factor in understanding the problems and the dangers of the world in which we live. The British empire, and its European counterparts, were 'wholly unprecedented in creating a global hierarchy of economic, physical and cultural power'; that is why their impact endures to a great extent. After all, as one commentator argues, 'the memory of European imperialism remains a live political factor everywhere from Casablanca to Jakarta, and whether one is talking nuclear power with Tehran or the future of the renminbi with the Chinese, contemporary diplomacy will fail if it does not take this into account.'

This, of course, is what Niall Ferguson does do. As we have seen, he sees in Empire cause for much that is good in the world, in particular the free movement of goods, capital and labour and the imposition of Western norms of law, order and governance. Without the spread of British rule around the planet, he argues, the success of liberal capitalism in so many economies today would not have been possible.

Even if this were arguably a defensible proposition, however, it is not necessarily, as Ferguson would put it, a Good Thing. The continuity of today's world with the world of the British empire, which he so celebrates, is most strikingly evident in the economic dependence of much of the postcolonial world on the former imperial states, a contemporary reality that hardly redounds to the credit of the colonizers. Empire might have gone, but it endures in the imitative elites it left behind in the developing world, the 'mimic men', in Naipaul's phrase, trying hard to be what the imperial power had not allowed them to be, while subjecting themselves and their societies to the persistent domination of corporations based mainly in the metropole. The East India Company has collapsed, but globalization has ensured that its modern-day successors in the former imperial states remain the predominant instruments of capitalism.

India is, to some degree, an exception, thanks to its decades of economic autarky; but, as Pankaj Mishra suggests, the liberal-capitalist 'rise of Asia' of which India is a contemporary epitome is also 'the bitter outcome of the universal triumph of western modernity, which turns the revenge of the East into something darkly ambiguous'. To Mishra and other left-leaning critics, it marks the triumph of materialist capitalism rather than Asian spiritualism; the Indian devil wears Prada too. The Left-wing British journalist Richard Gott was unsparing in his denunciation of his country's imperialism: '[T]he British empire was essentially a Hitlerian project on a grand scale, involving military conquest and dictatorship, extermination and genocide, martial law and "special courts", slavery and forced labour, and, of course, concentration camps and the transoceanic migration of peoples.' Though he was not wrong, perhaps a more complicated assessment is due. To look at the legacy of the Raj is also to examine the impact of the imperial enterprise on the societies it fractured and transformed, and the human beings it changed, exiled, made, destroyed and made anew; the rich intercourse of commerce and miscegenation, as British capitalists sought profit where they might; the inter-penetration of peoples, with the shattering of age-old barriers and the erection of new ones within India and, through the migration of Indians, elsewhere; the resultant mongrelization of language and culture; the tug of conflicting loyalties to family, caste, religion, country and Empire; and, above all, the irresistible lure of lucre, the most profound animating spirit of the colonial project. That is a vast project, one well beyond the scope of this book.

There was, of course, a somewhat more unfortunate agenda behind Ferguson's book: to use the history of the British empire to set the stage for the new American imperium he hoped was dawning. Ferguson argued in 2003, just as the US was embarking on its ultimately ill-fated Iraqi adventure with the intention of reshaping the Middle East, that 'the ultimate, if reluctant, heir of Britain's global power was not one of the evil empires of the East, but Britain's most successful former colony.' Ferguson saw America's imperial future in Britain's imperial past, and he sought quite explicitly to use his history of Empire to justify the proposition that just as Pax Britannica inaugurated an unprecedented period of global peace and prosperity, so too would Pax Americana revive the world of the twenty-first century. History is ill-served by such meretricious reasoning, and the years of chaos, anarchy, death and deinstitutionalization that have followed in Iraq (as well as in Libya and

Syria) since the publication of *Empire* seem to have given short shrift to Ferguson's arguments.

In this Ferguson is at least living up to the ethos of the colonial project, which primarily benefited the European imperialists in material, moral and intellectual terms. Imperialism elevated European notions of humanity to predominance in the world, posited the white male as the apotheosis of the ideal of the Enlightenment, and did so by fiat and military power. In the process imperial historians wrote the 'history' of their subject peoples in tendentious terms to explain and justify their own imperium. Ferguson merely continues a long-established colonial tradition of the writing of world history with his own people and their interests as the fixed, first and final point of reference.[16] It is best to see his work as a reflection of the spasm of imperial hubris that briefly jerked into life at the beginning of the twenty-first century, rather than as a definitive statement of the nature and implications of the experience of Empire for hundreds of millions of people around the globe.

Returning the Jewel in the Crown

So what do we do about colonialism, other than understand it? The issue of reparations, as I explained in the introduction, has been overblown: no accurate figure is payable and no payable figure is credible. My own suggestion of a symbolic pound a year may not be a practicable one to the finance ministries that would have to process it. An apology—an act of genuine contrition at Jallianwala Bagh, like Trudeau's over *Komagata Maru*, might work best as a significant gesture of atonement. And a determination, in the metropolitan country, to learn the

---

[16] There were some who asserted intellectual independence from this dominant imperial trope: thinkers who devised a view of life that was neither modern nor anti-modern, Marxist nor revolutionary, colonialist nor, strictly speaking, anti-colonialist. Some of these under-appreciated intellectual responses to Western dominance in the late nineteenth and early twentieth centuries are traced by Pankaj Mishra in *From the Ruins of Empire: The Revolt against the West and the Remaking of Asia*, London: Allen Lane, 2012. Mishra ruefully admits the East was 'subjugated by the people of the West that they had long considered upstarts, if not barbarians' (p. 3).

lessons of Empire—to teach British schoolchildren what built their homeland, just as German children are shepherded to concentration camps to see the awful reality of what their forefathers did.

Another, of course, is the return of some of the treasures looted from India in the course of colonialism. The money exacted in taxes and exploitation has already been spent, and cannot realistically be reclaimed. But individual pieces of statuary sitting in British museums could be, if for nothing else than their symbolic value. After all, if looted Nazi-era art can be (and now is being) returned to their rightful owners in various Western countries, why is the principle any different for looted colonial treasures? Which brings me, inevitably, to the vexed issue of the Kohinoor in the Queen's crown.

The Kohinoor was once the world's largest diamond, weighing 793 carats or 158.6 grams, when it was first mined near Guntur in India's present-day southern state of Andhra Pradesh by the Kakatiya dynasty in the thirteenth century. (It has been whittled down to a little over 100 carats over the centuries.) The Kakatiya kings installed it in a temple, which was raided by the Delhi Sultan Alauddin Khilji, who took it back to his capital along with other plundered treasures. It passed into the possession of the Mughal empire that established itself in Delhi in the sixteenth century, and in 1739 fell into the hands of the Persian invader Nadir Shah, whose loot from his conquest of Delhi (and decimation of its inhabitants) included the priceless Peacock Throne and the Kohinoor itself.

It was Nadir Shah himself, or so legend has it, who baptized the diamond the Kohinoor, or 'Mountain of Light'. An eighteenth-century Afghan queen memorably and colourfully stated, 'if a strong man were to throw four stones, one north, one south, one east, one west and a fifth stone up into the air, and if the space between them were to be filled with gold, it would not equal the value of the Kohinoor'. Upon Nadir Shah's death, the diamond fell into the hands of one of his generals, Ahmed Shah Durrani, who became the Emir of Afghanistan. One of Durrani's descendants was then obliged to cede the Kohinoor in tribute to the powerful Sikh Maharaja of Punjab, Ranjit Singh, in 1809. But Ranjit Singh's successors could not hold on to his kingdom and the Sikhs were defeated by the British in two wars, culminating in the annexation of the Sikh domains to the British empire in 1849. That was when the Kohinoor fell into British hands.

The startling statement in early 2016 by the solicitor general of India—an advocate for the government—that the Kohinoor diamond had been gifted to the British and that India would not therefore seek its return, helped unleash a passionate debate in the country. Responding to a suit filed by a non-governmental organization, the All-India Human Rights and Social Justice Front, demanding that the government seek the return of the famed diamond, that the erstwhile Sikh kingdom in Punjab had given the Kohinoor to the British as 'compensation' for the expenses of the Anglo-Sikh wars of the 1840s.

'It was neither forcibly stolen nor taken away' by the British, declared the Solicitor General; as such there was no basis for the Government of India to seek its return.

The resultant uproar has had government spokesmen back-pedalling furiously, asserting that the Solicitor General's was not the final official view and a claim might still be filed. Indians will not relinquish their moral claim to the world's most fabled diamond. For the Government of India to suggest that the diamond was paid as 'compensation' for British expenses in defeating the Sikhs is ridiculous, since any compensation by the losing side in a war to the winners is usually known as reparations. The diamond was formally handed over to Queen Victoria by the child Sikh heir Maharaja Duleep Singh, who simply had no choice in the matter. As I have pointed out in the Indian political debate on the issue, if you hold a gun to my head, I might 'gift' you my wallet—but that doesn't mean I don't want it back when your gun has been put away.

Reparations are in fact what many former colonies feel Britain owes them for centuries of rapacity in their lands. Returning priceless artefacts purloined at the height of imperial rule might be a good place to start. But the Kohinoor, which is part of the Crown Jewels displayed in the Tower of London, does pose special problems. While Indians consider their claim self-evident—the diamond, after all, has spent most of its existence on or under Indian soil—others have also asserted their claims. The Iranians say Nadir Shah stole it fair and square; the Afghans that they held it until being forced to surrender it to the Sikhs. The latest entrant into the Kohinoor sweepstakes is Pakistan, on the somewhat flimsy grounds that the capital of the Sikh empire, the undisputed last pre-British owners, was in Lahore, now in Pakistan. (The fact that hardly any Sikhs are left in Pakistan after decades of ethnic cleansing of minorities there tends to be glossed over in asserting this claim.)

The existence of contending claims comes as a major relief to Britain as it seeks to fend off a blizzard of demands to undo the manifold injustices of two centuries or more of colonial exploitation of far-flung lands. From the Parthenon Marbles to the Kohinoor, the British expropriation of the jewels of other countries' heritage is a particular point of contention. Giving in on any one item could, the British fear, open Pandora's box. As former Prime Minister David Cameron conceded on a visit to India in July 2010, 'If you say yes to one, you would suddenly find the British Museum would be empty. I'm afraid to say it [the Kohinoor] is going to have to stay put.'

And then there is a technical objection. In any case, the solicitor general averred, the Antiquities and Art Treasures Act of 1972 does not permit the government to seek the return of antiquities exported from the country before India's independence in 1947. Since the Kohinoor was lost to India a century before that date, there was nothing the government of independent India could do to reclaim it. (Of course, the law could also be amended, especially by a Parliament that is likely to vote unanimously in favour of such a change, but that does not seem to have occurred to the government, which perhaps understandably fears rocking the bilateral boat. For the same reason, it has not sought to move the Intergovernmental Committee for Promoting the Return of Cultural Property to its Countries of Origin or its Restitution in case of Illicit Appropriation, a UN body that could help its case.) The Indian solicitor general's stand seems to have taken the sail out of the winds of nationalists like myself who would like to have seen items of cultural significance in India returned as a way of expressing regret for centuries of British oppression and loot of India.

Still, flaunting the Kohinoor on the Queen Mother's crown in the Tower of London is a powerful reminder of the injustices perpetrated by the former imperial power. Until it is returned—at least as a symbolic gesture of expiation—it will remain evidence of the loot, plunder and misappropriation that colonialism was really all about. Perhaps that is the best argument for leaving the Kohinoor where it emphatically does not belong—in British hands.

Resisting Colonialism: The Appeal of Gandhism

Part of the legacy of colonialism is the worldwide impact of the methods used to resist it. The case for Mahatma Gandhi's global relevance, after the departure of the British from India, rests principally on his central tenet of non-violence and the followers it inspired. The major example is of Martin Luther King Jr., who attended a lecture on Gandhi, bought half a dozen books on him and adopted *satyagraha* as both precept and method. King, more than anyone else, used non-violence most effectively outside India in breaking down segregation in the southern states of the USA. 'Hate begets hate. Violence begets violence,' he memorably declared in echoing Gandhi: 'We must meet the forces of hate with soul force.' King later avowed that 'the Gandhian method of non-violent resistance…became the guiding light of our movement. Christ furnished the spirit and motivation and Gandhi furnished the method.'

So Gandhism arguably helped to change the American Deep South forever. But, despite a slew of Nobel Peace Prizes for self-declared Gandhians, from Rigobérta Menchú in Guatemala to Adolfo Pérez Esquivel in Argentina, it is difficult to find many other major instances of its effectiveness. (Gandhi, of course, never won the Peace Prize himself.) India's independence marked the dawn of the era of decolonization, but many nations still came to freedom only after bloody and violent struggles. Other peoples have fallen under the boots of invading armies, been dispossessed of their lands or forced to flee in terror from their homes. Non-violence has offered no solutions to them. It could only work against opponents vulnerable to a loss of moral authority, governments responsive to domestic and international public opinion, governments capable of being shamed into conceding defeat. The British, representing a democracy with a free press and conscious of their international image, were susceptible to such shaming. But in Mahatma Gandhi's own day non-violence could have done nothing for the Jews of Hitler's Germany, who disappeared into gas chambers far from the flashbulbs of a war-obsessed press. It is ironically to the credit of the British Raj that it faced an opponent like Mahatma Gandhi and allowed him to succeed.

The power of non-violence rests in being able to say, 'to show you that you are wrong, I punish myself'. But that has little effect on those who are not interested in whether they are wrong and are already seeking to punish you whether you disagree with them or not. For them your willingness to undergo punishment is the most convenient means of victory. No wonder Nelson Mandela, who wrote that Gandhi had 'always' been 'a great source of inspiration', explicitly disavowed non-violence as useless in his struggle against the ruthless apartheid regime.

On this subject Gandhi sounds frighteningly unrealistic: 'The willing sacrifice of the innocent is the most powerful answer to insolent tyranny that has yet been conceived by God or man. Disobedience to be "civil" must be sincere, respectful, restrained, never defiant, and it must have no ill-will or hatred behind it. Neither should there be excitement in civil disobedience, which is a preparation for mute suffering.'

For many smarting under injustice across the world, that would sound like a prescription for sainthood or for impotence. Mute suffering is all very well as a moral principle, but it has rarely brought about meaningful change. The sad truth is that the staying-power of organized violence is almost always greater than that of non-violence. It is increasingly argued that Gandhi could embarrass the British but not overthrow them. It was when soldiers who had sworn their loyalty to the British Crown rebelled during World War II, and when sailors of the Royal Indian Navy mutinied in 1945 and fired their own cannons at British port installations, that the British realized the game was up. They could jail an old man and allow him to fast, but they could not indefinitely suppress an armed rebellion that had 320 million people behind it. Gandhi won the moral case, the 'soft power' battle, in today's parlance; but even without a military victory, the rebels and mutineers in uniform won the 'hard-power' war.

And when right and wrong are less clear-cut, Gandhism flounders. The Mahatma, at the peak of his influence, was unable to prevent the partition of India even though, in his terms, he considered it morally 'wrong'. He believed in 'weaning an opponent from error by patience, sympathy and self-suffering' but if the opponent believes equally in the justice of his cause, or is conscious of his amorality and unconcerned by it, he is hardly going to accept that he is in 'error'. Gandhism is viable at its simplest and most profound in the service of a transcendent principle like independence from foreign rule. But in more complex situations it cannot and, more to the point, does not work as well.

The Mahatma's ideals had a tremendous intellectual impact on the founding fathers of the new India, who incorporated many of his convictions into the directive principles of state policy. Yet Gandhian solutions have not been found for many of the ills over which he agonized, from persistent sectarian (or 'communal') conflict to the ill treatment of Dalits. Instead, his methods (particularly the fast, the *hartal* or business shutdown, and the deliberate courting of arrest) have been abused and debased by far lesser men in the pursuit of petty sectarian ends. Outside India, too, Gandhian techniques have been perverted by such people as terrorists and bomb-throwers declaring hunger strikes when punished for their crimes. Gandhism without moral authority is like Marxism without a proletariat. Yet few who wish to use his methods have his personal integrity or moral stature.

Internationally, the Mahatma expressed ideals few can reject: he could virtually have written the United Nations Charter, except of course for the provisions of Chapter 7 authorizing the use of force. But the decades after his death have confirmed that there is no escape from the conflicting sovereignties of states. Some thirty million more lives have been lost in wars and insurrections since his passing. In a dismaying number of countries, including his own, governments spend more for military purposes than for education and healthcare combined. The current stockpile of nuclear weapons represents over a million times the explosive power of the atom bomb whose destruction of Hiroshima so grieved him. Universal peace, which the Mahatma considered so central to Truth, seems as illusionary as ever.

As governments compete, so religions contend. The ecumenist Mahatma Gandhi who declared, 'I am a Hindu, a Muslim, a Christian, a Zoroastrian, a Jew' would find it difficult to stomach the exclusivist revivalism of so many religions and cults the world over. But perhaps his approach was always inappropriate for the rest of the world. As his Muslim rival Muhammad Ali Jinnah retorted to his claim of eclectic belief—'only a Hindu could say that'.

And finally, the world of the spinning-wheel, of self-reliant families in contented village republics, is even more remote today than when the Mahatma first espoused it in *Hind Swaraj*. Despite the brief popularity of intermediate technology and 'small is beautiful', there does not appear to be much room for such ideas in an interdependent world.

Self-reliance is too often a cover for protectionism and a shelter for inefficiency in developing countries. The successful and prosperous countries are those who are able to look beyond spinning wheels to silicon chips—and who give their people the benefits of technological developments which free them from menial and repetitive chores and broaden the horizons of their lives. But today's urbanizing India is far removed from the idealized, self-sufficient village republics he envisaged, and its enthusiastic embrace of technology would have struck the Mahatma as selling its soul.

But if Gandhism has had its limitations exposed in the years after his assassination, there is no denying the Mahatma's greatness. While the world was disintegrating into fascism, violence and war, he taught the virtues of truth, non-violence and peace. He destroyed the credibility of colonialism by opposing principle to force. And he set and attained personal standards of conviction and courage which few will ever match. He was that rare kind of leader who was not confined by the inadequacies of his followers.

So Mahatma Gandhi stands as an icon of anti-colonialism, a figure of his times who transcended them. The ultimate tribute to the British Raj might lie in the quality of the 'Great Soul' who opposed it.

Cast a Long Shadow: The Residual Problems of Colonialism

The colonial era is over. And yet, residual problems from the end of the earlier era of colonization, usually the result of untidy departures by the colonial power, still remain dangerously stalemated. The prolonged state of chronic hostility between India and Pakistan, punctuated by four bloody wars and the repeated infliction of cross-border terrorism as a Pakistani tactic against India, is the most obvious example. But there are others. The dramatic events in East Timor in 1999 led to the last major transfer of power to an independence movement. Yet at least closure has occurred there, unlike in Western Sahara or in those old standbys of Cyprus and Palestine, all messy legacies of European colonialism. Fuses lit in the colonial era could ignite again, as they have done, much to everyone's surprise, in the Horn of Africa, between Ethiopia and Eritrea, where war broke out over a colonial border that the Italians of an earlier era of occupation had failed to define with enough precision and where peace simmers today amidst much uncertainty. The Sykes-Picot Agreement of 1916, by which the British and the French agreed to carve up the former Ottoman territories between themselves and which set the boundaries between independent Syria and Iraq, is another relic of colonial history that haunts us today. For when ISIS ('Daesh') advanced ruthlessly in those countries, it railed against the iniquities of that Anglo-French agreement and avowed its determination to reverse the Sykes-Picot legacy—making the imperial era compellingly current once more.

But it is not just the direct results of colonialism that remain relevant: there are the indirect ones as well. The intellectual history of colonialism is littered with many a wilful cause of more recent conflict. One is, quite simply, careless anthropology: the Belgian classification of Hutus and Tutsis in Rwanda and Burundi, which solidified a distinction that had not existed before, continues to haunt the region of the African Great Lakes. A related problem is that of motivated sociology: how much bloodshed do we owe, for instance, to the British invention of 'martial races' in India, which skewed recruitment into the armed forces and saddled some communities with the onerous burden of militarism? And one can never overlook the old colonial administrative habit of 'divide and rule', exemplified, again, by British policy in the subcontinent after 1857, systematically promoting political divisions between Hindus and Muslims, which led almost inexorably to the tragedy of Partition.

An ironic corollary to both the 'martial races' theory and the politics of *divide et impera* was the resultant militarization of Pakistan. At Partition, Pakistan received, thanks to the lopsided application of the 'martial races' theory by the British, a larger share of undivided India's military than of either its population or territory. With 21 per cent of India's population and 17 per cent of its revenue, Pakistan got 30 per cent of the Indian Army, 40 per cent of the Indian Navy and 20 per cent of the Indian Air Force, obliging its Government to devote 75 per cent of the country's first budget to cover the costs of maintaining this outsize force. The disproportionately large military establishment had a vested interest in its own perpetuation, since it needed to invent a military threat in order to justify its continuance. Therein lay the prosaic roots of Pakistan's obdurate hostility to India. Sadly, instead of cutting back on its commitments to the military, Pakistan kept feeding the monster till it devoured the country itself. Even when Pakistan lost half its territory in the disastrous Bangladesh War of 1971, the army continued to expand.

Such colonial-era distinctions as 'martial races' and religious divisions were not just pernicious; they were often accompanied by an unequal distribution of the resources of the state within the colonial society. Belgian colonialists favoured Tutsis, leading to Hutu rejection of them as alien interlopers; Sinhalese resentment of privileges enjoyed by the Tamils in the colonial era in Sri Lanka prompted the discriminatory policies after Independence that in turn fuelled the Tamil revolt. India still lives with the domestic legacy of divide and rule, with a Muslim population almost as large as Pakistan's, conscious of itself as a minority striving to find its place in the Indian sun.

A 'mixed' colonial history within one modern state is also a potential source of danger. When a state has more than one colonial past, its future is vulnerable. Secessionism, after all, can be prompted by a variety of factors, historical, geographical and cultural as well as 'ethnic'. Ethnicity or language hardly seem to be a factor in the secessions (one recognized, the other not) of Eritrea from Ethiopia and the 'Republic of Somaliland' from Somalia. Rather, it was different colonial experiences (Italian rule in Eritrea and British rule in Somaliland) that set them off, at least in their own self-perceptions, from the rest of their ethnic compatriots. A similar case can be made in respect of the former Yugoslavia, where parts of the country that had been under Austro-Hungarian rule for 800 years had been joined to parts that spent almost as long under Ottoman suzerainty. The war that erupted in 1991 was in no small measure a war that pitted those parts of Yugoslavia that had been ruled by German-speaking empires against those that had not (or had resisted such colonization).

Boundaries drawn in colonial times, even if unchanged after independence, still create enormous problems of national unity. We have been reminded of this in Iraq, whose creation from the ruins of the Ottoman empire welded various incompatibilities into a single state. But the issue is much more evident in Africa, where civil conflict along ethnic or regional lines can arise when the challenge of nation building within colonially drawn boundaries becomes insurmountable. Where colonial constructions force disparate peoples together by the arbitrariness of a colonial mapmaker's pen, nationhood becomes an elusive notion. Older ethnic and clan loyalties in Africa were mangled by the boundaries drawn, in such distant cities as Berlin, for colonially created states whose post-independence leaders had to invent new traditions and national identities out of whole cloth. The result was the manufacture of unconvincing political myths, as artificial as the countries they mythologize, which all too often cannot command genuine patriotic allegiance from the citizenry they aim to unite. Civil war is made that much easier for local leaders challenging a 'national' leader whose nationalism fails to resonate across his country. Rebellion against such a leader is, after all, merely the reassertion of history over 'his' story.

State failure in the wake of colonialism is another evident source of conflict, as the by-product of an unprepared newly independent state's inability to govern. The crisis of governance in many African countries is a real and abiding cause for concern in world affairs today. The collapse of effective central governments—as manifest in Darfur, South Sudan and eastern Congo today, and in Sierra Leone, Liberia and Somalia yesterday (and who knows where tomorrow?)—could unleash a torrent of alarming possibilities: a number of 'weak states', particularly in Africa, seem vulnerable to collapsing in a welter of conflict.

Underdevelopment in postcolonial societies is itself a cause of conflict. The uneven development of infrastructure in a poor country, as a result of priorities skewed for the benefit of the colonialists, can lead to resources being distributed unevenly, which in turn leads to increasing fissures in a society between those from 'neglected regions' and those who are better served by roads, railways, power stations, telecommunications, bridges and canals. Advancing underdevelopment in many countries of the South, which are faring poorly in their desperate struggle to remain players in the game of global capitalism, has created conditions of desperate poverty, ecological collapse and rootless, unemployed populations beyond the control of atrophying state systems—a portrait vividly painted by Robert Kaplan in his book *The Coming Anarchy*, which suggests the real danger of perpetual violence on the peripheries of our global village.

As we embark upon the twenty-first century, it seems ironically clear that tomorrow's anarchy might still be due, in no small part, to yesterday's colonial attempts at order. I have no wish to give those politicians in postcolonial countries whose leadership has been found wanting in the present, any reason to find excuses for their failures in the past. But in looking to understand the forces that have made us and nearly unmade us, and in hoping to recognize possible future sources of conflict in the new millennium, we have to realize that sometimes the best crystal ball is a rear-view mirror.

NOTES AND REFERENCES

PREFACE

xxii the attempt by one Indian commentator...to compute what a fair sum of reparations would amount to: Minhaz Merchant, 'Why Shashi Tharoor is right on Britain's colonial debt to India', www.dailyo.in, 23 July 2015. www.dailyo.in/politics/minhaz-merchant-shashi-tharoor-oxford-union-address-congress-britain-colonialism-monsoon-session-parliament/ story/1/5168.html.

xxiv Tharoor might have won the debate—but moral victory: Shikha Dalmia,'Perhaps India Shouldn't Get Too Excited About Reparations', *Time*, 3 August 2015.

xxiv One blogger added, for good measure: Sifar AKS, 'Dear Shashi, Your Accent Could Not Mask the Holes in Your Speech', www.akkarbakkar.com. www.akkarbakkar.com/dear-shashi-tharoor-your-accent-could-not-mask-the-holes-in-your-speech.

xxiv Commentator Jonathan Foreman put it most bluntly: Jonathan Foreman, 'Reparations for the Raj? You must be joking!', www.politico.eu, 3 August 2015. www.politico.eu/article/british-reparations-for-india-for-the-raj-oxford.

xxv One Indian commentator argued that the claim for reparation: Gouri Dange, 'For a few claps more...', *Pune Mirror*, 29 July 2015.

xxvi Historian John Keay put it best: John Keay, 'Tell it to the Dreaming Spires', *Outlook*, 15 August 2015.

xxvi According to a recent UN Population Division report: 'World Population Ageing 1950–2050' report, United Nations, www.un.org/esa/population/ publications/worldageing19502050/pdf/90chapter iv.pdf.

xxvii to start teaching unromanticized colonial history: Steven Swinford and Christopher Hope, 'Children should be taught about suffering under the British Empire, Jeremy Corbyn says', *The Telegraph*, 27 July 2015.

xxvii what the British-domiciled Dutch writer Ian Buruma saw as an attempt to remind the English: Ian Buruma, *Playing The Game*, New York: Farrar, Straus & Giroux, 1991, p. 258.

xxvii Buruma was, of course, echoing: Salman Rushdie, 'Outside the Whale', *Granta*, 1984, reproduced in *Imaginary Homelands*, New Delhi: Viking, 1993.

xxviii The Indian columnist Aakar Patel suggested: Aakar Patel, 'Dear Shashi, the fault was not in the Raj, but in ourselves', *Times of India*, 26 July 2015.

xxix '[W]hen we kill people,' a British sea-captain says: Amitav Ghosh, *Sea of Poppies*, New York: Farrar, Straus & Giroux, 2011, p. 242.

CHAPTER 1: THE LOOTING OF INDIA

1 The British conquest of India: Will Durant, *The Case for India*, New York: Simon & Schuster, 1930, p. 7.

2 'The little court disappears': John Sullivan, *A Plea for the Princes of India*, London: E. Wilson, 1853, p. 67.

2 'Nearly every kind of manufacture or product': Jabez T. Sunderland, *India in Bondage: Her Right to Freedom and a Place Among the Great Nations*, New York: Lewis Copeland, 1929, p. 367.

2 At the beginning of the eighteenth century, as the British economic historian Angus Maddison: Angus Maddison, *The World Economy*, Development Centre of the Organisation for Economic Co-operation and Development, 2006.

5 'What honour is left to us?': William Dalrymple, 'The East India Company: The Original Corporate Raiders', *The Guardian*, 4 March 2015.

6 Bengal's textiles were still being exported: Most of these details are from K. N. Chaudhuri, *The Trading World of Asia and the English East India Company: 1660–1760*, Cambridge: Cambridge University Press, 2006 and Sushil Chaudhury, *The Prelude to Empire: Plassey Revolution of 1757*, New Delhi: Manohar Publishers, 2000.

6 The soldiers of the East India Company obliged, systematically

NOTES AND REFERENCES

smashing the looms: William Bolts, *Considerations on Indian Affairs: Particularly Respecting the Present State of Bengal and its Dependencies*, London: J. Almon, P. Elmsly, and Brotherton and Sewell, 1772, p. vi.

7 India had enjoyed a 25 per cent share of the global trade in textiles: P. Bairoch and M. Levy-Leboyer, (eds), from 'The Main Trends in National Economic Disparities since the Industrial Revolution' in *Disparities in Economic Development since the Industrial Revolution*, New York: Macmillan, 1981.

7 British exports of textiles to India, of course, soared: Jon Wilson, *India Conquered: Britain's Raj and the Chaos of Empire*, London: Simon & Schuster, 2016, p. 321.

7 India's weavers were, thus, merely the victims of technological obsolescence: This argument is made by B. R. Tomlinson in *The Economy of Modern India, 1870–1970, The New Cambridge History of India*, Vol 3, 3, Cambridge: Cambridge University Press, 1996, p. 15.

8 In 1936, 62 per cent of the cloth sold in India: Gurcharan Das, *India Unbound: From Independence to the Global Information Age*, New York: Alfred A. Knopf, 2001.

9 at the end of British rule, modern industry employed only 2.5 million people: Ibid, p. 63.

9 'the redemption of a nation... a kind of gift from heaven': Owen Jones, 'William Hague is wrong... we must own up to our brutal colonial past', *The Independent*, 3 September 2012.

9 'There are few kings in Europe': Letter to the Duke of Choiseul, dt. London, 27 Feb. 1768. A.E./C.P., Angleterre, Vol. 477, 1768; quoted in Sudipta Das, 'British Reactions to the French Bugbear in India, 1763–83', *European History Quarterly*, 22 (1), 1992, pp. 39–65.

9 '[tax] defaulters were confined': Durant, *The Case for India*.

11 Nabobs, [Macaulay] wrote: *Historical Essays of Macaulay:William Pitt, Earl of Chatham, Lord Clive,Warren Hastings*, Samuel Thurber (ed.), Boston: Allyn and Bacon, 1894. The five paragraphs that follow draw extensively from Tillman W. Nechtman, 'A Jewel in the Crown? Indian Wealth in Domestic Britain in the Late Eighteenth Century', *Eighteenth-Century Studies*, 2007, Vol. 41 (1), pp. 71–86.

11 'India is a sure path to [prosperity]': James Holzman, *The Nabobs in England: A Study of the Returned Anglo-Indian, 1760–1785*, New York: Columbia University Press, 1926, pp. 27–28, quoted in Nechtman, 2007.

11 **'As your conduct and bravery is become the publick'**: Richard Clive to Robert Clive, 15 December 1752; OIOC Mss Eur G37/3 quoted in Nechtman, 2007.

11 **'Here was Lord Clive's diamond house'**: Walpole to Mann, 9 April 1772, quoted in Henry B. Wheatley, *London Past and Present: Its History, Associations, and Traditions*, London: John Murray, 1891, p. 2.

12 **The Cockerell brothers, John and Charles**: www.sezincote.co.uk.

13 **'the Company providentially brings us home'**: *The Gentleman's Magazine*, Vol. 56, Part 2, London: A. Dodd and A. Smith, 1786, p 750.

14 **'Today the Commons of Great Britain'**: Dalrymple, 'East India Company'.

14 **'combined the meanness of a pedlar with the profligacy of a pirate'**: R. B. Sheridan, 'Speech on the Begums of Oude, February 7, 1787', quoted in *British Rule in India: Condemned by the British Themselves*, issued by the Indian National Party, London, 1915, p. 15.

14 **'in the former capacity, they engross its trade'**: Minute of 18 June 1789, quoted in *'British Rule in India: Condemned by the British Themselves'*, issued by the Indian National Party, London, 1915, p. 17.

15 **Hastings duly informed the Council that he had received a 'gift'**: See the vivid accounts of the trial in Nicholas B. Dirks, *The Scandal of Empire: India and the Creation of Imperial Britain*, Cambridge, MA: Belknap Press/Harvard University Press, 2006; and Peter J. Marshall, *The Impeachment of Warren Hastings*, Oxford: Oxford University Press, 1965.

15 **He described in colourfully painful detail the violation of Bengali women**: Ibid.

15 **'the scene of exaction, rapacity, and plunder'**: William Howitt, *The English in India*, London: Longman, Orme, Brown, Green, and Longmans, 1839, pp. 42–43.

16 **'the misgovernment of the English was carried'**: Thomas Babington Macaulay, *Essays: Critical and Miscellaneous*, London: Carey and Hart, 1844.

16 **It is instructive to see both the extent to which House of Commons debates**: See, for instance, substance of Sir Arthur Wellesley's speech delivered in the Committee of the House of Commons on the India Budget on Thursday, 10 July 1806 in *Bristol Selected Pamphlets*, 1806, University of Bristol Library.

NOTES AND REFERENCES

16 The prelate Bishop Heber wrote in 1826: Bishop Heber, writing to Rt. Hon. Charles W. Wynne from the Karnatik, March 1826, quoted in *British Rule Condemned by the British*, p. 24.

16 In an extraordinary confession, a British administrator in Bengal, F. J. Shore: Hon. F. J. Shore's *Notes on Indian Affairs*, Vol. ii, London, 1837, p. 516, quoted in Romesh Chunder Dutt, *The Economic History India Under Early British Rule: From the Rise of the British Power in 1757 to the Accession of Queen Victoria in 1837*, London: K. Paul, Trench, Trubner & Co. Ltd, 1920.

17 Rueful voices had coined the catchphrase, 'Poor Nizzy pays for all': See John Zubrzycki, *The Last Nizam*, New Delhi: Picador India, 2007, p. 34.

18 The revenue had to be paid to the colonial state everywhere in cash: See Sugata Bose, *Peasant Labour and Colonial Capital*, Cambridge: Cambridge University Press, 1993.

18 'The ryots in the Districts outside the permanent settlement': H. M. Hyndman, *The Ruin of India by British Rule: Being the Report of the Social Democratic Federation to the Internationalist Congress at Stuttgart*, London: Twentieth Century Press, 1907, cited in *Histoire de la Ile Internationale*, Vol. 16, Geneva: Minkoff Reprint, 1978, pp. 513–33.

19 'the difference was this, that what the Mahomedan rulers claimed': Chunder Dutt, *The Economic History*, pp. xi–xii.

19 A committee of the House of Commons declared: Quoted in Howitt, *English in India*, p. 103.

19 Thereby abolishing century-old traditions and ties: Ibid, p 149.

20 'As India is to be bled, the lancet should be directed': *British Rule Condemned*, pp. 6–7.

20 Cecil Rhodes openly avowed that imperialism: Quoted in Zohreh T. Sullivan, *Narratives of Empire: The Fictions of Rudyard Kipling*, Cambridge: Cambridge University Press, 1993, p. 7.

20 Bengali novelist Bankim Chandra Chatterjee wrote of the English: Tapan Raychaudhuri, *Europe Reconsidered: Perceptions of the West in 19th Century Bengal*, Oxford: Oxford University Press, 1988, p. 185.

21 Paul Baran calculated that 8 per cent of India's GNP: Paul Baran, *The Political Economy of Growth*, New York, 1957, p. 148.

22 India was 'depleted', 'exhausted' and 'bled' by this drain of

resources: Dadabhai Naoriji, *Poverty and Un-British Rule in India*, London: Swan Sonnenschein, 1901.

22 The extensive and detailed calculations of William Digby: William Digby, *'Prosperous' British India: A Revelation from Official Records*, London: T. Fisher Unwin, 1901.

22 'There can be no denial that there was a substantial outflow': Angus Maddison, *Class Structure and Economic Growth: India and Pakistan Since the Moghuls*, New York: Routledge, 2013, p. 63.

22 In 1901, William Digby calculated the net amount: See William Digby, *Indian Problems for English Consideration*, London: National Liberal Federation, 1881 and *'Prosperous' British India*, 1901.

23 A list of Indian Army deployments overseas by the British: H. S. Bhatia (ed.), *Military History of British India, 1607–1947*, New Delhi: Deep & Deep Publications, 1977.

23 Sikh who named his Hurricane fighter 'Amritsar': Ibid, p. 101.

23 Every British soldier posted to India: Bill Nasson, *Britannia's Empire: Making a British World*, Stroud, Gloucestershire: Tempus, 2004.

24 Biscuits, rice…authorized to the European soldier, came from Indian production: Bhatia, *Military History*, p. 152.

24 'how little human life and human welfare': Howitt, pp. 40–41.

25 In the oft-quoted words of the Cambridge imperial historian John Seeley: John R. Seeley, *The Expansion of England: Two Courses of Lectures*, London: Macmillan, 1883, p. 243.

25 'The mode by which the East India Company': Howitt, *English in India*, p. 9.

26 'The British empire in India was the creation of merchants': Ferdinand Mount, *The Tears of the Rajas: Mutiny, Money and Marriage in India 1805–1905*, London: Simon & Schuster, 2015, p. 773.

26 Mr. Montgomery Martin, after examining: Dadabhai Naoroji, *Poverty and Un-British Rule in India*, London: Swan Sonnenschein, 1901.

28 Indian shipbuilding…offers a more complex but equally instructive story: This section relies heavily on Indrajit Ray, 1995, 'Shipbuilding in Bengal under Colonial Rule: A Case of "De-Industrialisation"', *The Journal of Transport History*, 16 (1), pp. 776–77.

30 India's once-thriving shipbuilding industry collapsed: Ibid

31 The total amount of cash in circulation in the Indian economy fell: Wilson, *India Conquered*, p. 433.

32 Even Miss Prism...could not fail to take note: Oscar Wilde, *The Importance of Being Earnest*, Act II, London: Leonard Smithers and Company, 1899.

32 English troopers in battle would often dismount and swap their own swords: Philip Mason, *A Matter of Honour: An Account of the Indian Army, its Officers and Men*, London: Penguin, 1974, p. 39.

33 India 'missed the bus' for industrialization, failing to catch up on the technological innovations: See, for instance, Akhilesh Pillalmarri, 'Sorry, the United Kingdom Does Not Owe India Reparations', *The Diplomat*, 24 July 2015; Raheen Kasam, 'Reparations for Colonial India? How about railways, roads, irrigation, and the space programme we still pay for', 22 July 2015, www.breitbart.com; and Foreman, 'Reparations for the Raj?.

35 The humming factories of Dundee, the thriving shipyards, and the remittances home: See *Scotland and the British Empire*, John M. MacKenzie and T. M. Devine (eds), Oxford: Oxford University Press, 2012. Also see Martha MacLaren, *British India and British Scotland 1780–1830*, Akron, Ohio: Akron University Press, 2012.

CHAPTER 2: DID THE BRITISH GIVE INDIA POLITICAL UNITY?

38 'considering its long history, India has had but a few hours': Diana Eck, *India: A Sacred Geography*, New York: Harmony Books. See also William Dalrymple's review of the book for *The Guardian*, 27 July 2012.

40 having once been a British colony is the variable most highly correlated with democracy: Taken from Seymour Martin Lipset, Kyoung-Ryung Seong and John Charles Torres, 'A Comparative Analysis of the Social Requisites of Democracy', *International Social Science Journal*, 1993, 45, pp. 155–75.

40 'every country with a population of at least 1 million': Myron Weiner, 'Empirical Democratic Theory', in E. Ozbudun and M. Weiner (ed.), *Competitive Elections in Developing Countries*, Durham, NC: Duke University, 1987, pp. 3–34.

41 'In India,' wrote an eminent English civil servant: H. Fielding-Hall, *Passing of the Empire*, London: Hurst & Blackett, 1913, p. 134.

42 'a society of little societies': Wilson, *India Conquered*, p. 14.

43 'Areas in which proprietary rights in land': See, for instance, Abhijit Banerjee and Lakshmi Iyer, 'History, Institutions, and Economic Performance: The Legacy of Colonial Land Tenure Systems in India', *The American Economic Review*, Vol. 95, No. 4, 2005, pp. 1190–1213.

43 'We may be regarded as the spring which': Forrest, 1918, p. 296.

44 William Bolts, a Dutch trader...wrote in 1772: Bolts, 1772, p. vi.

44 'Of all human conditions, perhaps the most brilliant': Dalrymple, 'The East India Company'.

46 The British charges against the rulers they overthrew: Hyndman: Report on India, 1907, *Ruin of India by British*, pp. 513–533.

47 'partly to amaze the indigenes, partly to fortify': Jan Morris, *Farewell the Trumpets: An Imperial Retreat*, London: Faber & Faber, 1978.

48 Years later, the management theorist C. Northcote Parkinson: C. Northcote Parkinson, *Parkinson's Law: The Pursuit of Progress*, London: John Murray, 1958.

49 Reflected what the British writer David Cannadine dubbed 'Ornamentalism': David Cannadine, *Ornamentalism: How the British Saw Their Empire*, London: Allen Lane, 2001.

50 'frivolous and sometimes vicious spendthrifts and idlers': David Gilmour, *Curzon: Imperial Statesman*, New York: Farrar, Straus & Giroux, 2003.

51 'neither Indian, nor civil, nor a service': Jawaharlal Nehru, *Glimpses of World History: Being Further Letters to his Daughter*, London: Lindsay Drummond Ltd., 1949, p. 94.

51 'a few hundred Englishmen should dominate India': For sympathetic accounts of the lives, careers and points of view of the British in India, see Philip Mason, *The Men Who Ruled India*, New York: W. W. Norton, 1985 and Charles Allen, *Plain Tales from the Raj*, London: Abacus, 1988.

52 The British in India were never more than 0.05 per cent: Figures from Maddison, 'The Economic and Social Impact of Colonial Rule in India', in *Class Structure*.

52 'so easily won, so narrowly based, so absurdly easily ruled': Eric Hobsbawm, *The Age of Empire*, Hachette, 2010, p. 82.

53 In David Gilmour's telling, they had no illusions: From David Gilmour, *The Ruling Caste: Imperial Lives in the Victorian Raj*, New York: Farrar, Straus & Giroux, 2006, pp. 5, 33, 19, 244.

53 'The whole attitude of Government to the people it governs': Fielding-Hall, *Passing of the Empire*, p. 54.

54 'constructed a world of letters, ledgers and account books': Wilson, *India Conquered*, p. 128.

54 He paid a Bengali clerk in the Collector's office to tell him: Ibid, p. 140.

55 'The new system was not designed': Ibid, pp. 128–129.

55 'allowed British officials to imagine': Ibid, p. 225.

55 'Collector of the Land Revenue. Registrar of the landed property': Hyndman, *Ruin of India by British*.

56 In the summer capital of Simla: Gilmour, *The Ruling Caste*, p. 271.

56 'ugly pallid bilious men': Gilmour, *The Ruling caste*, p. 104.

57 'A handful of people from a distant country': Henry W. Nevinson, *The New Spirit in India*, London: Harper & Brothers, 1908, p. 329.

57 'India is…administered by successive relays of English carpet-baggers': H. M. Hyndman, *Ruin of India by British*, pp. 513–33.

58 Insulated from India by their upbringing and new social circumstances: See a detailed account in Anne de Courcy, *The Fishing-Fleet: Husband-Hunting in the Raj*, London: Weidenfeld & Nicolson, 2012.

58 The places named for the British have mostly been renamed: Gilmour, *The Ruling Caste*.

58 'the Government of India is not Indian, it is English': Fielding-Hall, *Passing of Empire*, p. 182.

58 Government must do its work: Ibid, p. 194.

59 'it would be impossible to place Indian civilians': Ibid, p. 188.

59 'Socially he belongs to no world': Ibid, p. 193.

60 'educated Indians whose development the Government encourages': *British Rule Condemned*, p. 13.

61 On the verge of being dismissed, Mahmud…resigned in 1892: Jon Wilson, 'The Temperament of Empire. Law and Conquest in Late Nineteenth Century India', from Gunnel Cederlof and Sanjukta Das Gupta, *Subjects, Citizens and Law: Colonial and Postcolonial India*, Routledge, 2016.

62 'if an Indian in such a position tries to preserve his self-respect': Ibid.

62 In the first decades of the twentieth century, J. T. Sunderland observed: Sunderland, 1929.

62 'With the material wealth go also': Dadabhai Naoroji, 'The Moral Poverty of India and Native Thoughts on the Present British Indian Policy (Memorandum No. 2, 16th Nov, 1880)', 1880, reproduced in Naoroji, *Poverty and Un-British Rule in India*, London: Swan Sonnenschein, 1901.

63 It is instructive to note the initial attitudes of whites in India: Two books that cover this theme especially well are Jonathan Gil Harris, *The First Firangis*, New Delhi: Aleph Book Company, 2015 and William Dalrymple, *White Mughals: Love and Betrayal in Eighteenth-Century India*, London: Harper Perennial, 2002.

63 'it was almost as common for Westerners to take on the customs': Dalrymple, *White Mughals*.

63 'the wills of company officials show that one in three': Ibid.

64 'our Eastern empire...has been acquired': Quoted by Wilson, *India Conquered*, p. 163.

64 'a passive allegiance,' Malcolm added: Dalrymple, *White Mughals*.

64 'Hundreds, if not thousands, on their way from Burma perished': Quoted by Wilson, *India Conquered*, pp. 449–450.

64 This very metaphor pops up in the quarrel: E. M. Forster, *A Passage to India*, London: Allen Lane, 1924, pp. 50–51.

65 'Naboth is gone now, and his hut is ploughed into its native mud': Rudyard Kipling, 'Naboth', in *Life's Handicap* (1891), republished by Echo Books, London, 2007, p. 289.

65 'sometimes with a rare understanding, sometimes with crusty, stereotyped contempt': Philip Mason, *Kipling: The Glass, The Shadow and The Fire*, New York: Holt, Rinehart & Wilson, 1975, p. 27.

65 'part of the defining discourse of colonialism': Zohreh T. Sullivan, *Narratives of Empire: The Fictions of Rudyard Kipling*, Cambridge: Cambridge University Press, 1993, p. 25.

65 'brave island-fortress/of the storm-vexed sea': Sir Lewis Morris, 'Ode', *The Times*, London, 22 June 1897.

66 'be the father and the oppressor of the people': Zohreh T. Sullivan, *Narratives of Empire*, p. 4.

66 'Who hold Zam-Zammah, that "fire-breathing dragon"': Rudyard Kipling, *Kim*, New York: Oxford University Press, 2008, p. 1.

66 the imperial enterprise required men of courage: See the detailed discussion in M. Daphne Kurtzer, *Empire's Children: Empire and Imperialism in Classic British Children's Books*, London: Routledge, 2002, pp. 13–44.

66 'There is something noble in putting the hand of civilization': Quoted in C. J. Wan-ling Wee, *Culture, Empire, and the Question of Being Modern*, New York: Lexington Books, 2003, p. 80.

67 'the ennobling and invigorating stimulus': Ibid, pp. 80–81.

68 'Imperialism,' Robert Kaplan suggests: Robert Kaplan, 'In Defense of Empire' *The Atlantic*, April 2014.

69 '[if] this chapter of reform led directly or necessarily': Morley, *Indian Speeches* London, 1910, 91, in Ishtiaq Husain Qureshi, *The Struggle for Pakistan*, University of Karachi, 1969, p. 28.

69 C. A. Bayly makes an impressive case: Christopher A. Bayly, *Recovering Liberties: Indian Thought in the Age of Liberalism and Empire*, Cambridge: Cambridge University Press, 2011.

70 'it [the Congress] was a model of order': Nevinson, *The New Spirit in India*, p. 327.

70 The chairman...summarized the history of the last year: Ibid, pp. 129–30, 132.

74 The British government in India has not only deprived: www.gktoday. in/poorna-swaraj-resolution-declaration-of-independence.

74 Unrest in India was occasioned by...the contemptuous disregard: Nevinson, *The New Spirit in India*, p. 322.

74 In historical texts, it often appears: M. B. L. Bhargava, *India's Services in the War*, Allahabad: Bishambher Nath Bhargava, 1919.

77 Never in the history of the world: Cited in Durant, *The Case for India*.

CHAPTER 3: DEMOCRACY, THE PRESS, THE PARLIAMENTARY
SYSTEM AND THE RULE OF LAW

79 'evangelical imperialism': Niall Ferguson, *Empire: The Rise and Demise of the British World Order and the Lessons for Global Power*, New York: Basic Books, 2003, p. 125.

79 'the most distinctive feature of the Empire': Ibid, pp. xxiii, 56, 125.

80 'India, the world's largest democracy': Ibid, pp. 332, 326, 358.

80 'not only underwrites the free': Niall Fergusson, *Colossus: The Price of America's Empire*, New York: Penguin, 2004, p. 2.

85 'have I seen more deliberate attempts': Nevinson, *The New Spirit in India*, p. 206 et seq.

87 This is why I have repeatedly advocated a presidential system for India: See my essay on the subject in *India Shastra: Reflections on the Nation in our Times*, New Delhi: Aleph Book Company, 2015.

88 'they rejected it with great emphasis': Bernard Weatherill, 'Relations between Commonwealth Parliaments and the House of Commons', *RSA Journal*, Vol. 137 No. 5399, October 1989, pp. 735–741. Published by Royal Society for the Encouragement of Arts, Manufactures and Commerce.

89 'the crushing of human dignity': Jawaharlal Nehru, *A Bunch of Old Letters*, Bombay: Asia Publishing House, 1958, p. 236.

89 'the law that was erected can hardly be said': Diane Kirkby and Catherine Coleborne (eds), *Law, History and Colonialism: The Reach of Empire*, Manchester: Manchester University Press, 2001, cited in Richard Price, 'One Big Thing: Britain, Its Empire, and Their Imperial Culture' *Journal of British Studies*, Vol. 45, No. 3, July 2006, pp. 602–627. Published by Cambridge University Press on behalf of The North American Conference on British Studies. www.jstor.org/stable/10.1086/503593.

90 'a body of jurisprudence written': Wilson, *India Conquered*, pp. 213–4.

90 When Lord Ripon...attempted to allow Indian judges: These details may all be found in Durant, *The Case for India*, pp. 138–139.

91 When Robert Augustus Fuller fatally assaulted his servant: Jordanna Bailkin, 'The Boot and the Spleen: When Was Murder Possible in British India?', *Comparative Studies in Society and History*, 48 (2), 2006, pp. 462–93.

91 Punch wrote an entire ode to 'The Stout British Boot': 'The British Boot', *Punch* 68, (30 January 1875), p. 50, quoted in Jordanna Bailkin, 'The Boot and the Spleen: When Was Murder Possible in British India?', *Comparative Studies in Society and History*, 48 (2), 2006, pp. 462–93.

91 Martin Wiener proposed an 'export' model: Martin Wiener, *Men of Blood: Violence, Manliness and Criminal Justice in Victorian England*, Cambridge: Cambridge University Press, 2004, p. 11.

92 'I will not be a party to any scandalous hushings up': Nayana Goradia, *Lord Curzon: The Last of the British Moguls*, Oxford: Oxford University Press, 1993.

93 'there is a great and dangerous gap between the people and the Courts': Fielding-Hall, *Passing of the Empire*, p. 103.

93 'compelled to live permanently under a system of official surveillance': Nevinson, *The New Spirit in India*, p. 204.

94 women on the Malabar Coast: This is described brilliantly in Manu Pillai, *The Ivory Throne*, New Delhi: Harper Collins, 2015.

94 The Criminal Tribes Legislation, 1911, gave authority: D. M. Peers and N. Gooptu (eds), *India and the British Empire*, Oxford: Oxford University Press, 2012.

94 The scholar Sanjay Nigam's work has shown: Sanjay Nigam, 1990, 'Disciplining and Policing the 'Criminals by Birth', Part 1: The Making of a Colonial Stereotype The Criminal Tribes and Castes of North India', and 'Part 2: the Development of a Disciplinary System, 1871–1900', *Indian Economic Social History Review*, 27, p. 131–164 and 257–287.

95 We declare it Our royal will and pleasure: 'Her Majesty's Proclamation (1858)', India Office Records, Africa, Pacific and Asia collections, British Library, London: L/P&S/6/463 file 36, folios 215–16.

96 'Our religion is sublime, pure, and beneficent': Quoted in Lawrence James, *Raj: The Making and Unmaking of the British Empire in India*, New York: St Martin's Griffin, 1997, p. 223.

96 'The first, and often the only, purpose of British power in India': Wilson, *India Conquered*, p. 6.

96 'there were no major changes in village society, in the caste system': Maddison, *Class Structure*.

96 The fact is that the British interfered with social customs: See, for example, the impassioned appeals by anti-slavery campaigners for the British government to put an end to certain traditional practices of servitude, which were of course completely ignored by Company officialdom: Wilson Anti-Slavery Collection, *A Brief View of Slavery in British India*, 1841, Manchester, England: The University of Manchester, John Rylands University Library. URL: www.jstor.org/stable/60228274

NOTES AND REFERENCES

CHAPTER 4: DIVIDE ET IMPERA

102 In the only already-white country the British colonized, Ireland: Caesar Litton Falkiner, *Illustrations of Irish History and Topography, Mainly of the 17th Century*. London: Longmans, Green, & Co., 1904, p. 117.

102 Not only were ideas of community reified, but entire new communities: Norman G. Barrier, *The Census in British India: New Perspectives*, New Delhi: Manohar Publishers, 1981.

103 'Colonialism was made possible, and then sustained': Nicholas B. Dirks, *Castes of Mind: Colonialism and the Making of Modern India*, Princeton: Princeton University Press, 2001.

103 'In the conceptual scheme which the British created': Bernard S. Cohn, *An Anthropologist Among The Historians And Other Essays*, Oxford: Oxford University Press, 1987. See also Ranajit Guha, *Dominance without Hegemony: History and Power in Colonial India*, Cambridge, MA: Harvard University Press, 1998.

103 The path-breaking writer and thinker on nationalism: Benedict Anderson, *Imagined Communities: Reflections on the Origin and Spread of Nationalism, 2nd ed.* London: Verso, 1991.

104 'capable of expressing, organizing, and': Dirks, 2001.

105 Caste, he says, 'was just one category among many': Ibid.

105 In Partha Chatterjee's terms, the colonial argument for why civil society: For more details, see Partha Chatterjee, *Lineages of Political Society: Studies in Postcolonial Democracy*, Columbia University Press, 2011 and *The Nation and its Fragments: Colonial and Postcolonial Histories'*, Princeton University Press, 1993.

106 The pandits...cited doctrinal justifications: See, for instance, Madhu Kishwar, *Zealous Reformers, Deadly Laws*, New Delhi: Sage Publications, 2008.

106 'enumerate, categorize and assess': Christopher Bayly, *The Birth of the Modern World, 1780–1914: Global Connections and Comparisons*, London: Wiley-Blackwell, 2004, p. 275.

107 The American scholar Thomas Metcalfe has shown how race ideology: Thomas Metcalfe, *Ideologies of the Raj*, Cambridge: Cambridge University Press, 1995, p. 89.

108 The census in India was led by British: This discussion relies heavily on K. W. Jones, 'Religious Identity and Indian Census' in *The Census* in *British India: New Perspectives*, N. G. Barrier (ed.), New Delhi: Manohar Publishers, 1981, pp. 73–102.

108 This is underscored by the scholar Sudipta Kaviraj: Sudipta Kaviraj, 'The Imaginary Institution of India', *Subaltern Studies* VII, Partha Chatterjee and Gyanendra Pandey (eds), New Delhi: Oxford University Press, 1992, p. 26.

109 Risley's work helped the British use such classification both to affirm their own convictions: See E. M. Collingham, *Imperial Bodies: The Physical Experience of the Raj, 1800–1947*, Oxford: Polity Press, 2001; Christopher Pinney, 'Classification and Fantasy in the Photographic Construction of Caste and Tribe', *Visual Anthropology* 3, (1990), pp. 259–284, p. 267; and Peter Gottschalk, *Religion, Science and Empire: Classifying Hinduism and Islam in British India*, London: Oxford University Press, 2012, p. 213.

110 Such caste competition had been largely unknown in pre-British days: See M. N. Srinivas, *Social Change in Modern India*, Hyderabad: Orient Longman India, 1972, which describes how social change and caste mobility were practiced before the advent of the British.

110 'Nothing embraces the whole of India, nothing, nothing': Forster, *A Passage to India*, p. 160.

110 Both David Washbrook and David Lelyveld believe that: David Washbrook, 'To Each a Language of His Own: Language, Culture, and Society in Colonial India', in *Language, History and Class*, Penelope J. Corfield (ed.), London: Blackwell, 1991, pp. 179–203; David Lelyveld, 'The Fate of Hindustani: Colonial Knowledge and the Project of a National Language', in *Orientalism and the Postcolonial Predicament*, Carol A. Breckenridge and Peter van der Veer (eds), Philadelphia: University of Pennsylvania Press, 1993, pp. 189–214.

110 The British even subsumed ancient, and not dishonourable, professions: Ratnabali Chatterjee, 'The Queen's Daughters: Prostitutes as an Outcast Group in Colonial India', Chr. Michelsen Institute Report 1992: 8.

111 The Hindu-Muslim divide was, as the American scholar of religion: Peter Gottschalk, *Religion, Science, and Empire*, Oxford: Oxford University Press, 2012.

112 Gyanendra Pandey suggests that religious communalism: Gyanendra Pandey, *The Construction of Communalism in Colonial North India*, New Delhi: Oxford University Press, 1990.

112 The colonialists' efforts to catalogue, classify and categorize the Indians: Ibid, 204.

113 A temple in South Arcot, Tamil Nadu, hosts a deity: Muttaal Ravuttan can be found in Virapatti, Tirukoyilur Taluk, South Arcot, Tamil Nadu. See Alf Hiltebeitel, 'Draupadi's Two Guardians: Buffalo King & Muslim Devotee' in *Criminal Gods and Demon Devotees: Essays on the Guardians of Popular Hinduism*, Binghamton, NY: SUNY Press, 1989, p. 338 et seq.

113 The Mughal court, she points out: Romila Thapar, *On Nationalism*, New Delhi: Aleph Book Company, 2016, pp. 14–15.

114 Hindu generals in Mughal courts, or of Hindu and Muslim ministers in the Sikh ruler Ranjit Singh's entourage: Gyanendra Pandey, *Construction of Communalism*.

114 The colonial state loosened the bonds that had held them together: Romila Thapar, *On Nationalism*.

114 Large-scale conflicts between Hindus and Muslims…only began under colonial rule: See Sandria Freitag, *Collective Action and Community: Public Arenas and the Emergence of Communalism in North India*, Berkeley: University of California Press, 1989.

114 Hindu or Muslim identity existed in any meaningful sense: C. A. Bayly, 'The Pre-History of 'Communalism'? Religious Conflict in India, 1700–1860', *Modern Asian Studies*, Vol. 19(2), 1985, p. 202.

115 The portrayal of Muslims as Islamist idol-breakers…is far from the truth: Richard M. Eaton, 'Temple Desecration and the Image of the Holy Warrior in Indo-Muslim Historiography', (paper presented at the annual meeting of the Association for Asian Studies, Boston, April 1994), cited by Cynthia Talbot, 'Inscribing the Other, Inscribing the Self: Hindu-Muslim Identities in Pre-Colonial India', *Comparative Studies in Society and History*, Vol. 37 (4), 1995, p. 718.

116 Cynthia Talbot observed that since a majority of medieval South India's: Talbot, 'Inscribing the Other', pp. 692–722. Also see H. K. Sherwani, 'Cultural Synthesis in Medieval India,' *Journal of Indian History*, 41, 1963, pp. 239–59; W. H. Siddiqi, 'Religious Tolerance as Gleaned from Medieval Inscriptions', in *Proceedings of Seminar on Medieval Inscriptions*, Aligarh: Centre of Advanced Study, Dept. of History, Aligarh Muslim University, 1974, pp. 50–58.

117 'a new religious feud was established': Nevinson, *The New Spirit in India*, p. 192–193.

118 I have almost invariably found: Ibid, p. 202.

119 it is striking that…the Aga Khan articulated a vision of India: The Aga Khan, *India in Transition: A Study in Political Evolution*, (Philip Lee Warner for the Medici Society, London, 1918); see particularly Chapter I, pp. 1–15, for his civilizational theories; Chapter XIII, 'India's Claim to East Africa'; pp. 123–132, and Chapter XV on Islam, pp. 156–161.

119 'to counteract the forces of Hindu agitation': Dr B. R. Ambedkar, *Thoughts on Pakistan*, Bombay: Popular Prakashan, 1941, p. 89.

120 'predominant bias in British officialdom': Durant, *The Case for India*, pp. 137–138.

121 'By 1905, religious rhetoric between Shias and Sunnis': Keith Hjortshoj, 'Shi'i Identity and the Significance of Muharram in Lucknow, India', in Martin Kramer (ed.), *Shi'ism, Resistance and Revolution*, Boulder: Westview Press, 1987, p. 234.

122 Muslims have been together with the Hindus since they moved: Maulana Husain Ahmad Madani, quoted in Venkat Dhulipala, *Creating a New Medina*, Cambridge: Cambridge University Press, 2016, pp. 449–450.

124 'The British are not a spiritual people': Lala Lajpat Rai, 'The Swadeshi Movement', 1905, quoted in Nevinson, p. 301.

126 'We are different beings,' he declared: Cited in Nisid Hajari, *Midnight's Furies: The Deadly Legacy of India's Partition*, New York: Houghton Mifflin Harcourt, 2015, p. 9.

131 Clement Attlee persuaded his colleagues: The entire section on the events leading to Partition (including the pages that follow) is based on the following books: Phillips Talbot, *An American Witness to India's Partition*, New Delhi: Sage Books, 2007; Leonard Gordon, *Brothers Against the Raj*, New York: Columbia University Press, 1990; Penderel Moon, Mark Tully and Tapan Raychaudhuri, *Divide and Quit*, Oxford: Oxford University Press, 1998; Sugata Bose, *His Majesty's Opponent: Subhas Chandra Bose and India's Struggle Against Empire*, Cambridge, MA: Harvard University Press, 2011; Maulana Abul Azad Khan, *India Wins Freedom*, New Delhi: Orient Blackswan, 2004; Durga Das, *India: From Curzon to Nehru and After*, New Delhi: Rupa Publications, 1967; Bipan Chandra, *India's Struggle for Independence*, New Delhi: Viking, 1988; Jawaharlal Nehru, *The Discovery of India*, New Delhi: Viking, 2013; Sarvepalli Gopal, *Jawaharlal Nehru*, Vols. I & II, New Delhi: Vintage, 2005; Nisid Hajari, *Midnight's Furies*; Tunzelmann, *Indian Summer*; Alan Campbell-Johnson, *Mission with Mountbatten*, London: Macmillan, 1985; Larry Collins and Dominique Lapierre, *Mountbatten and the Partition of India*, New Delhi: Vikas, 1975; Michael Brecher, *Nehru: A*

Political Biography, London: Beacon Press, 1962; Stanley Wolpert, *Nehru: A Tryst with Destiny*, New York: Oxford University Press, 1995; M. J. Akbar, *Nehru*, New Delhi: Viking, 1988; H. V. Hodson, *The Great Divide*, Oxford: Oxford University Press, 1997; Yasmin Khan, *The Great Partition*, New Haven: Yale University Press, 2008; Louis Fischer, *The Life of Mahatma Gandhi*, New York: Harper Collins, 1997; Nicholas Mansergh, *The Transfer of Power 1942–47*, London: HM Stationery Office, 1983; and Lord Archibald Wavell, *Viceroy's Journal* (ed.), Penderel Moon, Oxford: Oxford University Press, 1973. For a short account, see also my own *Nehru: The Invention of India*, New York: Arcade Books, 2003.

132 'It is alarming and nauseating to see Mr Gandhi': Ramachandra Guha, 'Statues in a Square', *The Telegraph*, 21 March 2015.

132 'He put himself at the head of a movement': Boris Johnson, *The Churchill Factor: How One Man Made History*, New York: Riverhead Books, 2014, p. 178.

133 'bound hand and foot at the gates of Delhi': Alex Von Tunzelmann, *Indian Summer: The Secret History Of The End Of An Empire*, New York: Henry Holt & Company, 2007.

134 'he represents a minority': Hajari, *Midnight's Furies*, p. 41.

134 Its membership swelled from 112,000 in 1941 to over 2 million: Ibid, p. 42.

135 'are only technically a minority': For the opposite view, marshalling various sources of evidence for the idea that Muslim separatist consciousness had deep roots in society and religion, see Venkat Dhulipala, *Creating a New Medina: State Power, Islam and the Quest for Pakistan in Colonial North India*, Cambridge: Cambridge University Press, 2015.

136 The latter was serious, affecting seventy-eight ships and twenty shore establishments: Srinath Raghavan, *India's War: The Making of Modern South Asia 1939–1945*, London: Penguin, 2016.

137 Wavell's astonishingly candid diaries reveal his distaste for,: Lord Archibald Wavell, *Viceroy's Journal* (ed.), Penderel Moon, p. 283.

142 'I've never met anyone more in need of front-wheel brakes': Hajari, *Midnight's Furies*, p. 102.

147 'The British Empire did not decline, it simply fell': Tunzelmann, *Indian Summer*, 2007.

147 'stands testament to the follies of empire': Yasmin Khan, *The Great Partition*, New Haven: Yale University Press, 2007.

148 Far from introducing democracy to a country mired in despotism: This argument is laid out in convincing detail in Amartya Sen, *The Argumentative Indian*, New York: Farrar, Straus & Giroux, 2005.

CHAPTER 5: THE MYTH OF ENLIGHTENED DESPOTISM

150 There has never been a famine in a democracy with a free press: Amartya Sen, *Poverty and Famines: An Essay on Entitlements and Deprivation*, Oxford: Clarendon Press, 1982.

150 The fatality figures are horrifying: Durant, *The Case for India*.

151 'it was common economic wisdom that government intervention': Dinyar Patel, 'How Britain Let One Million Indians Die in Famine,' BBC News, 11 June 2016. www.bbc.com/news/world-asia-india-36339524.

152 'If I were to attempt to do this, I should consider myself no better': Ibid.

152 'complex economic crises induced by the market': Mike Davis, *Late Victorian Holocausts: El Niño Famines and the Making of the Third World*, London; New York: Verso Books, 2001, p. 19.

153 'We have criticized the Government of Bengal for their failure to control the famine': *Famine Inquiry Commission Final Report*, Famine Inquiry Commission, (John Woodhead, Chairman), India, 1945, pp. 105–106.

153 'Behind all these as the fundamental source of the terrible famines': Durant, *The Case for India*, pp. 36–37.

154 'There is to be no interference of any kind': Davis, 2001, pp. 31, 52.

154 Lytton's pronouncements were noteworthy: Ibid.

155 'it is the duty of the Government': Johann Hari, 'The Truth? Our Empire Killed Millions', *The Independent*, 19 June 2006.

155 'severely reprimanded, threatened with degradation': Ibid.

156 'Scores of corpses were tumbled into old wells': Ibid.

156 'When in August 1877 the leading citizens of Madras': Georgina Brewis, 'Fill full the Mouth of Famine: Voluntary action in famine relief in India 1877–1900', in Robbins, D. et al. (eds), Yearbook II PhD research in progress, London: University of East London, 2007, pp. 32–50.

157 'were humane men and, although hampered by inadequate': Ibid.

157 '[i]n its influence on agriculture, [cattle mortality]: J. C. Geddes, *Administrative Experience Recorded Former Famines*, Calcutta, 1874, p. 350. Another official noted that 'a loss that is likely to fall more heavily on the farmers than even the temporary loss of manual labour, is the loss by death of their plough and well bullocks'. Report of Colonel Baird Smith to Indian Government on Commercial Condition of North West Province of India and recent Famine, Parliamentary Papers, 8 May 1861, p. 29; and Report of the Same Officer to the Indian Government on the Recent Famine in the Same Province, House of Commons, 1862, p. 39.

158 'it falls to us to defend our Empire from the spectral armies: Cited in Chandrika Kaul, *Reporting the Raj: The British Press and India 1880–1922*, Manchester: Manchester University Press, 1922, p. 75.

159 'in the past 12 years the population of India': *Sydney Morning Herald*, 6 November 1943.

160 Richly-documented account of the Bengal Famine: Madhusree Mukerjee, *Churchill's Secret War: The British Empire and the Ravaging of India During World War II*, New York: Basic Books, 2010, p. 332.

160 The way in which Britain's wartime financial arrangements: Durant, p. 36. For famines in general and the Bengal Famine of 1943–44 in particular, see also Cormac Ó Gráda, *Eating People is Wrong, and Other Essays on Famine, its Past, and its Future*, Princeton, N.J.: Princeton University Press, 1950.

161 'a providential remedy for overpopulation': William Jennings Bryan, *British Rule in India*, reprinted by the British Committee of the Indian National Congress, London, 1906, p. 11.

161 which rests largely on the introduction of quinine as an anti-malarial drug: These claims are made in Ferguson, *Empire*, p. 215.

162 From 1787, Indian convicts were transported, initially to the penal colonies: These details are cited in G. S. V. Prasad and N. Kanakarathnam, 'Colonial India and Transportation: Indian Convicts in South East Asia and Elsewhere', *International Journal of Applied Research*, Vol. 1 (13), 2015, pp. 5–8.

162 Between 1825 to 1872, Indian convicts made up the bulk of the labour force: Ibid.

163 'Whether labour were predominantly enslaved, apprenticed

or indentured': Clare Anderson, *Convicts in the Indian Ocean*, London: Palgrave Macmillan, 2000, pp. 104–106.

164 The 'Brotherhood of the Boat' became the subject of poetry: See this song from the 1970s in the Carribean called 'Jahaji Bhai, Brotherhood of the Boat': www.youtu.be/DOh4fsIaTH8.

164 In the period 1519–1939, an estimated 5,300,000 people whom scholars delicately dub 'unfree migrants': G. S. V. Prasad and Dr N Kanakarathnam, 'Colonial India and transportation: Indian convicts in South East Asia and elsewhere', *International Journal of Applied Research*, 1(13), 2015.

165 'was as if fate had thrust its fist': Ghosh, *Sea of Poppies*, p. 367.

166 'Most of the time, the actions of British imperial administrators': Wilson, *India Conquered*, p. 5.

166 'their sense of vulnerability and inability': Ibid, pp 75–77.

166 'I can only [subdue resistance] by reprisals': Howitt, p. 21.

167 Delhi…was left a desolate ruin: Ferdinand Mount, *Tears of the Rajas*.

167 'I knowed what that meant': Denis Judd, *The Lion and the Tiger: The Rise and Fall of the British Raj, 1600–1947*, Oxford: Oxford University Press, 2005, p. 132.

168 'every mutiny, every danger, every terror, and every crime': John Ruskin, *The Pleasures of England: Lectures Given in Oxford*, London: G. Allen, 1884, p. 111.

171 'Peterloo massacre had claimed about 11 lives': Helen Fein, *Imperial Crime and Punishment*, Honolulu: The University Press of Hawaii, 1977, p. xii.

171 'the calumny…that frail English roses: Salman Rushdie, 'Outside the Whale'.

172 General Dyer issued an order that Hindus using the street: Durant, *The Case for India*, pp. 134–135.

174 'I know it is said in missionary meetings that we conquered India': Quoted in *British Rule Condemned*, p. 36.

CHAPTER 6: THE REMAINING CASE FOR EMPIRE

175 'In the beginning, there were two nations': Tunzelmann, *Indian Summer*, p. 6.

175 'led to the modernisation, development, protection, agrarian advance': Amit Singh, 'Think India should be grateful for colonialism? Here are five reasons why you're unbelievably ignorant', *The Independent*, 10 November 2015.

176 'Wherever they are allowed a free outlet': H. M. Hyndman, *Ruin of India by British*, pp. 513–33.

178 There were fourteen questions on this issue: Breakdown of questions figures based on Amba Prasad, *Indian Railways: A Study in Public Utility Administration*, Bombay: Asia Publishing House, 1960.

182 Indians also pointed out at the time that the argument that the railways: See, for instance, Horace Bell, *Railway Policy in India*, Rivington, Percival & Company, 1894 and Edward Davidson, *The Railways of India:With an Account of Their Rise, Progress, and Construction*, E. & F. N. Spon, 1868.

182 'sordid and selfish...': Bipan Chandra, *The Rise and Growth of Economic Nationalism in India: Economic Policies of Indian National Leadership, 1880–1905*, New Delhi: Har-Anand Publications, 2010.

183 'Britain provided India with the necessary tools': Jonathan Old, 'Why I think Shashi Tharoor's Speech is Populist, Oversimplified and Ignores the Problems', www.youthkiawaaz.com, 28 July 2015.

183 The British left India with a literacy rate of 16 per cent: The Census of India, 1951, New Delhi: Publications Division, 1952.

183 'When the British came, there was, throughout India, a system of communal schools: Durant, *The Case for India*, pp. 31–35.

186 'in pursuing a system, the tendency of which': Sir Thomas Munro, 'His Life', Vol. III, quoted in *British* Rule Condemned by British Themselves, p. 16.

187 Philosopher James Mill and his followers urged the promotion of western science: James Mill, *History of British India*, London: Baldwin, Cradock and Joy, 1817, p. 156.

188 'The fact that the Hindoo law is to be learned chiefly': Macaulay's *Minute on Education*, 2 Feb 1835, is published in Henry Sharp, *Selections from the Educational Records*, Bureau of Education, India, I, Calcutta, 1920.

189 'most fully admitted that the great body of the people': Quoted in Zastoupil and Moir, (1999), p. 140–141.

189 It is difficult to argue...that such education acquired as much reach: From Margrit Pernau (ed.), *Delhi College: Traditional Elites, the Colonial State and Education before 1857*, New Delhi: Oxford University Press, 2006.

190 'become a sort of hybrid': Fielding-Hall, *Passing of the Empire*, p. 298.

190 All Indian aspirations and development of strong character: *British Rule Condemned*, p 9.

190 European subordination of Asia was not merely economic: Pankaj Mishra, *From the Ruins of Empire: The Revolt Against the West and the Remaking of Asia*, London: Allen Lane, 2012.

191 To the memory of the British Empire in India: Nirad C. Chaudhuri, *Autobiography of an Unknown Indian*, London: Macmillan, 1951.

191 Made Chaudhuri a poster child for scholarly studies of how Empire creates: Ian Almond, *The Thought of Nirad C. Chaudhuri: Islam, Empire and Loss*, Cambridge: Cambridge University Press, 2015.

191 'these two processes of self-othering': Ibid, p. 115.

191 Moved to Oxford, there to live out his centenarian life: Ibid, p. 120.

192 Seeing even in Clive's rapacity...the 'counterbalancing grandeur' of the grand imperialist: Chaudhuri, *Autobiography*, p. 3; Chaudhuri, *Clive of India*, p. 11.

192 'Nirad Chaudhuri is a fiction created by the Indian writer: David Lelyveld, 'The Notorious Unknown Indian', *New York Times*, 13 November, 1988.

192 'all the squalid history of Indo-British personal relations': Chaudhuri, *Autobiography*, p. 15.

193 'mythological histories...where fable stands in the face of facts': Javed Majeed, *Ungoverned Imaginings: James Mill's The History of British India and Orientalism*, Clarendon Press, 1992.

194 Gauri Vishwanathan has done pioneering work on the role of: Gauri Viswanathan, *Masks of Conquest: Literary Study and British Rule in India*, New York: Columbia University Press, 1989.

194 Arguments made for propagating English literature through the English language: Charles E. Trevelyan, *On the Education of the People of India*, London: Longman, Orme, Brown, Green & Longmans, 1838.

196 'the rise of Raj revisionism': Rushdie, 'Outside the Whale'; see also Kathleen Wilson (ed.), *A New Imperial History: Culture, Identity and Modernity in Britain and the Empire 1660–1840* (2004); Antoinette Burton, *Empire in Question: Reading, Writing, and Teaching British Imperialism*, Durham: Duke University Press, 2011.

196 'it is impossible to make the English language the vernacular tongue': Howitt, p. 88.

196 'in our schools pupils imbibe sedition': J. D. Rees, *The Real India*, London: Methuen, 1908, pp. 162–163.

197 The study of which, even in Oxford, induces a regrettable tendency towards vain: Ibid, p. 343.

201 'That was the age when the English loved and treasured': Richard West, 'Wodehouse Sahib', Harpers and Queen, 1988, pp. 114–115.

204 'let the English who read this at home reflect': Quoted in *British Rule Condemned*, p. 19.

205 Large numbers of trees were chopped down since the opium poppy: Arupjyoti Saikia, 'State, peasants and land reclamation: The predicament of forest conservation in Assam, 1850s-1980s', *Indian Economic & Social History Review, 2008*, pp. 81–82.

206 The term Puliyur has lost its meaning: For details of India's environmental destruction under the British, see Mahesh Rangarajan, *India's Wildlife History*, New Delhi: Permanent Black, 2001; Madhav Gadgil and Ramachandra Guha, *Ecology and Equity: The Use and Abuse of Nature in Contemporary India*, New Delhi: Routledge, 1995.

207 Cricket is really, in the sociologist Ashis Nandy's phrase: Ashis Nandy, *The Tao of Cricket: On Games of Destiny and the Destiny of Games*, New Delhi: Oxford University Press, 2000, p. 1.

208 Why cricket acquired such a hold in Bengal society between 1880 and 1947: Anonymous, 'Cricket in Colonial Bengal (1880–1947): A lost history of nationalism', *The International Journal of the History of Sport*, Vol. 23 (6), 2006.

209 'saw cricket as an identifier of social status': Nandy, p. 53.

209 'an English cricketer and an Indian prince': Buruma, p. 234.

210 'attacked the political and economic aspects of British imperialism': Richard Cashman, *Patrons, Players, and the Crowd: The Phenomenon of Indian Cricket*, London: Orient Longman, 1980, p. 22–3.

210 Sports such as gymnastics and cricket were made compulsory to develop: Mrinalini Sinha, *Colonial Masculinity: The 'Manly Englishman' and the 'Effeminate Bengali' in the Late Nineteenth Century*, Manchester: Manchester University Press, 1995.

CHAPTER 7: THE (IM)BALANCE SHEET: A CODA

214 'an exercise in benign autocracy and an experiment in altruism': See www. andrewlownie.co.uk/authors/lawrence-james/books/raj-the-making-and-unmaking-of-british-empire.

214 Recent years have seen the rise of what the academic Paul Gilroy: Paul Gilroy, *Postcolonial Melancholia*, New York: Columbia University Press, 2005.

214 A 2014 YouGov poll revealed that 59 per cent of respondents: www.yougov.co.uk/news/2014/07/26/britain-proud-its-empire/

214 'the optimal allocation of labour, capital and goods': Ferguson, *Empire*, p. xx.

215 Human beings do not live in the long run; they live, and suffer, in the here and now: These arguments are cogently substantiated by Linda Colley, 'Into the Belly of the Beast', *The Guardian*, 18 January 2003, and Philip Pomper, 'The History and Theory of Empires', *History and Theory*, Vol. 44 (4), December 2005, Wiley for Wesleyan University, pp. 1–27.

216 Indian society has no history at all, at least no known history: Karl Marx, 'The Future Results of British Rule in India', in David McLellan, ed., *Karl Marx: Selected Writings*, Oxford: Oxford University Press, 1982, p. 362.

216 'whether all this has been for better or worse, is almost impossible to say': Denis Judd, *The Lion and the Tiger: The Rise and Fall of the British Raj, 1600–1947*, Oxford: Oxford University Press, 2005, p. 200.

216 'its operation was driven instead by narrow interests and visceral passions': Wilson, *India Conquered*, p. 500.

216 'between 1757 and 1900 British per capita gross domestic product': Ferguson, *Empire*, p. 216.

NOTES AND REFERENCES

217 The Indian government brought electricity to roughly 320 times as many villages: Paul Cotterrill, 'Niall Ferguson's Ignorant Defence of British Rule in India', *New Statesman*, 16 August 2012.

217 India was… an 'extractive colony': Daron Acemoglu and James Robinson, *Why Nations Fail*, New York: Crown Business, 2012.

217 Colonial exploitation happened instead: See Cotterrill, 'Ferguson's Ignorant Defence' and 'The Incomplete State: Charles Tilly and the Defence of Aid to India', www.thoughcowardsflinch.com/2012/02/07/the-incomplete-state-charles-tilly-and-the-defence-of-aid-to-india/, 7 Feb 2012.

218 'When the English came to India': William Jennings Bryan, *British Rule in India*, Westminster: British Committee of the Indian National Congress, 1906, p. 19.

218 'The empire was run on the cheap': Jon Wilson, 'False and dangerous', *The Guardian*, 8 February 2003.

218 'in return for its moment of greatness on the world stage': Lawrence James, *Raj: The Making and Unmaking of British India*, New York: St Martin's Griffin, 1997.

218 'Why, for example, should one assume that eighteenth-century India': Professor Andrew Porter's review of *Empire: How Britain Made the Modern World*, (History review no. 325) www.history.ac.uk/ reviews/review/325.

219 He talked admiringly of spices and jewels, precious stones: Sanjay Subrahmanyam, *The Career and Legend of Vasco da Gama*, Cambridge: Cambridge University Press, 1997.

219 The annual revenues of the Mughal Emperor Aurangzeb: John Kautsky, *The Politics of Aristocratic Empires*, Chapel Hill: University of North Carolina Press, 1982, p. 188.

219 The India that succumbed to British rule enjoyed an enormous financial surplus: Chunder Dutt, *Economic History of India*, p. xxv.

219 'In 1750, Indians had a similar standard of living to people in Britain': Wilson, 'False and Dangerous'.

220 'a flabby, pretending, weak-eyed devil of a rapacious and pitiless folly': Joseph Conrad, *Heart of Darkness*, London: Dover Thrift Editions, 1990, originally published in the volume *Youth: A Narrative, and Two Other Stories*, Edinburgh and London: William Blackwood & Sons, 1902.

220 'The question…': Ferguson, *Empire*, p. xxix.

221 'The industrial revolution did not occur because': Das, 'India: How a rich nation'; see also Das, *India Unbound*, pp. 228–243.

224 'Ten per cent of the army expenditure applied to irrigation': William Jennings Bryan, p. 12.

224 'temperate, respectful, patient, subordinate, and faithful': Ibid, p. 187.

225 'Our force does not operate so much by its actual strength': Mason, *A Matter of Honour*.

228 [It was] the practice of the miserable tyrants whom we found in India: Thomas Babington Macaulay, *Miscellaneous Writings and Speeches—Volume 4*, Project Gutenberg, 2008. www.gutenberg. org/files/21 70/2170-h/2170-h.htm.

228 British interfered with social customs only when it suited them: See, for example, the impassioned appeals by anti-slavery campaigners for the British government to put an end to certain traditional practices of servitude, which were of course completely ignored by Company officialdom: Wilson Anti-Slavery Collection, *A Brief View of Slavery in British India*, 1841, Manchester: The University of Manchester, John Rylands University Library. URL: www.jstor.org/stable/60228274.

229 'Unlike Stalin's Russia, the British empire': Lawrence James, *The Making and Unmaking of British India*, New York: St. Martin's Press, 2000; also published as *Raj: The Making and Unmaking of British India*, London: Little, Brown &Co., 1997.

229 For whom was the British empire an open society?: See the essays in Philippa Levine, ed., *Gender and Empire*, Oxford History of the British Empire Companion Series, Oxford University Press, 2004.

230 Let's look at the numbers one last time, widening the lens a little: See https:// infogr.am/Share-of-world-GDP-throughout-history.

231 As of 2014 Britain accounted for 2.4 per cent of global GDP: www.quandl.com/collections/economics/gdp-as-share-of-world-gdp-at-pp-by-country.

231 'Ferguson's "history" is a fairy tale for our times': Priyamvada Gopal, 'The story peddled by imperial apologists is a poisonous fairytale', *The Guardian*, 28 June 2006.

231 Henry Labouchère, published an immediate rejoinder: Henry Labouchère, 'The Brown Man's Burden' was first published in the London magazine, *Truth*, edited by Labouchère, in February 1899.

CHAPTER 8: THE MESSY AFTERLIFE OF COLONIALISM

235 A 1997 Gallup Poll in Britain revealed: Stuart Ward, ed., *British Culture and the End of Empire* (Manchester, 2001), 28, 128, cited in Richard Price, 'One Big Thing: Britain, Its Empire, and Their Imperial Culture', *Journal of British Studies*, Vol. 45, No. 3, July 2006, pp. 602–627. Published by: Cambridge University Press on behalf of The North American Conference on British Studies www.jstor.org/stable/10.1086/503593.

236 'wholly unprecedented in creating a global hierarchy': Pankaj Mishra, *From the Ruins of Empire. The Revolt against the West and the Remaking of Asia*, London: Allen Lane, 2012, p. 42.

236 'the memory of European imperialism remains a live political factor': Mark Mazower, 'From the Ruins of Empire', *Financial Times*, 27 July 2012.

236 He sees in Empire cause for much that is good: Ferguson, *Empire*, p xxv.

236 Without the spread of British rule around the planet: Ibid, p. 358.

236 The East India Company has collapsed, but globalization: Philip Pomper, 'The History and Theory of Empires', *History and Theory*, Vol. 44, No. 4, December 2005, pp. 1–27, published by Wiley for Wesleyan University. www.jstor.org/stable/3590855.

237 The liberal-capitalist 'rise of Asia' of which India is a contemporary epitome: Mishra, *From the Ruins of Empire*, p 42 et seq.

237 '[T]he British empire was essentially a Hitlerian project on a grand scale': Richard Gott, 'White wash' (book review of *Ornamentalism: How the British saw their Empire* by David Cannadine), *The Guardian*, 5 May 2001.

239 if looted Nazi-era art can be (and now is being) returned to their rightful owners: See the discussion in Erin Johnson, 'If we return Nazi-looted art, the same goes for empire-looted,' Aeon. www.aeon.co/ideas/if-we-r etur n-nazi-looted-art-the-same-goes-for-empir e-looted?utm_source=twitter&utm_medium=oupphilosophy&utm_campaign=oupphilosophy.

239 'if a strong man were to throw four stones': 'The Koh-i-noor diamond is in Britain illegally. But it should still stay there', *The Guardian*, 16 February 2016.

242 Part of the legacy of colonialism is…the worldwide impact

of the methods: For a searching political analysis of the Empire and its continuing implications, see two books by John Darwin, *The Empire Project*, London: Penguin, 2010; and *Unfinished Empire: The Global Expansion of Britain*, London: Allen Lane, 2013.

246 The militarization of Pakistan and the disproportionate size of its armed forces: Husain Haqqani, *India vs Pakistan: Why Can't we Just Be Friends?* (New Delhi: Juggernaut Books, 2016).

BIBLIOGRAPHY

Acemoglu, Daron and Robinson, James, *Why Nations Fail*, New York: Crown Business, 2012. Akbar, M. J., *Nehru*, New Delhi: Viking, 1988.

Ali, Abeerah, 'The Role of the British Colonial/Imperial Rule in the Introduction of Representative Institutions in India (1857–1947)', *Journal of European Studies*, *29*, 2013.

Allen, Charles, *Plain Tales from the Raj*, London: Abacus, 1988.

Almond, Ian, *The Thought of Nirad C. Chaudhuri: Islam, Empire and Loss*, Cambridge: Cambridge University Press, 2015.

Anderson, Benedict, *Imagined Communities: Reflections on the Origin and Spread of Nationalism*, 2nd edn, London: Verso, 1991.

Anderson, Clare, *Convicts in the Indian Ocean*, London: Palgrave Macmillan, 2000.

Azad, Maulana Abul Kalam, *India Wins Freedom*, New Delhi: Orient Blackswan, 2004.

Bailkin, Jordanna, 'The Boot and the Spleen: When Was Murder Possible in British India?', *Comparative Studies in Society and History*, *48 (2)*, 2006.

Barrier, Norman G. (ed.), *The Census in British India: New Perspectives*, New Delhi: Manohar Publishers, 1981.

Bayly, Christopher A., *Recovering Liberties: Indian Thought in the Age of Liberalism and Empire*, Cambridge: Cambridge University Press, 2011.

————, *The Birth of the Modern World, 1780–1914: Global Connections and Comparisons*, London: Wiley-Blackwell, 2004.

Bhargava, M. B. L., *India's Services in the War*, Mukat Bihari Lal Bharagava, 1919.

Bhatia, H. S. (ed.), *Military History of British India, 1607–1947*, New Delhi: Deep & Deep Publications, 1977.

Bolts, William, *Considerations on Indian Affairs: Particularly Respecting the Present State of Bengal and its Dependencies*, London: Printed for J. Almon, 1772.

BIBLIOGRAPHY

Bose, Sugata, 'Starvation amidst Plenty: The Making of Famine in Bengal, Honan and Tonkin', 1942–45, *Modern Asian Studies*, *24*, 1990.

———, *His Majesty's Opponent: Subhash Chandra Bose and India's Struggle Against Empire*, Cambridge, MA: Harvard University Press, 2011.

Brecher, Michael, *Nehru: A Political Biography*, London: Beacon Press, 1962.

Breckenridge, Carol A. and van der Veer, Peter (eds), *Orientalism and the Postcolonial Predicament*, Philadelphia: University of Pennsylvania Press, 1993.

Burton, Antoinette, *Empire in Question: Reading, Writing, and Teaching British Imperialism*, Durham and London: Duke University Press, 2011.

Campbell-Johnson, Alan, *Mission with Mountbatten*, London: Macmillan, 1985.

Cannadine, David, *Ornamentalism: How the British saw their Empire*, London: Allen Lane, 2001.

Cashman, Richard, *Patrons, Players, and the Crowd: The Phenomenon of Indian Cricket*, London: Orient Longman, 1980.

Chandra, Bipan, *India's Struggle for Independence*, New Delhi: Viking, 1988.

———, *The Rise and Growth of Economic Nationalism in India: Economic Policies of Indian National Leadership, 1880–1905*, New Delhi: Har-Anand Publications, 2010.

Chatterjee, Partha, and Pandey, Gyanendra (eds), *Subaltern Studies VII*, Delhi: Oxford University Press, 1992.

Chatterjee, Partha, *Lineages of Political Society: Studies in Postcolonial Democracy*, New York: Columbia University Press, 2011.

———, *The Nation and its Fragments: Colonial and Postcolonial Histories*, Princeton: Princeton University Press, 1993.

Chaudhuri, K. N., *The Trading World of Asia and the English East India Company, 1660–1760*, Cambridge: Cambridge University Press, 2006.

Chaudhuri, Nirad C., *Autobiography of an Unknown Indian*, London: Macmillan, 1951.

———, *A Passage to England*, London: St. Martin's Press, 1960.

Chaudhury, Sushil, *The Prelude to Empire: Plassey Revolution of 1757*, New Delhi: Manohar Publishers, 2000.

Cohn, Bernard S., *An Anthropologist Among The Historians and Other Essays*, Oxford: Oxford University Press, 1987.

Collingham, E. M., *Imperial Bodies: The Physical Experience of the Raj, 1800–1947*, Oxford: Polity Press, 2001.

Collins, Larry and Lapierre, Dominique, *Mountbatten and the Partition of India*, New Delhi: Vikas, 1975.

Corfield, Penelope J. (ed.), *Language, History and Class*, London: Blackwell, 1991.

Dalrymple, William, *White Mughals*, London: Harper Perennial, 2002.

Darwin, John, *The Empire Project: The Rise and Fall of the British World-System, 1830–1970*, Cambridge: Cambridge University Press, 2009.

BIBLIOGRAPHY

Darwin, John, *Unfinished Empire:The Global Expansion of Britain*, London: Allen Lane, 2013.

Das, Durga, *India: From Curzon to Nehru and After*, New Delhi: Rupa Publications, 1967.

Das, Sudipta, 'British Reactions to the French Bugbear in India, 1763–83', *European History Quarterly, 22 (1)*, 1992.

Davis, Mike, *LateVictorian Holocausts: El Niño Famines and the Making of theThird World*, London; NewYork:Verso Books, 2001.

de Courcy, Anne, *The Fishing-Fleet: Husband-Hunting In the Raj*, London: Weidenfeld & Nicolson, 2012.

Dhulipala,Venkat, *Creating a New Medina*, Cambridge: Cambridge University Press, 2016.

Digby, William, *Indian Problems for English Consideration, published for the National Liberal Federation*, London, 1881.

————, *'Prosperous' British India: A Revelation from Official Records*, London: T. Fisher Unwin, 1901.

Dirks, Nicholas B., *Castes of Mind: Colonialism and the Making of Modern India*, Princeton: Princeton University Press, 2001.

Durant,Will, *The Case for India*, NewYork: Simon & Schuster, 1930, reissued in a limited edition by Strand Book Stall, Mumbai, 2015.

Dutt, Romesh Chunder, *The Economic History of India under Early British Rule: From the Rise of the British Power in 1757 to the Accession of Queen Victoria in 1837*, New Delhi: Routledge, 1950, reprinted by the Government of India, 1963.

Eck, Diana, *India: A Sacred Geography*, NewYork: Harmony Books, 2012.

Falkiner, Caesar Litton, *Illustrations of Irish history and topography, mainly of the 17th century*, London: Longmans, Green, & Co., 1904.

Ferguson, Niall, *Colossus:The Price of America's Empire*, New York: Penguin, 2004.

————, *Empire:The Rise and Demise of the BritishWorld Order and the Lessons for Global Power*, NewYork: Basic Books, 2003.

Fielding-Hall, H., *Passing of the Empire*, London: Hurst & Blackett, 1913.

Fischer, Louis, *The Life of Mahatma Gandhi*, NewYork: Harper Collins, 1997.

Forrest, George, *The Life of Lord Clive:Volume 2*, London: Frank Cassell, 1918.

Forster, E. M., *A Passage to India*, London: Penguin/Allen Lane, 1924.

Freitag, Sandria, *Collective Action and Community: Public Arenas and the Emergence of Communalism in North India*, Berkeley: University of California Press, 1989.

Gadgil, Madhav, and Guha, Ramachandra, *Ecology and Equity:The Use and Abuse of Nature in Contemporary India*, New Delhi: Routledge, 1995.

Geddes, J. C., *Administrative Experience Recorded Former Famines*, Calcutta, 1874.

Ghosh, Amitav, *Sea of Poppies*, NewYork: Farrar, Straus & Giroux, 2011.

BIBLIOGRAPHY

Gilmour, David, *Curzon: Imperial Statesman*, New York: Farrar, Straus & Giroux, 2003.

———, *The Ruling Caste: Imperial Lives in the Victorian Raj*, New York: Farrar, Straus & Giroux, 2006. Gopal, Sarvepalli, *Jawaharlal Nehru, Volumes I & II*, New Delhi: Vintage, 2005.

Goradia, Nayana, *Lord Curzon: The Last of the British Moguls*, Oxford: Oxford University Press, 1993.

Gordon, Leonard, *Brothers Against the Raj*, New York: Columbia University Press, 1990.

Gottschalk, Peter, *Religion, Science and Empire: Classifying Hinduism and Islam in British India*, London, 2012, Oxford University Press

Guha, Ranajit, *Dominance without Hegemony: History and Power in Colonial India*, Cambridge, MA: Harvard University Press, 1998.

Hajari, Nisid, *Midnight's Furies*, Boston: Houghton Mifflin Harcourt, 2015.

Haqqani, Husain, *India vs Pakistan: Why Can't we Just Be Friends?* (New Delhi: Juggernaut Books, 2016)

Harris, Jonathan Gil, *The First Firangis*, New Delhi: Aleph Book Company, 2015.

Hiltebeitel, Alf, *Criminal Gods and Demon Devotees: Essays on the Guardians of Popular Hinduism*, Binghamton NY: SUNY Press, 1989.

Hobsbawm, Eric, *The Age of Empire*, London: George Weidenfeld and Nicolson, 1987.

Hobson, J. M., *The Eastern Origins of Western Civilisation*, Cambridge: Cambridge University Press, 2004.

Hodson, H. V., *The Great Divide*, Oxford: Oxford University Press, 1997.

Holzman, James, *The Nabobs in England: A Study of the Returned Anglo-Indian, 1760–1785*, New York: Columbia University Press, 1926.

Howitt, William, *The English in India*, London: Longman, Orme, Brown, Green, and Longmans, 1839.

Indian National Party, *British Rule in India: Condemned by the British Themselves*, issued by the Indian National Party, London, 1915.

James, Lawrence, *Raj: The Making and Unmaking of British India*, New York: St Martin's Griffin, 1997.

Judd, Denis, *The Lion and the Tiger: The Rise and Fall of the British Raj, 1600– 1947*, Oxford: Oxford University Press, 2005.

Khan, Yasmin, *The Great Partition*, New Haven: Yale University Press, 2008.

Kipling, Rudyard, 'Naboth' in *Life's Handicap* (1891), republished by Echo Books, London, 2007.

———, *Kim*, New York: Oxford University Press, 2008.

Kishwar, Madhu, *Zealous Reformers, Deadly Laws*, New Delhi: SAGE Publications, 2008.

Kramer, Martin (ed.), *Shi'ism, Resistance, and Revolution*, Boulder, CO: Westview Press, 1987.

BIBLIOGRAPHY

Kurtzer, M. Daphne, *Empire's Children: Empire and Imperialism in Classic British Children's Books*, London: Routledge, 2002.

Levine, Philippa (ed.), *Gender and Empire, Oxford History of the British Empire Companion Series*, Oxford: Oxford University Press, 2004.

Lipset, Seymour Martin, Seong, Kyoung-Ryung and Torres, John Charles, 'A Comparative Analysis of the Social Requisites of Democracy', *International Social Science Journal, 45*, 1993.

Macaulay, Thomas Babington, *Historical Essays of Macaulay:William Pitt, Earl of Chatham, Lord Clive,Warren Hastings*, ed. by Samuel Thurber, Boston: Allyn and Bacon, 1894.

MacMillan, Margaret, *Women of the Raj: The Mothers,Wives, and Daughters of the British Empire in India*, New York: Random House, 2007.

Maddison, Angus, *Class Structure and Economic Growth: India & Pakistan since the Moghuls*, London: Routledge, 2013.

————, *The World Economy*, Development Centre of the Organisation for Economic Co-operation and Development, 2006.

Majeed, Javed, *Ungoverned Imaginings: James Mill's The History of British India and Orientalism*, Oxford: Clarendon Press, 1992.

Majumdar, R. C., *The History and Culture of the Indian People: The Maratha Supremacy*, Bombay: Bharatiya Vidya Bhavan, 1977.

Mansergh, Nicholas, *The Transfer of Power 1942–47*, London: HM Stationery Office, 1983.

Marshall, Peter J., *The Impeachment of Warren Hastings*, Oxford: Oxford University Press, 1965.

Mason, Philip, *A Matter of Honour: An Account of the Indian Army, its Officers and Men*, London: Penguin, 1974.

————, *Kipling: The Glass, the Shadow and the Fire*, New York: Holt, Rinehart & Wilson, 1975.

————, *Men Who Ruled India*, New Delhi: Rupa Publications, 1992.

Metcalfe, Thomas, *Ideologies of the Raj*, Cambridge: Cambridge University Press, 1995.

Mishra, Pankaj, *From the Ruins of Empire: The Revolt against the West and the Remaking of Asia*, London: Allen Lane, 2012.

Moon, Penderel, *The British Conquest and Dominion of India*, India Research Press, 1989.

Moon, Penderel, Tully, Mark and Raychaudhuri, Tapan, *Divide and Quit*, Oxford: Oxford University Press, 1998.

Moorhouse, Geoffrey, *India Brittanica*, New York: Harper & Row, 1983.

Morris, Jan, *Farewell the Trumpets: An Imperial Retreat*, London: Faber & Faber, 1978.

Mount, Ferdinand, *Tears of the Rajas*, London: Simon and Schuster, 2015.

Mukerjee, Madhusree, *Churchill's Secret War: The British Empire and the Ravaging of India During World > War II*, New York: Basic Books 2010.

BIBLIOGRAPHY

Naipaul, V. S., *An Area of Darkness*, London: André Deutsch, 1964.

————, *India: A Wounded Civilization*, London: André Deutsch, 1976.

Nandy, Ashis, *The Tao of Cricket: On Games of Destiny and the Destiny of Games*, Oxford: Oxford University Press, 2000.

Naoroji, Dadabhai, *Poverty and Un-British Rule in India*, London: Swan Sonnenschein, 1901.

Nasson, Bill, *Britannia's Empire: Making a British World*, Stroud, Gloucestershire: Tempus Publishing, 2004.

Nechtman, Tillman W., 'A Jewel in the Crown? Indian Wealth in Domestic Britain in the Late Eighteenth Century', *Eighteenth-Century Studies, 41 (1)*, 2007.

Nehru, Jawaharlal, *Glimpses of World History*, New Delhi: Oxford University Press, 1989.

————, *Jawaharlal Nehru: An Autobiography*, New Delhi: Oxford University Press, 1989.

————, *The Discovery of India*, New Delhi: Oxford University Press, 1989.

Nevinson, Henry W., *The New Spirit in India*, London: Harper & Brothers, 1908.

Ó Gráda, Cormac, *Eating People is Wrong, and Other Essays on Famine, its Past, and its Future*, Princeton, NJ: Princeton University Press, 2015.

Ozbudun, E. and Weiner, M. (eds), *Competitive Elections in Developing Countries*, Durham, NC: Duke University, 1987.

Pandey, Gyanendra, *The Construction of Communalism in Colonial North India*, New Delhi: Oxford University Press, 1990.

Parkinson, C. Northcote, *Parkinson's Law: The Pursuit of Progress*, London, John Murray, 1958.

Peers, D. M. and Gooptu, N. (eds), *India and the British Empire*, Oxford: Oxford University Press, 2012.

Pernau, Margrit (ed.), *Delhi College: Traditional Elites, the Colonial State and Education before 1857*, New Delhi: Oxford University Press, 2006.

Pillai, Manu, *The Ivory Throne*, New Delhi: Harper Collins, 2015.

Prasad, Amba, *Indian Railways: A Study in Public Utility Administration*, Bombay: Asia Publishing House, 1960.

Qureshi, Ishtiaq Husain, *The Struggle for Pakistan*, University of Karachi, 1969.

Rai, Lala Lajpat, *Unhappy India*, Calcutta: Banna Publishing Company, 1928.

Rangarajan, Mahesh, *India's Wildlife History*, New Delhi: Permanent Black, 2001.

Ray, Indrajit, 'Shipbuilding in Bengal under Colonial Rule: A Case of 'De-Industrialisation'', *The Journal of Transport History*, 16 (1), 1995.

Raychaudhuri, Tapan, *Europe Reconsidered: Perceptions of the West in 19th Century Bengal*, Oxford: Oxford University Press, 1988.

BIBLIOGRAPHY

Rees, J. D., *The Real India*, London: Methuen, 1908.

Scott, Paul, *The Jewel in the Crown*, London: Heinemann, 1966.

————, *The Day of the Scorpion*, London: Heinemann, 1968.

————, *The Towers of Silence*, London: Heinemann, 1971.

————, *A Division of the Spoils*, London: Heinemann, 1975.

Sen, Amartya, *Poverty and Famines: An Essay on Entitlements and Deprivation*, Oxford: Oxford University Press, 1983.

————, *The Argumentative Indian*, New York: Farrar, Straus & Giroux, 2005.

Sinha, Mrinalini, *Colonial Masculinity: The 'Manly Englishman' and the 'Effeminate Bengali' in the Late Nineteenth Century*, Manchester: Manchester University Press, 1995.

Srinivas, M. N., *Social Change in Modern India*, 1972, Orient Longman India: Hyderabad.

Sullivan, Zohreh T., *Narratives of Empire: The Fictions of Rudyard Kipling*, Cambridge: Cambridge University Press, 1993.

Sunderland, J. T., *India in Bondage: Her Right to Freedom And a Place Among the Great Nations*, New York: Lewis Copeland Company, 1929.

Tagore, Rabindranath, *Crisis in Civilization (1941)*, in *The Essential Tagore*, Cambridge, MA: Harvard University Press, 2011.

Talbot, Phillips, *An American Witness to India's Partition*, New Delhi: SAGE Publications, 2007.

Taylor, A. J. P., *English History 1914–45*, Oxford: Oxford University Press, 1965.

Telford, Judith, *British Foreign Policy, 1870–1914*, Glasgow: Blackie, 1978.

Tharoor, Shashi, *Nehru: The Invention of India*, New York: Arcade Books, 2003.

Trevelyan, C. E., *On the Education of the People of India*, London: Longman, Orme, Brown, Green & Longmans, 1838.

Viswanathan, Gauri, *Masks of Conquest: Literary Study and British Rule in India*, New York: Columbia University Press, 1989.

Wan-ling, C. J. Wee, *Culture, Empire, and the Question of Being Modern*, New York: Lexington Books, 2003.

Ward, Stuart (ed.), *British Culture and the End of Empire*, Manchester: Manchester University Press, 2001.

Wavell, Lord Archibald, *Viceroy's Journal* (ed.), Penderel Moon, Oxford: Oxford University Press, 1973.

Weiner, M. and Ozbudun, E. (eds), *Competitive Elections in Developing Countries*, Durham, NC: Duke University Press, 1987.

Wiener, Martin, *Men of Blood: Violence, Manliness and Criminal Justice in Victorian England*, Cambridge: Cambridge University Press, 2004.

Wilson, Jon, *India Conquered*, London: Simon & Schuster, 2016.

Wilson, Kathleen (ed.), *A New Imperial History: Culture, Identity and Modernity in Britain and the Empire 1660–1840*, Cambridge: Cambridge University Press, 2004.

Wolpert, Stanley, *Nehru: A Tryst with Destiny*, New York: Oxford University Press, 1995.

Zastoupil, L., and Moir, M. (eds), *The Great Indian Education Debate: Documents Relating to the Orientalist-Anglicist Controversy, 1781–1843*, Richmond: Curzon Press, 1999.

Zubrzycki, John, *The Last Nizam*, New Delhi: Picador India, 2007.

INDEX

INDEX

INDEX

INDEX